George Butte

SUTURE AND NARRATIVE

DEEP INTERSUBJECTIVITY IN FICTION AND FILM

The Ohio State University Press | Columbus

Copyright © 2017 by The Ohio State University.
All rights reserved.

Library of Congress Cataloging-in-Publication Data
Names: Butte, George, 1947– author.
Title: Suture and narrative : deep intersubjectivity in fiction and film / George Butte.
Other titles: Theory and interpretation of narrative series.
Description: Columbus : The Ohio State University Press, [2017] | Series: Theory and
 interpretation of narrative | Includes bibliographical references.
Identifiers: LCCN 2016045083 | ISBN 9780814213292 (cloth ; alk. paper) |
 ISBN 0814213294 (cloth ; alk. paper)
Subjects: LCSH: Narration (Rhetoric) | Intersubjectivity in literature. | Intersubjectivity. |
 Fiction—Technique. | Motion pictures—Philosophy.
Classification: LCC PN3383.N35 B88 2017 | DDC 809/.923—dc23
LC record available at https://lccn.loc.gov/2016045083

Cover design by Laurence J. Nozik
Text design by Juliet Williams
Type set in Sabon and Myriad

♾ The paper used in this publication meets the minimum requirements of the American National Standard for Information Sciences—Permanence of Paper for Printed Library Materials. ANSI Z39.48–1992.

9 8 7 6 5 4 3 2 1

CONTENTS

	Acknowledgments	v
CHAPTER 1	**Introduction: Why Suture?**	1
CHAPTER 2	**Suture and the Narration of Experience**	20
	i. Suture Theory: The Origins in Film Theory	20
	ii. Revising Suture Theory: Merleau-Ponty and Deep Intersubjectivity	31
	iii. Chiasmus and *Nothing But a Man*	38
	iv. The Mystery of the Oblique Angle and *The Silence of the Lambs*	51
	v. The Politics of Suture, Again	69
CHAPTER 3	**The Case of Henry James: Suture and Deep Intersubjectivity**	73
	i. Theory I: Suturing Consciousnessses	73
	ii. Practice: Reading Looking	84
	iii. Theory II: Suture and Free Indirect Discourse	92
	iv. The Oblique Angle Again: James in Film	100
CHAPTER 4	**The Wounds of Peter Pan: Suture and Loss**	120
	i. Barrie's Peter Pans: "Would Not" or "Could Not"?	123
	ii. *Peter and Wendy* and Barrie's Multiple Narratees: Who Is Listening to This Story?	128

iii. Eavesdropping: Targeting Children in
"Wendy's Story"—Practice I 139
iv. Eavesdropping: Free Indirect Discourse and
Mothers, the Toads—Practice II 146
v. Eavesdropping and the Ricochet Effect: Theory 154
vi. The Peter Pan Films: Narrating Loss and Anxiety 161

CHAPTER 5 **Suture and Film Comedy: *Raising Arizona* and the Derridean *Komos*** 176
i. Ethan and Joel's Pharmacy 180
ii. Postmodern Sutures 189

EPILOGUE **Suture and Community in *Why Be Happy When You Could Be Normal?* and *(500) Days of Summer*** 207

Appendix: The Ricochet Effect: Narrative Theory and Boundary Ethics 219
Works Cited 227
Index 237

ACKNOWLEDGMENTS

Once again, a book about intersubjectivity has benefited from the contributions of many people. Here at Colorado College, I am grateful for extensive support: to the dean's office for a Benezet grant for a summer when I wrote the Henry James chapter; for two sabbaticals; for a generous grant to cover expenses for the book's index; and for multiple travel grants to attend Narrative Society conventions. Thanks go to the English Department for a MacLean grant for time to write (and a quiet thank you to the spirit of Dorothy J. MacLean, Colorado College class of 1922, who years ago told me as we sat in her Winnetka living room that she wanted to endow support for intellectual life in our department; and thanks to her children and grandchildren who have continued this support. I think often of D. J. when I look at her senior essay in my office on the then "new" poets Vachel Lindsay and T. S. Eliot. I hope she would be pleased with this book.) I also received a very helpful grant from the department's Miller fund.

Several kinds of thanks go to Paula Pyne, our department's superb staff assistant, not only for solving all kinds of computer and software problems but for designing the Ricochet Effect chart, and for long conversations on the riddles of Peter Pan, which interested her almost as much as they do me. I also want to thank Diane Armock, librarian extraordinaire, who tracked down an elusive copy of the 1913 edition of *The Coral Island*, which contained Barrie's preface (until then un-reprinted). And I want to thank Chad Schonewill, IT magus, and his colleagues Weston Taylor and Tulio Wolford, for creating files for my screenshots. Thanks also to Dan Wiencek for his media savvy.

Once again the wonderful conversation with editors and outside readers for the Theory and Interpretation of Narrative series at The Ohio State University Press has enormously improved this book. It's difficult to describe how deeply Jim Phelan and Robyn Warhol, especially, and the two anonymous outside readers entered into the labyrinths of the manuscript, and escaped out the other side with their sanity intact, and with wonderful suggestions to make the journey better for future readers. Responding to their questions and ideas has been a significant pleasure in completing this work.

Some sections of this book have already appeared in print. Parts of chapter 2 were originally published in *Poetics Today*, vol. 29, no. 2 (2008), pp. 277–308, copyright 2008 by the Porter Institute for Poetics and Semiotics, Tel Aviv University, and reprinted by permission of the copyrightholder and the present publisher, Duke University Press. Parts of chapter 3 were first published in *The Henry James Review*, vol. 30, no. 2 (2009), pp. 129–43, copyright 2009 by the Johns Hopkins University Press, and reprinted with their permission.

Finally, I want to give thanks again to the patience and warm support of my wife Billie, our children Kate and Read, as well as the canine scholars Lucy, Biscuit, and Cinnamon—who have watched this project grow. They are proud—and perhaps a little relieved—that its journey is almost done.

CHAPTER 1

Introduction

Why Suture?

What a thrill—
My thumb instead of an onion.
The top quite gone
Except for a sort of a hinge

Of skin,
A flap like a hat,
Dead white
Then that red plush.
 —Sylvia Plath, "Cut," *Ariel*

The surgeon drew a six-inch dotted line with a marking pen across a sleeping patient's abdomen and then, to my surprise, had the nurse hand me the knife. It was, I remember, still warm from the sterilizing autoclave. The surgeon had me stretch the skin taut with the thumb and forefinger of my free hand. He told me to make one smooth slice down to the fat. I put the belly of the blade to the skin and cut. The experience was odd and addictive, mixing exhilaration from the calculated violence of the act, anxiety about getting it right, and a righteous faith that it was somehow good for the person. There was also the slightly nauseating feeling of finding that it took more force than I'd realized. (Skin is thick and springy, and on my first pass I did not go nearly deep enough; I had to cut twice to get through.)
 —Atul Gawande, "Education of a Knife," *Complications*

> "Our habits of expence make us too dependent, and there are not many in my rank of life who can afford to marry without some attention to money."
>
> "Is this," thought Elizabeth, "meant for me?" and she coloured at the idea; but recovering herself, said in a lively tone, "and what is the price of an Earl's younger son? Unless the elder brother is very sickly, I suppose you would not ask above fifty thousand pounds."
>
> He answered her in the same style, and the subject dropped. To interrupt a silence which might make him fancy her affected with what had passed, she soon afterwards said,
>
> "I imagine your cousin brought you down with him chiefly for the sake of having somebody at his disposal. I wonder he does not marry, to secure a lasting convenience of that kind."
>
> —Jane Austen, *Pride and Prejudice* (II/10)

> Then suddenly he lifted his head and looked straight at Ursula with dark, almost vengeful eyes.
>
> "He should have loved me," he said. "I offered him."
>
> She, afraid, white, with mute lips, answered:
>
> "What difference would it have made!"
>
> "It would!" he said. "It would."
>
> He forgot her and turned to look at Gerald. . . . Gerald's father had looked wistful, to break the heart: but not this last terrible look of cold, mute Matter. Birkin watched and watched.
>
> Ursula stood aside and watched the living man stare at the frozen face of the dead man. Both faces were unmoved and unmoving.
>
> —D. H. Lawrence, *Women in Love* (chapter 31)

"I put the belly of the blade to the skin and cut": Atul Gawande's account is a dramatic example of the story behind *suture*. The word is about cutting and sewing the body. Because the cutting leads to the sewing, *suture* also embodies the intention to heal, or at least to put back together the pieces taken apart. Gawande's language alerts us to the paradox here: the "belly" of the blade cuts into the patient's abdomen, arc into arc, and invades in an act of "calculated violence" to make whole. The violence functions within a network of intention, including observation (the supervising surgeon) and need (the patient): it articulates "calculation" in the midst of a network of consciousnesses. In one thread of twentieth-century narrative theory, sewing together has become a figure for narrative construction, for putting together the pieces of a tale. In its journey from medicine to storytelling, *suture* retained some of its implications in narrative theory, and lost some: constructing remained, for example, but the body of the patient and the intentionality of the blade did not. The calculation of author and narrator did, but the calculation of actors and observers attending to each other, the network of subjectivities, did not. The purpose of this book is to examine what remains in the notion of suture in narrative theory, to recover what was lost, and to explain why this matters.

Suture is an image that knits together threads from several topics in narrative theory. The image originated as a narratological concept in Lacanian film theory of the late 1960s and early 1970s; it functioned to figure the lack at the core of intersubjectivity in narrative film. In this early chapter of film theory, suture's primal story was a tale of absences, about the something missing at the core of selfhood, of subjectivity, and of discourse. In my alternative view, suture is another example of the narrative practice of what I call deep intersubjectivity. As a narrative form, suture in this account is not about emptiness but about the formation of consciousness, or rather the formation of consciousn*esses*, the dance—tragic, comic, ironic, duplicitous, even traumatized *by* emptiness—of multiple centers of awareness in narrative. Recasting suture in new phenomenological terms has a broad usefulness for many aspects of storytelling: it offers a reframed approach to narrators, narratees, implied viewers and readers, and most importantly, to character, and especially to characters in the plural, to the webs of multiple consciousnesses represented in print as well as in film narratives. Rethinking suture is the occasion for an exemplary exercise of this book's primary strategy, the connection of resources in film theory and phenomenology to enrich narrative theory and our interpretation of stories.

For me the major task is to bring the body (and its subjectivity) back to suture. By embedding (and embodying) suture in what will be multiple forms, from shot / reverse shot editing in film to free indirect discourse in fiction and the chiasmus of what I will call the ricochet effect, we can trace multiple kinds of embodiments in looking and touching, caressing and wounding and betraying, and especially in the embodiments of other embodiments, or the failure of such embodiments, in the multiple rhetorics and plots of deep intersubjectivity. My fundamental thread throughout is to show how telling the story of human experience is indeed complexly intersubjective, and to track some of the implications of that how. My theme is the story of subjectivities experiencing or not experiencing or partially experiencing or mis-experiencing or believing they experience themselves by way of the other's similar perception or misperception or both. Deep intersubjectivity is the form in narrative of self-knowledge by way of others in an intricate series of encounters: how stories tell about others encountering yet others to reencounter or revise or mistake themselves and the other too.[1]

To embody this telling as a version of suture, even when the tale embodies failure and misperception of misperception, is to move from one phenomenology to another, from one model of the human interworld to another, in particular from Jean-Paul Sartre and Jacques Lacan to Maurice Merleau-Ponty. This is a shift from an ontology of absence to an ontology of loss and occasional and partial presence. In this new paradigm, stories of loss, and some stories of encounter and espousal, are part of a chiasmus, a looping around the body and the consciousness of the other or others, and as a result these stories are more complex than usually conceived, with many layers, nestings inside nestings, and degrees: tales of losses and gains that are partial in subtly new and different ways. This theory of suture thus returns the wounded body to narrative by conceiving narrative in a new framework *as* embodied intersubjectivities, so that we can measure better, with greater narratological precision, what can and what cannot be stitched together in our stories.

Among the many forms of suture are the first two examples with which I began, Plath's "hinge of skin" with its thrill at loosing her own blood, and the disciplined scalpel (and needle) of Gawande's surgeon: in a broad sense, that is, narratives of cutting and stitching. Unlike the Lacanian model of Jacques-Alain Miller and Jean-Pierre Oudart, this model of suture allows for the possibility of comedy, of an espousal (to use Merleau-Ponty's word) that is always imperfect, never transcendental, and even then only a possibility. Also, this model allows for a range of types, from what I call elementary suture, a more one-dimensional wound, as in the Plath poem; to stitchings across other threads, in a midrange of linked intersubjectivities, as in Gawande's surgeon threading his work between the observing master and the sleeping patient; to the most profound and recursive examples of deep suture in my last two examples, as Elizabeth blushes before what she thinks Colonel Fitzgerald thinks she is thinking, and as Ursula watches Birkin watch the frozen, unwatching face of Gerald (here the loops of subjectivities include the still gaze of death). All suture is not deeply intersubjective, but all deep

---

1. See Butte, chapter 1, for an extended discussion of deep intersubjectivity as a narratological, phenomenological, and historical concept.

intersubjectivity makes some use of the strategies of suture. The range of examples I have chosen in this book will begin to make the case for that claim.

Suture is an ancient image borrowed from surgery to illuminate forms of consciousness*es* in narrative. Its complementary image, drawn from classical rhetoric and contemporary phenomenology, is the chiasmus. Like the intertwining syntax of the chiasmus ("love is flowerlike, the flower is loverly"), intersubjectivity in the work of the French phenomenologist Merleau-Ponty is an exchange of perceptions of perceptions that weaves a kind of knowledge about self and others that is neither transcendental, transparent, nor entirely illusory. My earlier book, *I Know That You Know That I Know,* was devoted to an exploration of multiple versions of this ambiguous terrain in stories about multiple consciousnessses. Deep intersubjectivity, as I studied it there, ranged from the complex mis-taking of another's mis-taking of one's own language and gestures to partial confirmations by each of the other's adoption of one's own mirroring gesture to them. The key change in "deep" intersubjectivity around the time of Jane Austen, as I argue in that book, was the addition in narrative of new layers of perceptions of perceptions perceived.[2] It is possible to trace further dolls inside Russian dolls, well beyond these first three or four exchanges and interpretations of interpretation, but the shift in the classical phenomenological paradigm has occurred with the move beyond "I know that you know," and the thematic implications for selfhood and community are similar once intersubjectivity has become so intricate. Further recessions of perceptions perceived certainly amplify the theme of uncertainty and error, to the point where, as Lisa Zunshine points out, cognitive control of the nestings becomes unsustainable.[3]

---

2. I make no claim that real people's consciousness or experience of others actually changed at the same time. Our narratives demonstrably changed, but *why* is a difficult question to answer. See Brian McHale's recent essay in *Narrative* (on Dorrit Cohn's *Transparent Minds* thirty-five years later), in which he comments on the dangers of assuming changes in representations of subjectivity are proof of changes in real persons. He compares the tautological quality of such arguments in recent cognitive narrative criticism to the "perfect *circularity*" of Julian Jayne's now-forgotten claims in *The Origin of Consciousness of the Bicameral Mind* (1976) for the nature of ancient consciousness (122; emphasis in original).

3. Zunshine's example of this "cognitive vertigo" is an episode from the TV show *Friends,* in which a group extends the embeddings in a *reductio ad absurdum*: Phoebe sums it up, "They're trying to mess with *us*? They don't know that we know they know we know!" (See below, chapter 3, note 2.) This is a good moment to observe that Zunshine has applied my notion of deep intersubjectivity to *Clarissa* (and perhaps Rousseau:

One way to figure the range of story rhetorics in this new paradigm is to set the ontology of others in Sartre against that of his one-time friend Merleau-Ponty. On one end of the spectrum lies Sartre's notion that the look of the other always wounds, always produces a hemorrhage in the person gazed at; he writes in *Being and Nothingness*, "'Being-seen-by-the-Other' is the *truth* of 'seeing-the-Other.' . . . He is that object in the world which determines an internal flow of the universe, an internal hemorrhage" (345). Because of the gaze of the Other, "I am *in danger*. This danger is not an accident, but the permanent structure of my being-for-others" (358). At the other end of the spectrum is Merleau-Ponty's paradigm for one person's possible responses to the other's gestures that inflect one's own, in an extending series of adoptions that are always mediated and partial and sometimes threatening—but *not* illusory, or not entirely, or very rarely such. And they are not always or inherently hostile or the results of bad faith. The extreme version of the conflict between these two phenomenologists sets shame against espousal. Merleau-Ponty's wonderful image for his always-embodied, never transcendental chiasmus of consciousnesses is the building of a wall that connects and separates: "There is said to be a wall between us and others, but it is a wall we build together, each putting a stone in the niche left by the other" (*Signs* 19). This book adds the image of suture to extend this understanding of deep intersubjectivity. Borrowed from that classical period of film theory in the 1960s and 1970s, suture serves to return the body and a chiasmus of intentionalities to stories by looking at a series of strategies for stitching together (or for unstitching) characters in narrative.

Here is an initial definition of narrative suture, reconceived by way of existentialist phenomenology and its nuanced approach to intersubjectivity. Each of these claims will be the subject of development in the chapters that follow, and my goal here (and there) is suggestion and illustration, not completeness. First, suture's purpose is the stitching together of human consciousnesses in narrative. (Other kinds of "stitching" occur in storytelling—think of cross-cutting between plots in Francis Ford Coppola's *The Godfather*—but my focus is phenomenological: how subjectivities connect—or don't.) And the narrative form of this suture at its most characteristic involves obliqueness, because its form narrates the connection of selves in a chiasmus of approach and retreat. The exemplary forms I will return to repeatedly are the shot / reverse shot in narrative

---

see her endnote 3) to suggest that the paradigm shift I argue for in *I Know That You Know That I Know* appears before Jane Austen (Zunshine, "Can We Teach").

film, with the strangeness of the oblique angle that links them, and free indirect discourse in print fiction. Narrating deep intersubjectivity—how Elizabeth believes she sees that Colonel Fitzwilliam perceives how she thinks he feels about her and has seen (she blushes to think) that she sees he sees—narrating these phenomenological complexities works best with the strategies of suture: indirection, looking at looking over the shoulder of the observer, and linking bodies and minds imperfectly and sometimes dangerously to other bodies and minds that read and misread in loops of chiastic error and sometimes not. The misreadings may be only partial: Ursula cannot read fully Birkin's reading of Gerald's frozen face, as she "stood aside" and watches from the wings of the scene, in this typical sidelines position, but she reads something, and not entirely in error.

This example suggests the second characteristic of narrative suture: the degree of error is a major theme suggested by suture's forms of indirection. Consciousness of consciousness(es) is never entirely transparent, nor entirely opaque in our stories. Only idealists, utopians, and young lovers could believe in complete transparency, but I want to be clear on this point, since my model has been accused of such confidence.[4] On the other end of the spectrum, the opaque is also never absolute. Even the thickest mask allows some reading of its surfaces and its deflected intentionality, and masks facing other masks maneuver in a dance of deception that itself can still be read. Deeply intersubjective narrative tells the stories of these intentionalities, these gestures (however hidden or avoided or misunderstood) to and from others. The suturing between others always leaves gaps, but these gaps are signs of presence, not the reverse. Suture leaves a trail of blood, as Merleau-Ponty understood, and Lacan did not. Suture is selves as embodied, not as shadows; as presence, not lack; but never transcendentally connected. And so suture raises complex questions about community. These loops describe the arcs of bodies and consciousnesses gesturing to each other, even if the arcs embody shame and aggression and misreadings of misreadings. The threads of suture can strangle as well as knit together, but the stories of knots that imprison or stories of broken threads and failed connection are still examples of the themes of suture, examples of the textures of multiple consciousnesses.

A third implication of these indirections is their presumption of an enunciator, an agency directing the camera and the over-the-shoulder

---

4. See, for example, footnote 21 on pp. 334–35 in *Literature as Conduct: Speech Acts in Henry James*, by J. Hillis Miller, who claims that my use of "know" (as in *I Know That You Know That I Know*) refers to a transparent, unmediated knowledge.

perception of perception perceived. Because suture loops together representations of consciousnesses with threads that however oblique or indirect never disappear from sight, some degree of defamiliarization is typical of this form. The oblique angle, the indirection of the chiasmus's loops, the over-the-shoulder stance of free indirect discourse: all allow for a gap, a space between diegesis and narration that alerts a thoughtful audience to its choices and allows space for commentary by that narrating agency. Of course, no narration is ever natural, innocent, ever not a choice. But suture's complexities permit many choices in form and subject. Suture narrates the whole range of human subjectivities and their intentions, conscious or not, aggressive, violent, and controlling, or not, and its indirections frame and comment on those choices.

Suture works so well—in ironic contrast to the use of the image in classical film theory—because its image conjures up bodies (and hence a grounding presence, not absence, for consciousness), because its operation is a threading through, a chiasmus (as both Merleau-Ponty and Derrida understand), and because its work reminds us of the wounds that generate narrative. And so, fourth: suture as form enunciates especially well suture as theme in many stories. Indeed, the wounds that suture narrates sometimes lie in the background throughout this book, but they are finally what it is about: the death of Clarice Starling's father in *The Silence of the Lambs, Peter Pan*'s loss of mothers, Maggie's shattered bowl in Henry James, Ed's unborn—that is, unconceived—child in *Raising Arizona*, the way Jeanette's adoption is a kind of abuse in *Why Be Happy When You Could Be Normal?* The intricacy of these themes and their narrative form varies in part because not all suture enunciates deep intersubjectivity. In the scale of sutures, my primary interest indeed will be deep suture, the complex form necessary to tell the stories of deep intersubjectivity, but we will look at times at less intricate connections, in which the loops articulate a sparer chiasmus, perhaps only *I know that you know,* with smaller or no recursive circles of minds' perceptions. Some angles of the ricochet effect, in chapter 3 for example, entail fewer threads of consciousnesses, and free indirect discourse can be less layered too, when the filtering mind is observing not another person or persons but, say, a golden bowl or a landscape. Elementary suture can be profound storytelling, whose simpler scale still echoes some of the more elaborate effects of *The Wings of the Dove* or *The Silence of the Lambs*. A reminder about boundaries to this concept might be useful: as I said before, all stitching together in narrative is not suture as a phenomenological concept. My focus is telling the stories of characters and their subjectivities. So, for example, cross-cutting of narrative threads, in, say, Dickens's *Bleak House* or D. W. Griffith's *Intolerance,* would not count as chiasmus or suture here, except to the degree the cross-cutting produces at least an elementary intersubjectivity.

The book that follows traces a series of problems and their venues in three case studies: its agenda is typological, and more illustrative than encyclopedic. The sequence is chronological, from Henry James's turn-of-the-twentieth-century fiction, to various iterations of Barrie's story from 1904 to the 1950s and later, and concluding with a classic of 1980s postmodernism. This one hundred years of narrative begins with the intensity of indirection in James's late novels that launches a century-long exploration (that continues as I write) of the difficulties of suture. The threads of suture could be named, with a whimsical Seussian logic, Oblique I (the indirections of free indirect discourse), Oblique II (the ricochet effect), and Oblique III (the chiasmus), with one case study focused on each, though the major examples will exhibit elements of all three versions of the oblique. The meditations on specifics are sometimes extensive, and each reader will have to judge how representative the texts are for each iteration of the oblique, which I first theorize in chapter 2 as a revised and embodied version of film theory's Absent Other in continuity editing. *The Wings of the Dove* and *The Golden Bowl* provide dazzling examples of free indirect discourse's over-the-shoulder indirection for (paradoxically) embodying the subtle confusions of family life and marriage: this is Oblique I in the first case study (chapter 3). The second thread connects free indirect discourse's over-the-shoulder stance to shot / reverse shot's evasions, first examined in Michael Roemer's *Nothing But a Man* (1964) and *The Silence of the Lambs* (1991) in chapter 2, but now extended to James Barrie's Peter Pan texts and the Peter Pan films; the particularly poignant consequence here is what I call the ricochet effect. These examples are Oblique II in chapter 4. The third form of the oblique connects suture's indirection to Derrida's notion of the chiasmus as expressing the doubleness of the *pharmakon,* and by extension of the *komos,* the narrative archetype of comedy. The case study here is the Coen Brothers' *Raising Arizona* (1987), in chapter 5, which tests the power of chiasmus as suture to close wounds in the particularly difficult setting of postmodern comedy.

These three studies of suture as oblique angle open up space for a phenomenological approach to narrative attuned to the rhetorical richness of deep intersubjectivity, of consciousnesses inside phenomenologically intricate story-worlds. In each case study, the oblique becomes more evasive, more skeptical, more attuned to the difficulties of what Merleau-Ponty called "espousal." Other examples would work—Edith Wharton instead of Henry James, for example, or John Cassavetes's *Faces* instead of *Nothing But a Man*—but my intent has been to offer not a survey of all similar narratives but a close study of especially rich examples of suture that suggest this arc of progression into difficulty. To me this progression continues through all of my examples, because my argument about *Raising Arizona* claims that its *komos* defines itself in a context of enormous (postmodern) skepticism about the promises of suture.

The primary theoretical work occurs in chapter 2, where I describe the features of classical suture theory that arose in the 1960s in approaches to film narrative. This description sets the stage for my alternative approach to suture. The classical theory, true to its origins in the work of Jacques-Alain Miller, a student of Lacan, tells a story of absence. The French film theorist Jean-Pierre Oudart begins with the mystery of shot / reverse shot editing in film narrative, and I end with that mystery at the conclusion of chapter 2. Continuity editing in film creates time and space, and always raises questions of agency and audience: who tells, how, why, for whom? I will argue throughout this book that these questions are fundamentally similar for print and film narrative: who controls the construction of a diegesis, who moves across a fabula to piece together a specific syuzhet from its broader canvas, who shifts from one image to another, from one frame to the next, to shape a rhetoric for a viewer or reader? For Oudart, a single shot in film gets stitched to its subsequent piece of film in order to hide the gap between the shots and, more importantly, the emptiness behind the first shot; suture provides the illusion of plenitude to fill this emptiness that haunts the viewing subject. In Oudart's approach, the source of the first shot is always mysterious, in an imponderable Absent One; the suture to the second shot masks that absence and tames the terror it threatens.

Film theory after Miller and Oudart extends the neediness and passivity of the audience. In the work of Daniel Dayan and Kaja Silverman, suture provides lost and empty human consciousness with a source (for that first shot) and an implied compensatory (and illusory) narrative that are fundamentally ideological. Because suture in film editing is so closely connected to looking, gaze theory and gender came to play large roles in understanding the ways film seduces its audience, and suture theory is especially important in the history of feminist approaches to narrative film theory.

Chapter 2 then offers my alternative approach to suture, which argues for presence, not absence, in this narrative form, though never full presence or unproblematic presence. The primary theoretical source for this model is indeed the work of Merleau-Ponty, and my critique of the Lacanian paradigm for suture theory mirrors Merleau-Ponty's critique of Lacan. For Merleau-Ponty, who rejects Lacan's theory of the mirror stage, the child is always already embodied, with a presence prior to the fragmentation of the gaze that knits together at least in some degree its individual perceptions. This self is also not as supremely passive as the subject in classic suture theory, which, according to Silverman, is so needy it will pay almost any price for the consolations of suture. In contrast, this alternative approach returns to suture its intentionality, its "aboutness" that guides the scalpel of the surgeon, as in that account of his training by Atul Gawande with which I began. But this intentionality does not work simply or transcendentally; it is always mediated, and the best exploration of that mediation is the notion of chiasmus that Merleau-Ponty developed in his late work *The Visible and the Invisible*. Chiasmus expresses the form of "identity at a distance"; whether it is the body of the child before a mirror or film's stitching together of frames, especially in shot / reverse shot sequences, chiasmus is an image for the linkages *and* the separations, across a loop, of consciousnesses (*Visible* 139). Like shot / reverse shots, chiasmus is about intersubjectivity, and like suture chiasmus works along a continuum from elementary to deep, but is always oblique and incomplete, always partial.

The absence at the core of suture in the classic Lacanian theory was most visible, so to speak, in film narrative's shot / reverse shot sequences, a convention in continuity editing with many complex implications. For Oudart, this convention, properly understood, bared the wound of the Absent One, a figure who sabotages the dream of wholeness promised by narrative, at least film narrative. In the remainder of chapter 2, I develop a different reading of shot / reverse shot conventions in film editing. My first test cases are exemplary moments from Michael Roemer's 1964 classic film of African-American life, *Nothing But a Man*, in which I explore the presence, not absence, of subjectivity and subjectivities in deeply tangled versions and revisions of others and others' version of yet others. In a second test case, Jonathan Demme's *The Silence of the Lambs*, I explore the mystery of the oblique angle in shot / reverse shot sequences in order to uncover a core motivation for this narrative form of intersubjectivity. (The mystery at hand is the odd fact that almost all reverse shots in these sequences sit at an oblique angle to the previous shot, often emphasizing this angle by capturing at the edge of the frame a shoulder or the back of the head of the person watching the speaker; the sequence, in other words, does not use strictly eyeline matches swiveling at the endpoint of each character's gaze.) This classic example in suture theory—gazes meeting but not meeting gazes (of characters or viewers)—is in my argument exactly an account of intention, embodiment, presence (and terror, yes, sometimes), not castration, absence, or erasure. Finally, I initiate the argument that this oblique angle in shot / reverse shot editing points to another example of suture, in print narrative, the narrative practice called free indirect discourse (the strategy of writers since Austen, especially James and Joyce, for representing character thoughts in a intimately indirect way: not "He thought, 'I will love her,'" not "He thought he would love her," but "He would love her"). The argument claims, that is, that the obliqueness of shot / reverse shot editing mirrors the obliqueness of free indirect discourse, and that the obliqueness in both cases is about something important.

In chapter 3, my first case study examines a primary form of narrative suture, the embodied obliqueness of free indirect discourse, in key scenes in the work of the great master of free indirect discourse, Henry James. These scenes come from *The Wings of the Dove* and *The Golden Bowl,* with asides on *The Portrait of a Lady* and *What Maisie Knew*. Free indirect discourse in James dances through the same arabesques of approach and avoidance that occur in our film examples in chapter 2, with similar thematic payoffs. Desire and the gaze become labyrinths of deeply intersubjective intentionality; furthermore, the way these labyrinths explore human *failures* does not make the labyrinths any less deeply intersubjective. James measures with great delicacy layers of failure and degrees of opacity in human relationships, because failures differ greatly, and opacities can be more or less transparent. Furthermore, violation and aggression occur in complex moments of deep intimacy. Loss and failure still require James to unravel the way misperception of misperception builds on gestures and words circling, espousing, hiding, and sabotaging the other's gestures and words. James explores betrayal so stunningly in Maggie's mis-reading of the Prince's mis-reading of her, and in the Prince's of Maggie's, in *The Golden Bowl*, because their layerings of error and bad faith (not necessarily only the Prince's) get told through the obliquely sutured long shots of James's free indirect discourse.

Suture in both film and print narratives also requires a restoration of confidence in a narrating agency (if not a "narrator") and an addressee for the narrative, whether an implied or authorial reader or viewer, and chapters 2 and 3 make the case for restoring this confidence, against skeptics in narrative theory for both print and film. James's fiction makes the need for this confidence especially clear because of the extreme intricacy of the workings of human consciousnesses in these novels. And this intricacy, especially as constructed through free indirect discourse, requires the support of an authorizing agency. In a kind of backhanded way, J. Hillis Miller describes the need for this authorization for free indirect discourse because it is "so extraordinary a gift of language that it remains to some degree unfathomable." Part of its mysteriousness is the way "the narrator can place himself (or itself, since it is an impersonal agency) directly, without intermediary, within the consciousness, the feelings, the very body of a character and speak for that character's most intimate experience" (*Literature as Conduct* 166–67). But narrative theory has witnessed strong disagreements over the role of a narrator in free indirect discourse (FID). What is at stake is the nature of narrative agency: who (or what, to avoid personification) controls tone and rhetoric in these narrative labyrinths?

On one side of the ring are narrative theorists like Ann Banfield, who argues in *Unspeakable Sentences* that no enabling voice lies behind the multiple layers of free indirect discourse, in contrast to Daniel Gunn, who argues there is such a voice. For Banfield, sentences in FID express the self of the character, with no traceable source in the text's narrator. In contrast, Gunn makes the case that FID expresses two voices, with echoes of a narrator mimicking the rhetoric and imagery of one or more characters.[5] Banfield distances the narrator whom Gunn foregrounds, or at least brings forward from the shadows. In film narrative, the opponents are David Bordwell, who makes the case in *Narration in the Fiction Film* against a narrator in film (unless an explicit voice-over presence), in contrast to Seymour Chatman, who makes the case for such a narrating agency in *Coming to Terms*, and to Nick Browne, who made a similar case in an exemplary reading of John Ford's *Stagecoach*. My vote of confidence goes to Gunn and Chatman and Browne, and to the correlative claim for an implied or authorial reader or viewer ("authorial" in Peter Rabinowitz's sense), and I explain these votes, and why the choices really matter for reading subjectivities in narrative (Rabinowitz, *Before Reading* 21*ff.*). The final section of chapter 3 addresses versions of these issues of narrative authority and the oblique (indirect) angle in several key James films, especially films of the novels and scenes I have previously discussed. One especially interesting example will be the 1972 BBC version of *The Golden Bowl* and its complex use of Cyril Cusack's Bob Assingham as narrator.

---

5. For Gunn's argument, see "Free Indirect Discourse." Banfield's book is *Unspeakable Sentences*.

In chapter 4, I turn to different implications of suture as narrative form in a particular body of work, J. M. Barrie's Peter Pan stories that appeared in their original formats in the early twentieth century, and took on new life in important film versions more than fifty years later. I choose the Peter Pan corpus for this, the longest chapter in the book, because these texts explore suture theory's obliqueness in both print and film more fully than almost any other examples. This exploration occurs in a wonderful match of form and content as well. This case study follows an expansion of forms of indirection into what I call the ricochet effect. One explanation of this richness in the Peter Pan texts goes back to the roots of *suture*: the word begins with *sew*, the presence of whose root in the mists of Indo-European ur-languages leads to cognates in almost all western vocabularies, and its application to the body begins immediately, in the deeply resonant words of the OED's first definition: "the joining of the lips of a wound." The lips of wounds need to be sutured throughout the Peter Pan tales, in form and theme. (One reason my introduction leads off with the Plath poem is to underscore this link between form and theme, between suture, the body, and the edges of the wound that need to be sewn together.) The body is a mouth that speaks here, often in telling silences and gestures. In both Barrie's work (short story, play, novella) and the subsequent film interpretations, the narrative forms of suture explore the complex secrets of family and loss and then the evasions of those secrets that are the center of the Peter Pan narratives.

Specifically, free indirect discourse and shot / reverse shot editing both enunciate an "over the shoulder" stance for characters that Barrie's tales develop in remarkable ways. Eavesdropping among multiple narratees opens the door for Barrie's study of family, eros, and abandonment. Furthermore, free indirect discourse enables a special and stunning experience among Barrie's attending children and adults (inside and outside the diegesis). At its most serious, this experience, the ricochet effect, seems to target child listeners, with a result that Jacqueline Rose has famously argued was *"molestation"* of the children (70; emphasis in original). In Rose's view, Barrie arranges the chairs for his readers so that younger children will necessarily overhear the shaming and wounding commentary of his adult narrator (for Rose these are primarily flesh-and-blood children too young to read themselves). Even if "molesting" children did not quite mean in 1983 what it means in 2011, Rose raises the fundamental question about sutured narrative in Barrie: how deep intersubjectivity can work to expose, frighten, and wound, as well as enclose and protect vulnerable subjects.

Indeed, what *is* children's literature, a vexed subject of much recent theoretical work, and is *Peter Pan* in some fraught sense an example of it? A hint of the issues here lies in the title of an important book theorizing children's literature, Perry Nodelman's *The Hidden Adult*: perhaps an adult grasp of the wounds inflicted by family and eros is *not* hidden, deeply enough or at all, in the Peter Pan tales. A correlative, equally fraught question is, what is the role of the touch in *Peter Pan*? Our responses to the previous questions will guide our reflections on this one, and also our response to Rose's accusation. The issues are so difficult because touching is the paramount example of a phenomenological doubleness in *Peter Pan*: it (touching) is both a wound and a caress. Early in Barrie's play, Peter explains to Wendy that he doesn't have a mother, and when Wendy immediately tries to hug Peter, he pulls back and says, "You mustn't touch me," and Wendy replies, "No wonder you were crying" (98). From the beginning, Barrie links touching with both consolation and pain.

The missing touch of the mother is the fundamental loss in Barrie, and part of most lives for Barrie, so that he writes elsewhere, "To be born is to be wrecked upon an island" (preface to *The Coral Island* [1913]; Alton 380). A key possibility and fear in *Peter Pan* is that mothers by their nature abandon children. Touching, then, is loss and wound as well as the memory of a desire (not to be abandoned). Peter's response to this ambiguity appears in the doubleness of Barrie's own subtitles for the play: "The Boy Who Would Not Grow Up" or "The Boy Who Could Not Grow Up." Merleau-Ponty's image of the chiasmus becomes deeply and similarly ambiguous, measuring dream and loss as well as recovery and espousal. Although elements of the Barrie texts (especially the versions he licensed for schools) and the Pan films displace these ambiguities, traces of their trouble and rupture remain, perhaps most powerfully in the Disney film (1953), followed closely by P. J. Hogan's live-action version (2003). Since the Peter Pan stories are about eros and family, they provide useful examples—in print and film—of what is at stake in thinking about suture in its many forms in narrative.

My final case study, in chapter 5, turns to a more hopeful version of suture, to connections after rupture, to rebirth in the midst of death in film comedy, and to suture as chiasmus, now not Merleau-Ponty's image, but Jacques Derrida's figure for the paradox of the *pharmakos* that is both medicine and poison. However, because my final example is a film, *Raising Arizona,* which seems to subvert narrative conventions in a way that used to be called postmodern but perhaps now we can simply call

Derridean, suture's role will be appropriately oblique. To remember for a moment the uncertainties named by "postmodern" or "poststructuralist," I will choose Lyotard's focus on the absence of the grand narratives as master paradigms for a particular story.[6] In the case of comedy, the apparently absent meta-fiction is the story of the *komos*, the ancient Greek rite of the sacrifice of the scapegoat, the *pharmakos*, to exorcise death and permit the return of spring. The role of the *pharmakos*, as medicine and poison, was deeply ambiguous in classical Greece, and a certain "play" in the signifier is already at work. So linking Derrida and the *komos* of the Cambridge Ritualists emphasizes a kind of high-wire act of redemption.[7] I invoke important words in Derrida's writing in a couple of ways here: first, his notion of "play" from "Structure, Sign and Play in the Human Sciences," which outlines what elsewhere he calls language's "undecidability"; second, his meditation in "Plato's Pharmacy" on the different poles of meaning to *pharmakon/pharmakos*; and third, Derrida's specific use of chiasmus to "authorize," even "prescribe" (his words) this play (*Limited, Inc.* 148; "Plato's Pharmacy" 117, 127). In close readings of *Raising Arizona*'s shot / reverse shot language of chiasmus, the chapter echoes our beginning in Lacanian theory, to measure how far we've come, from the narrative of absence to a paradigmatic comedy, a story of wounds that might, against all doubts, be stitched together. Rene Girard's discussion of the role of the scapegoat will remind us how much suffering and loss this figure has permitted, and how difficult it can be even to conceive of the healing of communities.

Concluding on theory of comedy, on the role of suture in the *komos*, and using a film as fractured and self-aware as *Raising Arizona* as the example provide a new perspective on theories of suture. It is possible to admit (and even celebrate) the fissures and dislocations of the Lacanian model without accepting the assumptions behind that model. For me, its very gaps and dissonances underscore the richness and subtlety of a deep intersubjectivity modeled on the ambiguities *and* promises of Merleau-Ponty's chiasmus of embodiment. My three studies of indirection and obliqueness may come, as this book progresses, to represent fundamental strategies of stories about characters entangled with other characters in

---

6. For a good survey of the meanings (and confusions) of the term *postmodern*, see (again) Brian McHale (*Postmodernist Fiction* 4–5) and J. Hillis Miller's more recent overview (*Conflagration* 232).

7. See Cornford, part 1, and Butte, *I Know*, chapter 3, for more discussion of the *komos*. Linking Derrida and Cornford is new in theory of comedy and underscores the importance of the wounds of suture.

multiple layers of consciousness. If I am correct that "espousal," however mediated and imperfect, becomes more difficult in the last hundred years, then concluding on comedy, on *Raising Arizona* rather than, say, Bergman's *Scenes from a Marriage* (a cousin to *The Golden Bowl*), is a choice that gives the book a certain spin, one that may suit those contrarian readers with more hopeful temperaments.

The fundamental controversy here, as the epilogue says again, concerns the nature of communities and the role of alterity, of the other (or Other) and others. There has been at least a threefold debate across the history of phenomenological thought, from Hegel and Husserl to Ricoeur, Nancy, and Levinas: One, how does one lay to rest the specter of aloneness, of solipsism? Two, what is the power and presence of another, or others? And three, if consciousness is indeed embedded even if only in the edge of the other(s), what are the politics of such contingencies? One strategy, in Husserl and early Merleau-Ponty and Heidegger, is to resolve one and two together, by arguing from analogy: the other has a hand, an eye, as I do, and so the comparison gives me access to some kind of knowledge of the other. A good example of the conversation over this move is Paul Ricoeur's response to Husserl, over "the decisive theme: the analogical grasping of the Other as another ego" by means of the body. Ricoeur asks, "Is this the squaring of the circle?" And replies, "But recourse to analogy creates as many problems as it solves" (*Husserl* 124–26). And then Levinas rejects the usefulness of the analogy with equal vigor; it cannot do the work of an effective bridge. Ricoeur, with a nice even-handedness, writes that Levinas's rejection of the analogical argument "employs even greater hyperbole, to the point of paroxysm" (*Oneself* 338).

The argument is profound because the yearning for a transcendental link to the other, to or toward community, recurs throughout the phenomenological tradition. Most current phenomenology accepts the failure of Husserl's ambition to clarify a transcendental connection between selves, or as Paul Armstrong writes in *The Johns Hopkins Guide to Literary Theory and Criticism*, "Contemporary phenomenology has for the most part abandoned Husserl's dream of finding indubitable foundations for knowledge" ("Phenomenology" 734), including knowledge of the other. But reminders of this idealism do surface in influential writers like Georges Poulet and the early J. Hillis Miller, and suspicions of its possible revival recur, as in Derrida's late meditations on Merleau-Ponty and Nancy in *On Touching* (2005) (see chapter 5 and the epilogue). Even as subtle a phenomenologist as Paul Armstrong, whom I just cited, can fall into the old binary when he talks about reading (in this case, the reading of flesh-and-blood readers) as oscillating between "self-transcendence" and "solipsism" because "reading is both an intersubjective and a solipsistic process" (*Challenge* 217). The transcendence Armstrong talks about is fleeting, but it still demonstrates how Husserlian ambition can haunt phenomenology.

Merleau-Ponty incorporates both tendencies—the transcendental and the skeptical—in his work: an early text like *The Phenomenology of Perception* (1944) can use language like this: "Transcendental subjectivity is a revealed subjectivity, revealed to itself and to others, and is for that reason an intersubjectivity" (361). This language surely echoes an important phrase—"transcendental intersubjectivity"—from *Cartesian Meditations* by Husserl (150), Merleau-Ponty's implied interlocutor often in his writing, and indicates his sometimes closeness to his predecessor. But the later Merleau-Ponty of *The Visible and the Invisible* does not use such language. Consciousnesses interconnect by means of "thick" threads without transcendental revelation, but in bodies that also mitigate their aloneness (*Visible* 264). From this debate about others stem all of the issues of this book, about stories that incorporate and suture bodies and multiple consciousnesses in a dazzling array of paradigms. This book will reason primarily from the framework of Merleau-Ponty's later writing and its elaboration of intersubjectivity as embedded and embodied. My intent is not to write a broader phenomenology of narrative. But I will engage in a conversation at appropriate moments with other voices, both those of the earlier Merleau-Ponty and of other phenomenological theorists, to complicate and also clarify these paradigms of suture.

As in *I Know That You Know That I Know*, my aim here is not to make claims about what is really true for consciousness or intersubjectivities, although I make use of writers who make such claims. My aim is to use their claims, their models, even their images or metaphors (such as "chiasmus" in Merleau-Ponty and Derrida), to suggest new depths to narratives. These claims and images are a means to an end. Of course, the claims about what is true by writers like Heidegger and Ricoeur and Goffman are often passionate, and I do not regret the spillover from these passions as we discuss *The Golden Bowl* or *Peter and Wendy*. What is at stake here, as J. Hillis Miller will suggest at the end of the book, is very serious, and not simply a rhetorical or structural topic (which is not to say those topics are not serious). My ideal readers are people who will work through the film theory, the phenomenology, and the narratology, keeping their eye on the light at the end of the tunnel (but enjoying the journey). One payoff is the series of close readings, some extended, that comprise a significant portion of this study.

The method here is to mine film theory and phenomenology for some approaches that will be helpful for narrative theory and can provide deeper understanding of some really good stories in print and in film. The organizing principle is an image stolen from film theory (suture). If this argument works, and the sample readings as well, then the notion of suture will be useful beyond these examples and beyond its early appearance in Jacques-Alain Miller and Jean-Pierre Oudart and French film theory, which is where we begin.

CHAPTER 2

Suture and the Narration of Experience

Suture first appeared as a significant concept in thinking about narrative about fifty years ago, in Lacanian film theory of the late 1960s. I want to raid that work and seize its image to adapt it to a new approach to the narration of human experience in both film and print narrative. Despite the limitations of its early use, suture from the beginning was an image to describe the representation of consciousness in narration in montage, and so the idea contains the seeds of possibilities beyond the Lacanian, and also beyond film. In this chapter, I want to accomplish four tasks: first, identify shortcomings in classical suture theory's approach to film's narration of subjectivity; second, offer a new model for a phenomenology of suture and narration; third, apply that model to two paradigmatic sequences from Michael Roemer's film about African-American life, *Nothing But a Man* (1964); and fourth, extend this model to address the mystery of the oblique angle in shot / reverse shot sequences, with close reading of test cases, especially from *The Silence of the Lambs* (1991). This theory of the oblique angle prepares for the argument that suture also functions in print fiction in the form of free indirect discourse, an idea I develop in the following chapter on Henry James. These arguments then provide the foundation for my larger claims about forms of obliqueness and indirection in suture.

i. SUTURE THEORY: THE ORIGINS IN FILM THEORY

Suture has been a significant topic in meditations on the representation of subjectivity in film narrative; the process of editing, of stitching together pieces of film, became, in the hands of these theorists, more than simply a device of continuity editing—that is, more than a subset of conventional editing strategies for telling stories efficiently in film time and space. Instead, suture theory came to presume and frame an ontology of the human subject. Classical suture theory needs rethinking, as I wrote in chapter 1, because its widely influential view of subjectivity and narrative in film is significantly misguided. My alternative approach to suture begins with an observation about what is missing from most writing about suture in film narrative: the cut, the wound; the body and its blood. The image of suture in medicine calls attention to the fullness of bodies practicing and practiced upon, to embodied consciousnesses acting and reacting in a web of relation that only begins with the blade, the taut skin, the "plush" red blood in Sylvia Plath's poem, and the institutions of discipline and licensure represented in Atul Gawande's supervising surgeon, in the examples that opened chapter 1. Suture implies a narrative of embodied subjectivities that *intend*; this is a narrative of intervention, and almost always of the interventions of several consciousnesses, in what Maurice Merleau-Ponty called a chiasmus, an interweaving of bodies and subjectivities. To understand the importance of this embodiment and intentionality, we need to return to our starting point, classical suture theory and its theory of lack.

The story of the idea of suture in film narrative, in the powerful and influential series of writings than began in the 1960s, has been a story of absence and evasion. I will begin with Jean-Pierre Oudart because he first used a notion of suture to explore the nature of film narrative, in a pair of essays in *Cahiers du Cinema* in 1969. His idea of suture, however, as a gap in discourse, draws explicitly from Jacques-Alain Miller's article "La Suture (elements de la logique du significant)" presented to Lacan's seminar on February 24, 1965, so in another sense Miller is the beginning (J.-A. Miller 23). Because the publication of Oudart's articles in 1969 became a seminal event in several stories, each with a different dominant theme, I have a multiply plotted tale to tell with crisscrossing threads that will resemble a screenplay by Quentin Tarantino or Alejandro Inarritu. One story thread tracks the theme of discourse in Lacanian thought as it influences film theory; it reaches back to the Miller article that Oudart cites, and continues in Stephen Heath's expansion of Oudart's idea of suture, with ripples throughout feminist film criticism in writers like Laura Mulvey (1975) and Linda Williams (2004). The second plot strand recounts the emergence of suture theory in English, with its interpellation of Althusser and ideology; this story line begins with Daniel

Dayan's widely read essay in *Film Quarterly* (Fall 1974), the first text in Anglo-American film theory to draw attention to Oudart's work, even before it had been translated into English. Dayan took an important and influential step, to argue an ideological function for the gap in discourse that Lacanian analysis saw suture as mystifying. Dayan's essay provoked an important response from William Rothman in *Film Quarterly* in 1975, and another critique by Benjamin Salt, also in *Film Quarterly,* in 1977. Subsequently in 1978 *Screen* collected translations of Miller's 1965 essay and Oudart's 1969 articles and added the response to both by Stephen Heath. In the years since 1978, this canon of core articulations has gathered a large body of commentary, including "friendly" extensions, such as those by feminist critics Kaja Silverman (1983) and Judith Halberstam (2001), who followed Dayan's Althusserian lead. This canon has also accumulated critiques of its fundamental assumptions—especially of its ideology of ideology, and its psychoanalytically inflected notion of passive spectatorship—by writers like David Bordwell (1985) and Noel Carroll (1996). Silverman tells the first chapters of these stories, from Miller to Heath, elegantly and extensively in *The Subject of Semiotics* (chapter 5).

A third narrative would situate Oudart's study of suture, and its particular example of shot / reverse shot edits, within a history of theorizing about montage, from Eisenstein to Bazin. One relevant example of Eisenstein's approach is his 1929 essay "Beyond the Shot" and his argument with the "Kuleshov school" over its view that a montage of shots is a "series . . . in a chain," in contrast to Eisenstein's notion of "montage as a *collision* . . . of two factors [that] gives rise to an idea" (87). The Kuleshov effect, with its argument about viewers connecting visual fields, bears an uncanny resemblance to Oudart's notion of looking at, or mislooking at, the Absent One.[1] An appropriate example of Bazin's thought is his identification of "shot-reverse-shot" as a "characteristic procedure" of pre-1940 films that "the shot in depth introduced by Orson Welles and William Wyler" challenged (33). Bazin's dislike, expressed in the same essay, for "chopping the world up into little fragments" provides a

---

1. Since I discuss the Kuleshov effect in section ii of this chapter, a brief definition is in order: The famous experiment intercut a shot of the same neutral face with different objects in an eyeline match, so that the resulting strips of film presented the same face looking at a baby, a coffin, for example, or a meal. When these different strips of film were exhibited to various audiences, they interpreted that face as happy, sad, or hungry. The Kuleshov effect has become shorthand for the notion that editing creates interpretations.

proleptic gloss on the issues of suture: should film narrative, as it cuts and juxtaposes pieces of film, emphasize fragments or larger wholes (38)?

Yet a fourth narrative might emphasize the phenomenological elements in Oudart that, before the articulation of reception theory in the 1970s and 1980s, began to speculate on the construction of consciousness in film. It does not occur to Oudart to distinguish between implied and real or flesh-and-blood viewers, for example, so that some of his analysis of spectatorship is confusing, a little premodern, so to speak, to our ears. Oudart's analysis of the phenomenology of watching explicitly describes the experience of flesh-and-blood viewers: "the spectator experiences with vertiginous delight . . . : he is at the cinema"; or in this example: "the spectator recuperates his difference, an operation by which he is himself placed outside the frame" (41, 45). Yet Oudart's account of experiencing gaps in film also focuses on that spectator's "mode of participation," on the conventions by which "the spectator's imagination" functions inside the text (41). Even though the spectator of interest to classic suture theorists was primarily the flesh-and-blood spectator, Oudart's essay opens the door for a study of the structures of consciousness *within* a text as well as a study of the structures of consciousness reading or viewing the text in the extrinsic world.[2]

Oudart's essay is incomplete because it never provides a taxonomy of "the variations of angle" of the camera and the gaze that they construct, whether intrinsic or extrinsic (39). The essay does not do so partly because Oudart's goal is not systematic in a narratological way. Nonetheless, his keen eye for structures of consciousness represented in film narrative adds important angles to Merleau-Ponty's understanding of intersubjectivity that frames much of this book. As I seek to rewrite suture theory, I will return to these four threads to explore missteps along the way, and also to acknowledge promising elements in earlier texts.

From the first, Oudart theorized suture as a narrative device in film that promoted an illusion that comforted spectators by closing a gap in their experience of film's space and narrativity. The nature of the gap, the nature of the illusion, and the nature of the comfort varied among writers

---

2. The distinction between implied and real viewers matters in my argument because, as will become clearer later, I take the position that film narrative, like other narratives, constructs an implied viewer. Later I use Peter Rabinowitz's term "authorial audience," which is similar to Iser's older term "implied reader" (or viewer) for the reception that a text's conventions seem to assume (Rabinowitz, *Before Reading* 21–29). Iser's "implied reader" lumps together several reader functions that Rabinowitz teases out more subtly.

following Oudart along this first, the Lacanian, pathway, but the interest in gaps and their mystification remained largely constant. For Oudart, who begins with a phenomenological study of montage, it is the shot / reverse shot chain that reveals how suture forms subjectivity in film narrative, because any visual field in a film frame implies a consciousness from which it could arise: "every filmic field is echoed by an absent field, the place of a character who is put there by the viewer's imaginary, and which we shall call the Absent One" (36). This "representation," however, is "burdened with a lack—the lack of someone," and so for Oudart, the logic of the shot sequence is to provide, in the second shot, a comforting source for what the screen sees in the first shot: "suture" is "the abolition of the Absent One and its resurrection in someone" (38, 37). Or, as Daniel Dayan later rephrased the notion, "the reverse shot has 'sutured' the hole opened in the spectator's imaginary relationship with the filmic field by his perception of the absent-one" (30). So in *Vertigo*, Hitchcock's camera does not simply record Madeleine's odyssey driving through San Francisco's streets; lest the gaze become unmoored, "decentered" (in Oudart's word), Hitchcock frames Madeleine's Jaguar specifically inside another car window, and consistently returns to Scottie's hands and face to "resurrect" the consciousness that owns this visual field (38).

William Rothman then replied to Dayan that this model ignores the common practice of beginning these sequences with a *prior* establishing shot that banishes absence before it is suggested: "in fact the point-of-view shot is ordinarily (that is to say: *always*, except in special cases) part of a three-shot (viewer/view/viewer) sequence" (46). In the essay that probably represents the high-water mark in suture's colonization of film form, Stephen Heath replied that Rothman's correct observations do not "render the concept of suture . . . no longer pertinent; rather, they suggest a necessary displacement" of suture into other film functions (66). Heath's argument is that Rothman, like Barry Salt (see footnote 5 in this chapter), "narrows the field of debate" by referring to a "very strictly defined point-of-view shot succession," as if the ontological absence at the core of film narrative could be erased by that extra establishing shot, and so (says Heath) Rothman misses the point. Suture is really about much more than shot / reverse shot cutting; suture functions in a "multiplicity" of "layerings and times and advances" (of which shot / reverse shot sequences are only one example), and the deeper function of suture is to articulate "the organization and hold of the look and looks in film" (66–67).

However untenable were some of Heath's larger claims for suture, he was correct that Oudart survived Rothman. The power of the idea of absence in Oudart's model of gazing at gazing was irresistible. Despite the accuracy of Rothman's observations about an establishing shot before the first perspective shot, Oudart's notion of absence as prior to any narrative origin for a strip of film remains important because Oudart's idea reflects an attractive ontology of the self that his essay cites from Jacques-Alain Miller's reflections on suture. Miller seeks to extend Lacan's thought, in which suture "stitches over," so to speak, the subject's experience of absence (of many kinds, but particularly the subject's experience of exclusion from the very discourse that forms its illusions of selfhood). One of Miller's images is especially analogous to Oudart's use of the reverse shot: it ("the o member of the series" of numbers) is "the standing-in-place" in that series of signifiers (again, numbers, in Miller's own example), which "suture[s] the absence (of the absolute zero)." For Miller, "the restored relation of the zero to the series of numbers" figures "the subject's relation to the signifying chain." But the restoration is fragile and temporary; suture confesses the truth of the subject's position, which is "its exclusion from the discourse which internally it intimates" (32). Suture has become a figure of absence.

The evasion this account identifies is deep and pervasive: the reverse shot of the gazer (Scottie at his steering wheel in *Vertigo*) sutures over that profound wound in our being, the absence of the truly Absent One (the "absolute zero," in Jacques-Alain Miller's terms), a shadowy Observer for whose gaze we need a safe, diegetic source: suture, in other words, provides to film spectators the illusion of an origin of what they see. Film's construction of seeing (and by implication narrative's construction of seeing) needs to be naturalized. More importantly, the construction of seeing seeing needs to be naturalized. The project, in Dayan and those who follow him in the subplot of interpellation, is to mislead the passive film viewer (implied or flesh and blood). This understanding of the gap in Oudart leads Dayan to predict only "entrapment" for the interpellated viewer (27). Dayan explains this effect further: "Unable to see the workings of the code, the spectator is at its mercy. His imaginary is sealed into the film; the spectator thus absorbs an ideological effect without being aware of it" (30). Kaja Silverman turns the screw even more subtly on that viewer:

> Suture can be understood as the process whereby the inadequacy of the [viewing] subject's position is exposed in order to create the desire for new insertions into a cultural discourse which promises to make good that lack.... The viewing subject's position is a supremely passive one,

> a fact which is carefully concealed through cinematic sleight-of-hand. (231–32)

This intense promotion of the viewer as "supremely passive" in Dayan and Silverman provokes some of the strongest and most effective criticism of their account of suture in writers like David Bordwell and Noel Carroll, who believe that viewers can be, and usually are, deeply active. In rare cases, Silverman admits, films like *Psycho* and *Lola Montes* defamiliarize the deceptions of suture. *Psycho* is an especially poignant example, from its opening relentless zoom shot (with no reverse shot to locate its origin) to the loss of Marion's gaze and the viewers' forced relocation to Norman:

> What *Psycho* forces us to understand is that we want suture so badly we'll take it at any price, even with the fullest knowledge of what it entails—passive insertions into pre-existing discursive positions (both mythically potent and mythically impotent); threatened losses and false recoveries; and subordination to the castrating gaze of a symbolic Other. (212–13)

But *Psycho* is the exception. Normally film's "multiple cuts" produce not only a plenitude that is illusory but a "castrating coherence" that violates again the already abused subject (205).

Even Oudart believed his viewer was "burdened with a lack" when experiencing a shot, a visual field, with no source (38). Consequently, that viewer will yearn for the resurrection of the Absent One in order to escape the "real terrorism of the sign," experienced when "signification actually penetrates the spectator as a sovereign speech" (43). Denied this resurrection, Oudart's viewer must settle for the reverse shot that identifies a source for that shot within the film's diegesis. Silverman's subjects, however, face a much bleaker outlook. For her, the film viewer is twice a victim. First, the viewers' "inadequacy"—that lack at the core of all identity—gets exposed in order to stimulate a desire for compensation, for repair of the self, and then the narrative product for sale conveniently turns up promising what is hopeless, to "make good that lack." For the viewer who yearns for wholeness, this promised but hollow plenitude is another betrayal: hence it is in Silverman's eyes paradoxically that "castrating coherence." To extend the Lacanian theme that gaps call for sutures that only emphasize the ironies of absence, in Miller the logic of suture is "the logic of the signifier, a displacement whose effect is the emergence of signification" (33). The signifier is another gap, whose suturing is always already too late.

To turn the screw a final time: because the logic of suture includes the displacement effect of signification, one of those effects is "the consciousness of the subject, [which] is to be situated on the level of the effects of signification" (33). That is, consciousness is another example of a displaced signified. So a reader like Judith Halberstam can approach the complexities of transgendered identities in the film *Boys Don't Cry* (2001) as an example of destabilized subjectivities constructed by conventions like shot / reverse shot cutting. "The inadequacy of the [transgendered] subject's position" is "a precondition of the narrative," an inadequacy that Halberstam, citing Silverman, finds enunciated by suture: in one example, "this shot/reverse shot involving the two Brandons now serves both to destabilize the spectator's sense of gender stability and also to confirm Brandon's manhood at the very moment that he has been exposed as female/castrated" (296). Halberstam's reading of subjectivity illustrates the staying power of classical suture theory. In this logic of suture, subject positions—that is, human consciousnesses—have become an effect of an effect of a displacement of an absence.

The configuration of the absence varies from Oudart and Dayan to Heath, or Silverman. But I want to emphasize here a common thread in these classic suture theorists, of suture as an *evasion* of their experience of absence offered to film characters, implied viewers, and particularly to real-world film spectators. Because that absence, that abyss, is so disturbing, film characters and viewers fasten desperately on these deceptive consolations: on the "tricks" of editing especially by which "the cinematographic level fools the spectator" (Dayan 30, 31). For those who are not fooled, suture is then about the interpellation of subjects into film narrative and its "discourse without an origin," and for Dayan and Silverman, true to their Althusserian roots, of subjects into ideology (Dayan 31).

Criticism of this understanding of suture began to surface in the 1980s. Much of this dissent concentrated on the extensive debt of classic suture theorists to Lacanian psychoanalysis; this debt led them to read actual audience response as a "repression" of "ghostly operations in the spectator's unconscious" (Carroll, *Theorizing* 414–15). In contrast, writers like Noel Carroll and David Bordwell suggested other models for audience experience for which no resort to psychoanalysis was necessary. Instead, "our normal experience of films" gives viewers "certain strategies for comprehending a shot chain, not only in virtue of familiarity with films, but also perhaps even more importantly, on the basis of knowledge of a broader culture that employs narrative, simile and metaphor in ways that can be mimed in editing" (Carroll, *Theorizing* 415). For David Bordwell, his "Constructivist" model of perception sees viewers as "already 'tuned,' prepared to test spatial, temporal and 'logical' schemata against what the shot represents"; again, no recourse to psychoanalysis is necessary to explain how viewers understand a shot chain (Bordwell, *Narration* 112).

Oudart's suture becomes for Bordwell a useful if somewhat murky early effort to map film spectators' cognition of space in film texts. Bordwell stresses each shot in Oudart not as a "*point of vision*, only as an offscreen *field or zone*"; Bordwell's imagery for the importance of this sequence is not phenomenological, but topological (not vision, but field or zone). The purpose of this sequence is cognitive: "Oudart wants to prove that this backing-and-filling movement, this process of stitching across a gap, helps narration construct space" (Bordwell, *Narration* 111). As a corollary, Oudart's method "plays down narration" because in the shot / reverse shot sequence, "there is no place for the narrator to hide," and with no "phantom narrator," there is no "invisible-observer account whereby the camera is the eye of an observer" (Bordwell, *Narration* 111). Bordwell sees in Oudart support for his project to erase narrators from cinema narrative.[3] In contrast, my own reading of Oudart will find in his examples a model for a layering of consciousnesses in film that supports a return to the idea of narrators in film (in contrast to Bordwell's project), and also to the idea of implied viewers (in contrast to the focus on real audiences in classical suture theory).[4] In order to model spectator activity better, Bordwell later added to his "principles of cognitive psychology" another explanatory matrix, "rational-agent social theory" in his model for a "constructivist theory of interpretation" (Bordwell, *Making Meaning* xiv). Despite Bordwell's cognitive use of Oudart, he recognizes in a backhanded kind of way the phenomenological complexity of Oudart's early study of multiple frames that record multiple looks in film. For my part, I acknowledge in Oudart a suggestion of the nested frames

---

3. For more on the return of the narrator in film, see page 46 and footnote 14 below.

4. In theory, the insights about spectators in both classical suture and cognitive models can apply to implied viewers, but in practice, both approaches concentrate on flesh-and-blood spectators, at a cost, especially in classical suture theory: a focus on real effects on flesh-and-blood viewers in the real world distracted suture theory from attending to the phenomenological and formal complexity of narrative texts.

of consciousnesses responding to consciousnesses in narrative that I call deep intersubjectivity (see Butte, chapter 1).

The differences between Bordwell and Carroll on the one side and Oudart on the other are in part differences in the work they seek to do: their projects and their foundational logics reflect deeply different topics and kinds of evidence. Bordwell praises Oudart's work as "a start toward characterizing the viewing activities that the spectator often engages in— anticipation, recollection and recognition of the spaces which narration represents" (Bordwell, *Narration* 111). But Oudart's project is not systematically narratological, nor is it cognitive in Bordwell's topological sense. That is, it does not seek to outline a series of activities and processes in a carefully reasoned taxonomy. It is also not about space and protocols for making sense of it by viewers; it is about layers of experience. Alongside Oudart's interest in Lacanian discourse and the defamiliarization of signifiers, his other fundamental purpose is phenomenological, to describe layers of consciousness, initially as presented inside a story, and then also, more clumsily and with more ontological apparatus, outside the story. Bordwell, Carroll, and Barry Salt sought outcomes from Oudart's account of experience in and of film that it was never designed to provide.[5] Dayan and Silverman and other Althusserian students of film as ideology have also misread, or underread Oudart, seizing on the Lacanian threads in his essays at the expense of their phenomenological richness.

I wish to dissent from the model of suture as absence, but my dissent does not emerge from cognitive psychology's reading of readers (or spectators) as in Bordwell, Carroll, or Salt, or from their expectations of a narratological poetics in Oudart. Instead I want to restore the body and its consciousness to suture by way of a phenomenological understanding of narrative linked to Merleau-Ponty's early reflections on film (that anticipate his critique of Lacan), and to his late notions of chiasmus. Along the way, this approach will acknowledge certain similar elements in Oudart as well. Something else, however, is missing in classical suture theory: a full respect for and attention to the narrative text (and here my criticism shares common ground with Bordwell, Carroll, and Salt, who also wanted to study the body of the story closely). Suture theory came to be about the phenomenology of film spectatorship in flesh-and-blood audiences. In virtually every instance, an account of experience represented by

---

5. Salt surveyed a sampling of films from the 1930s and 1940s and produced a chart with percentages of angled shot / reverse shot sequences. He concluded that these shot chains are a small number of total shot transitions in mainstream films and do not require much study (50).

suture inside film narrative slips quickly into an account of the experience of the film's real-world spectator that serves to illustrate some angle of psychoanalytic film theory as a theory of reception.

As a result, suture theory abdicated its opportunity to contribute to a poetics of film narrative, as it could well have done, even from its Lacanian foundation. For example, when Dayan discusses Lacanian "psychoanalysis [as] a theory of intersubjectivity," and wants to see film as a "tutor-code" for ideological formation, the intersubjective linkage he maps occurs from screen to audience, not within the film narrative. For Dayan, the payoff to suture theory is an understanding of what happens in the cinema audience, not in the film narrative: "falling under the control of the cinematographic system, the spectator loses access to the present" (31). For critics like Bordwell, Carroll, and me, such ideologically driven psychoanalytic theories of reception are abstract and tendentious, as well as rhetorically naïve in practice (no students of Wayne Booth hereabouts). Suture theorists had turned away from a poetics of film narrative, and at the same time came to seem irrelevant in their work on extrinsic reception. In the words of Robert Burgoyne, "the analytic category of the audience, with its concrete historical and contextual dimensions, has in large part replaced the psychoanalytic category of the spectator in current theory" (Stam, Burgoyne, and Flitterman-Lewis 86).[6] These words from 1992 are still true. The study of real-world audiences and spectators has fallen to cultural studies scholars, for whom empirical and archival research are the route to understanding flesh-and-blood readers, and narratological work has never returned to suture.[7] As one sign of which way the wind is blowing, the sixth edition of the canonical anthology *Film Theory and Criticism,* published by Oxford in 2004, dropped two of the three suture essays (deleting Rothman and Silverman, retaining Dayan) that it had published since at least 1992.

The move from a focus on film narrative to its effects on real-world spectators in suture theorists was unfortunate, because it disabled a useful set of questions and analytic tools that can help us think about what often is at stake in film narrative: how it represents the formation of human subjectivities (including, yes, a film's flesh-and-blood spectators as well as its implied viewers). Oudart's essays themselves enact the movement away from the text, but only after significant analysis of consciousnesses

---

6. See page iv for identification of the author (Burgoyne) of this quotation.

7. An example of the study of real audiences is Jackie Stacey's *Star Gazing: Hollywood Cinema and Female Spectatorship,* which tellingly is dedicated to "all women who wrote to me with their memories of Hollywood stars of the 1940's and 1950's" (v).

represented within a text. It has been easy to overlook the intersubjective implication of famous Oudart's formulation: "Every filmic field is echoed by an absent field, the place of a character who is put there by the viewer's imaginary, and which we shall call the Absent One" (Oudart 36). Although Oudart becomes most interested in the inner life of his spectator in the theater, he still begins by noticing the construction of an intrinsic subjectivity—"a character"—as source of the first "filmic field." Furthermore, the logic of the second shot (even if it is the third, as Rothman says) does not erase this first subjectivity represented in a text, but to the contrary multiplies subjectivities.

Oudart's focus on the spectator's experience of emptiness does not erase these representations. Neither does Dayan's and Silverman's analysis of narrative as ideology. Since like Seymour Chatman I want to reclaim an implied narrating agency for these shots, and will assume an implied spectator inside the text also, I will argue in section ii below that the result of these shot sequences is not a suturing of absence, but a suturing of presences.[8]

ii. REVISING SUTURE THEORY: MERLEAU-PONTY AND DEEP INTERSUBJECTIVITY

In this project to recover what was always already implicit in the image but denied by theorists, suture now is a narrative of embodied consciousnesses in scenarios of cutting and stitching and sometimes loss and sometimes healing. This model will return to suture those implications, originating in medical practice, of "aboutness," of intentionality and intersections in the world. That "aboutness" will surprise those for

---

8. My own interest in intersubjectivities in narrative concentrates on the formal dimensions of the text, including its cues for its authorial audience *inside* a film's diegesis. "Intersubjectivity" certainly can also include links to real-world audiences, from particularly gendered or ethnically identified or competent and informed audiences to other audience groups whom empirical study can learn much about, and who are necessary to create the narrative that otherwise is only a signal. I am not writing a broader phenomenology of reading of the kind that Paul Armstrong offers in *Play and the Politics of Reading*. Armstrong proposes a model for the reading by flesh-and-blood persons that can "mediat[e] epistemological, cultural, and social differences" in a process of dialogue as a kind of "play" (from Hans Georg Gadamer's "spiel") (21). For Armstrong, reading's "nonconsensual reciprocity" can become a kind of paradigm for effective liberal education (175–92). However, thoughts about these kinds of "flesh-and-blood" intersubjectivities lie outside the scope of this book.

whom phenomenology wears the aura of idealism.⁹ But a phenomenology of suture in the tradition of Merleau-Ponty need not be essentialist or transcendental, as Laura Doyle has argued. Doyle acknowledges the traditional accusation that the phenomenology of Husserl, for example, presumes a deeply ideological "transcendental subject," enabled by naturalized class, gender, and racial privileges (Doyle xvii–xviii). Such an idealist phenomenology would not provide a useful antidote to the drama of Lacanian absence; suture as an idealist narratological strategy would trade one emptiness (of the Lacanian signifier) for another (the transcendentally Human). In contrast, Doyle offers her claim for a politically intelligent phenomenology that seeks to "name . . . how it is that we live a not-at-all simple coexistence with others, an involuted resistance to and with ourselves and others, a knowing of, against, and through others" and yet "does not merely recolonize the world in the image of those who can afford to dream of their own harmony with it" (xxv). Doyle's own example in her book illustrates such a "knowing of, against, and through others" by way of tales of terrorized consciousnesses in prison narratives, where, for example, she explains how "witnessing" is "an intersubjective, intercorporeal form of involuntary agency" (96).

---

9. *Phenomenology* is a word that has often suggested various transcendental idealisms about human consciousness: the notion that identity expresses itself transparently in various signifiers and texts, or that identity's essence transcends class, gender, and ethnicity, or that intersubjectivity is not problematic because minds can grasp directly the experiences of other selves. A similar idealism has seemed to tarnish what I call first-wave phenomenological narrative readings, in, for example, Georges Poulet (who claimed that "because of the strange invasion of my person" that occurs when he reads, "I am the subject of thoughts other than my own" [59]) and in J. Hillis Miller's works of the 1950s and 1960s, like *The Disappearance of God* (1963). My framework grows out of Merleau-Ponty's critique of such transcendental phenomenology, which nonetheless seeks to describe a deeply embodied intersubjectivity. See Butte, chapter 1, for a review of these issues, and for more on "deep intersubjectivity" and my effort to read narrative by way of a phenomenology neither transcendental nor Derridean, but still attentive to poststructuralist critiques.

Two prior efforts in this direction deserve mention: Vivian Sobchack's *The Address of the Eye: A Phenomenology of Film Experience* (1992), which, despite its thoughtful readings of Merleau-Ponty, is somewhat compromised by a Husserlian idealism, and Wheeler Winston Dixon's *It Looks At You: The Returned Gaze of Cinema* (1995), which is not. A recent study, *Cinematic Interfaces: Film Theory After New Media* (2013), by Seung-Hoon Jeong, offers an extensive theory of suture as dis/connection in the tradition of Lacan/Silverman (the spectator is relatively passive: "film as a whole is nothing but a fantasy that constitutes the spectator as a desiring subject") and Sobchack's phenomenology (film establishes "a congruency between diegetic and extradiegetic subjects") (49).

Like Doyle, I promote a phenomenological strategy, in this case toward a poetics of narrative in film and also in print, that is neither entirely contingent nor transcendental. Ideology still matters in this model, and interpellation still occurs—Dayan and Silverman were not entirely wrong—but in an interworld of consciousnesses that are by no means "supremely passive," to repeat Silverman's words (232). Oudart's essays themselves offer a rich vein of phenomenological observations that in fact turn away from absence and the passive. Particularly important is his emphasis on the necessary obliqueness of camera angles for the suturing of deeply intersubjective consciousnesses in film narrative (37, 39, 45). That obliqueness will be fundamental in redirecting our thinking toward what really matters about suture, the narration of intersubjectivity in all its rhetorical and ideological complexity.

What, then, would it mean to consider film's narration of human consciousnesses by way of the devices of suture? Two different yet complementary notions from Merleau-Ponty suggest how we could frame suture's narration of subjectivities. The first notion, or cluster of notions, occurs in his 1948 essay on film, in which he claims (in an eerie anticipation of Stanley Cavell) that film is a natural topic for philosophical reflection.[10] The key thread in "The Film and the New Psychology" is the wholeness, simultaneity, and relatedness of human perceptions. Merleau-Ponty's first illustration of this relatedness comes not from film, but from everyday experience: "A sick person contemplating the wallpaper in his room will suddenly see it transformed if the pattern and figure become the ground while what is usually seen as ground becomes the figure" ("Film" 48). His conclusion: "Such a perception of the whole is more natural and more primary than the perception of isolated elements" ("Film" 49). Merleau-Ponty's major example of this principle is the experiments in editing that we usually attribute to Lev Kuleshov (but Merleau-Ponty attributes to Pudovkin): "the meaning of the shot depends on what precedes it in the movie, and the succession of scenes creates a new reality which is not merely the sum of its parts" ("Film" 54–55). Merleau-Ponty then recalls a sequence from the film *Broadway Melody* in which two actors onstage address first their audience, in a medium shot, and then each other, sotto voce, in a close-up. He concludes from this example of the Kuleshov effect, "The expressive force of this montage lies in its

---

10. For Cavell's claim that film and philosophical interrogation are natural companions, see books like *The World Viewed: Reflections on the Ontology of Film* (1979) and *Pursuits of Happiness: The Hollywood Comedy of Remarriage* (1981).

ability to make us sense the coexistence, the simultaneity of lives in the same world" ("Film" 55). And so, for Merleau-Ponty, film understands "the common feature of presenting consciousness thrown into the world" ("Film" 58).

This conception of montage, achieved of course by suturing strips of film together, helps Merleau-Ponty explain a notion of human consciousness and intersubjectivity that anticipates his critique of the mirror-stage in Lacan's thought.[11] Since classic suture theory owes much to a version of Lacan, this critique will clarify what is different in the idea of suture I am offering. Here is one fragment from Merleau-Ponty's restatement of Lacan's notion of the mirror-stage, in the essay "The Child's Relation with Others."

> To use Dr. Lacan's terms, I am "captured, caught up" by my spatial image. Thereupon I leave the reality of my lived *me* in order to refer myself constantly to the ideal, fictitious, or imaginary *me*, of which the specular image is the first outline. In this sense I am torn from myself.... The general function of the specular image would be to tear us away from our immediate reality; it would be a "de-realizing" function. (136–37)

In reply to Lacan, Merleau-Ponty develops a notion of selfhood as chiasmus, using a figure that I cited in chapter 1: he argues that

> in the case of the specular image, instead of a second body which the child would have and would be located elsewhere than his tactile body, there is a kind of *identity at a distance* ... ; the body is at once present in the mirror and present at the point where I feel it tactually.... The two aspects that are to be coordinated are not really separated in the child. (139–40; emphasis in original)

This notion of the child as already one body echoes closely Merleau-Ponty's account of the representation of consciousness in film, in what he calls "the ensemble" of images and music in time ("Film" 56). What

---

11. Lacan's influential 1949 seminar on the mirror-stage emphasized the experience of a small child, at twelve to eighteen months, before its mirror image as one of the "*meconnaissances* that constitute the ego, the illusion of autonomy" (6). This illusion born of the mirror seduces the child because the image's wholeness promises more than the small child's experience of its own "fragmented body" but leads in fact to the "assumption of the armour of an alienating identity" (4).

Lacan saw as separation, a fragmentation of feeling in the child before the always impossible promise of fullness in the mirror, is for Merleau-Ponty connectedness in the body that is "at once present in the mirror and . . . where I feel it." Sutured pieces of film illustrate the same principle of "coexistence" and "simultaneity" that Merleau-Ponty sees in the child's body. The construction of montage in film—that is, sutured narrative—is another example of how human consciousness works for Merleau-Ponty:

> I do not think the world in the act of perception. . . . The objects behind my back are not represented to me by some operation of memory or judgment; they are present, they *count* for me, just as the ground which I do not see continues nonetheless to be present beneath the figure which partially hides it. ("Film" 51)

Merleau-Ponty's example is almost exactly contrary in structure and function to Jacques-Alain Miller's for the ensemble of suture. For Merleau-Ponty the objects behind one's back that one does not remember are present in one's consciousness, in contrast to Miller's series of numbers/signifiers whose suturing confesses the subject's "exclusion from the discourse" that nonetheless constitutes it (32). Here lies the usefulness of Merleau-Ponty's phenomenology of coexistence: it offers an alternative to those notions of exclusion and loss that are fundamental to classic suture theory in film narrative. In Merleau-Ponty "identity at a distance," whether in the body of a child before a mirror or in film's spliced sequences, is evidence for the linkages in and between consciousnesses, however oblique and imperfect, not for their gaps, as it is for Miller and Dayan and Silverman ("Child's" 139).

For Merleau-Ponty the Kuleshov effect is another reminder that consciousness, intersubjectivity, and narrative are ensemble acts that add up to more than a sum of their parts. This "more than" sounds an alarm bell to skeptics, and Merleau-Ponty himself consistently criticized the idealism of earlier phenomenologies. I do not want at all to claim for film narrative's representations of sutured consciousnesses a full presence to themselves or to others. Merleau-Ponty's own notions of slippage and absence will become clearer in our discussion of chiasmus, but there as here I want to steer a middle course between an archaic transcendentalism and Lacanian absence. I certainly want to avoid the skepticism of Levinas, who critiqued Merleau-Ponty's famous image of reciprocity in hands touching hands touching (from *The Visible and the Invisible*: "There is a circle of the touched and the touching, the touched takes hold of the touching" [143]):

> One may especially wonder, then, whether such a "relation," the ethical relation, is not imposed across a *radical separation* between the two hands, which precisely do not belong to the same body, nor to a hypothetical or only metaphorical intercorporeality. (Levinas, "Intersubjectivity" 59)

For Merleau-Ponty, this linkage, whether or not ethical, is neither hypothetical or metaphorical. Of course two persons' hands do not belong to the same body, but when they touch, each touching the other's touching as an embodied and mirrored intention, their linkage is neither only a metaphor nor only a hypothesis. It is an example of chiasmus.

The second idea to help us reconceptualize suture's work in film narrative is indeed Merleau-Ponty's late notion of chiasmus, and together with the approach to perceptions as simultaneous and interconnecting/constructing, it provides a new understanding of suture in film narrative. Chiasm is originally a rhetorical device, X-shaped, so to speak, like the Greek letter *chi*, which features the reversibility of symmetrical grammatical elements, as in this example, courtesy of Oscar Hammerstein: "Do I love you because you're beautiful, or are you beautiful because I love you?" In Merleau-Ponty's thought, chiasm becomes an image for the interweaving between the partially reversible perceptions of two (or more) consciousnesses. That is, chiasm is a paradigm for embodied intersubjectivity. The late essay "The Intertwining—The Chiasm" in *The Visible and the Invisible* (1964) offers the just-cited image: "there is a circle of the touched and the touching, the touched takes hold of the touching." Merleau-Ponty continues, the circle that includes seeing others see oneself seeing "betray[s] the solipsist illusion . . . that every going beyond is a surpassing accomplished [only] by oneself" (*Visible* 143). Although this self-transcending, this "going-beyond," is not a self-delusion, neither does the circle of perceptions achieve a pure transcendence of subjectivity, as Merleau-Ponty's notes to his essay explain: the chiasm "does not realize a surpassing, a dialectic in the Hegelian sense, [this] is realized on the spot, by encroachment, thickness, *spatiality*" (264). Neither solipsist nor transcendentalist: the image of chiasmus expresses quite precisely Merleau-Ponty's sense of consciousnesses, of intersubjectivity, in the world; the thickness and spatiality of crisscrossing threads anchor each self in its body, but also touch the other body whose gestures mirror back one's gestures to oneself, in a chain of intercorporeal responses that cannot be entirely hypothetical nor entirely a delusion.

Merleau-Ponty is the poet of such ambiguities, of a human "interworld" (Merleau-Ponty's word for an imperfectly joined web of experiences) in which subjects are never entirely present nor entirely absent to each other (*Adventures* 200). An image from *Signs* that I cited in chapter 1 expresses this complexity: "there is said to be a wall between us, but it is a wall we build together, each putting a stone in the niche left by the other" (19). Or in a earlier essay: "there is woven between us an 'exchange,' a 'chiasm between two destinies,' in which there are never quite two of us, and yet one is never alone" (*In Praise* 82). Chiasm as suture, suture as chiasm—one more image opens up this possibility even more clearly: "chiasm . . . the insertion of the world between the two leaves of my body / the insertion of my body between the 2 leaves of each thing and of the world" (*Visible* 264). I argue that suture in this view is an interleaving of embodiments (even in terrifying or invasive versions: shame, violation, abuse, surveillance), in a reversal of the absences of classic suture theorists. I add shame and violation, because Merleau-Ponty usually figures intersubjectivity as "espousal," and that optimism needs muting in the face of the aggression that human presences, however truly yet partially chiasmatic, can wreak on each other.[12] Luce Irigaray emphasized the dark side of the chiasm in her reading of Merleau-Ponty: "Weaving the visible and my look in this way, I could just as well say that I close them off from myself. The texture becomes increasingly tight, taking me into it, sheltering me there but imprisoning me as well" (183). Imprisonment, absence, and Silverman's "castrating coherence," unleaving as well as interleaving, are always possible in a corporeal interworld, whether perceived in the real world or in a narrative text. But they are not the only possibilities.

I propose that suture in narrative articulates such a chiasmus of consciousnesses and embodiments, a chiasmus that is implicit in film's narrative practices and to which classical suture theory was blinded by its absorption in the Lacanian drama of absence. In this understanding of the representation of consciousnesses in storytelling, even cutting apart may be a deeply intersubjective narrative. A suture that enables the narration of both unleaving and interleaving is nonetheless about threading subjects, not about triumphant emptiness.

---

12. See Butte 24–28 on the quarrel between Merleau-Ponty and Sartre over intersubjectivity as espousal or shame.

iii. CHIASMUS AND *NOTHING BUT A MAN*

To explore suture as chiasmus in what I intend as an exemplary exercise, I have chosen two brief sequences from a film that is almost entirely two-shots and three-shots, in extended shot / reverse shot sequences of the kind so important to Oudart and other classical suture theorists. This brilliant 1964 film, *Nothing But a Man*, by Michael Roemer and Robert Young, which explores the struggles of one African-American couple in the tumultuous early 1960s in the rural American South, is austere in a way that is effective but deceptive, because its formal style deepens vertiginously on reflection from what seem its simple shape and materials. I want to make large claims for these two sequences: that understanding suture in two forms (one for each sequence) illuminates *presence,* not absence, in the frame, and illuminates the narration of multiple consciousnesses in the context of intense personal, social, and political violence.[13]

The tensions that threaten to erupt inside the frames of *Nothing But a Man* had parallels outside those frames. The film was shot in Cape May, New Jersey, between June and September, 1963. In June NAACP field secretary Medgar Evers was killed in Jackson, Mississippi; in August Martin Luther King Jr. led the massive demonstration in Washington where he delivered his "I Have a Dream" speech; on September 15, a bomb killed four girls at the Sixteenth Street Baptist Church in Birmingham. According to Jim Davidson's account of the production, each of these events challenged the cast and crew to maintain focus on the film. And segregation was not dead in New Jersey: "the black cast and crew remember precisely where they stayed, in their own hotel, the Planter," which may

---

13. Let me set the scene briefly for readers who have not seen this film, or not seen it recently. Duff (played by Ivan Dixon) is a skilled African-American worker on the railway who meets the local preacher's daughter (played by Abbey Lincoln), who is a schoolteacher, while working near a small town not far from Birmingham, Alabama. Duff, a veteran who has lived in the North, is tough, angry, rebellious, and the father of a small boy whom he has left in unsavory circumstances in Birmingham. After a rare visit to see the boy, and his own alcoholic, angry father, Duff meets Josie in the Birmingham bus station and proposes marriage. Josie's father opposes the marriage, fearing Duff's anger and difference in class. After the marriage, Josie and Duff continue to struggle with the racism of the Jim Crow South, whose violence simmers under the surface of their lives. (Josie remarks that the last lynching occurred only eight years earlier.) Duff loses various jobs, despite his effort to be less confrontational. After his father's death, and with Josie's encouragement, Duff brings his son to live with them.

For more cultural contexts, from the civil rights movement to Italian neorealism, see the extensive discussions in *Black Camera*'s Spring 2012 number (vol. 3, no. 2), edited by Michael T. Martin and David Wall, about half of which is devoted to *Nothing But a Man.*

FIGURE 2.1. *Nothing But a Man* (39:19)

have been the first black-owned business in Cape May (14). As a result, "the Planter was their oasis in a Jim Crow setting. 'I went into restaurants where I was not served,' [Ivan] Dixon says. 'With my whole family, six or eight people'" (14).

This film, and the two scenes I have chosen, are designed to make the case against cinema as gaps, and the case for phenomenological readings that acknowledge embeddedness in class, race, gender, and history. Our first sequence will offer, in its apparently uncomplicated structure, an almost categorical denial of the claims to emptiness or castration in earlier suture theory that I discussed in sections i and ii of this chapter. Instead we will find layer upon layer of narration, voice and consciousnesses, as this brief scene, a marriage proposal, becomes a dance of subjectivities that are fearful yet attentive to each other, hostile and yearning. These are the structural elements: eighty seconds of film, eight shots; four are two-shots that are the same medium close-up of our lovers, Josie and Duff (figure 2.1). Simple as the framing seems to be, between them in the distance (in the bus station) is a middle-class, middle-aged white man, in coat and tie. The other four shots are divided evenly: two of Josie, with Duff partially out of focus on the right edge of the frame looking at her (figure 2.2), and two of the classic reverse-shot, angled toward Duff with Josie slightly out of focus on the left edge of the frame looking at him (figure 2.3). Here is the scene's dialogue, with the shot selection at the right.

FIGURE 2.2. *Nothing But a Man* (39:26)

The cuts between shots, say from 1 to 2, occur at the beginning of the line of dialogue marked at the right with "1," "2," or "3."

DUFF:	Y'know, I been thinking. How 'bout us gettin' married?	1
JOSIE:	What do you mean?	
DUFF:	Just what I said. (Pause.) Don't look so scared.	2
	How about it?	1
JOSIE:	What happened, Duff?	
DUFF:	Look, baby, I don't know about you,	3
	but it's the right thing for me, I just know it is. What do you say?	
JOSIE:	Don't push me, Duff.	
DUFF:	Wouldn't be no picnic for you. I ain't exactly housebroken.	1
JOSIE:	What about that girl?	2
DUFF:	She ain't nothin' to me. That's all over.	
	Baby, I'm asking you to *marry* me.	3
	I guess you want a big scene.	
JOSIE:	No—but a small one. (tight smile)	
(Bus announcer's voice: "Now boarding....")		1
(38:58–40:40)		

The argument that suture—here, deep suture—is chiasmus as deeply intersubjective narrative hinges on the extended reciprocal exchange

FIGURE 2.3. *Nothing But a Man* (40:25)

between subjectivities, in their perceptions in this scene of the other's perceptions (an interleaving, not an unleaving, of words and gestures). The architecture of the scene involves the interweaving of specific close-ups that link consciousnesses by means of their reciprocal gestures strung like beads on the rigorous geometry of the sequence's eyeline matches. (Every edit cuts to the next shot on the line of a gaze from the first shot.) The unspoken feeling beneath both voices is fear, and here as elsewhere Duff watches Josie's tightness (2), as we watch her watching him watch her trying to understand and manage that fear (3). For Josie to marry Duff means rebellion and danger, abandoning the protections of her father's laboriously constructed world, and accepting risks she would face inside and outside Duff's home: inside, because Duff, as he admits, "ain't exactly housebroken," and outside because as a privileged, attractive, educated African-American woman, Josie knows that white folk are always watching her. Note that Duff says, "Don't *look* so scared," not "Don't be scared" (emphasis added). The danger is showing fear in the midst of such intense supervision in their world (and not just from white people: there are also fathers, schoolchildren, former lovers). In the matrix of Jim Crow and shot / reverse shots, Duff and Josie never touch; the space in the master shot (1) is open between them, with white Birmingham in the interstices, yet they look and return looks and return looks yet again, answer and do not answer, across that space *inside* the frame (1) and across the frames that divide them (2 and 3). The result is a partial grasp by each of the other's grasp of their fear, even if unnarrated ("What happened?"), undefined (what is Duff refusing to promise when he says he isn't "exactly housebroken"?), and underdramatized (how is a marriage proposal to be taken seriously if its agent rejects the genre's requirements for the big scene?). (For a more traditional view of these close-ups—as individual shots, not parts of a sequence—in this scene and in the film, see Robert Young's interview in *Black Camera,* where he celebrates looking at Josie's and Duff's faces: "they were beautiful people"[Wall 122]. Also see Judith E. Smith's commentary on the close-up's role in the film's "foregrounding of black subjectivity" [166]).

The relations between shots, the formal devices of suture, also articulate a chiasmus of consciousnesses. The layering of subjectivities within each frame is mirrored by the suturing together of shots. Merleau-Ponty described chiasmus as that process of mutual interleaving: "the insertion of the world between the two leaves of my body / the insertion of my body between the 2 leaves ... of the world" (*Visible* 264). In our sequence, Roemer's editing inserts close-ups (figures 2.2 and 2.3) between master shots (figure 2.1), and master shots (figure 2.1) between close-ups (figures 2.2 and 2.3). Furthermore, the edges are not tightly aligned, because slippage between consciousnesses is fundamental to intersubjectivity in the world, as Merleau-Ponty always argued. Remember his line that I quoted above, "There is woven between us an 'exchange,' a 'chiasm between two destinies,' in which there are never quite two of us, and yet one is never alone" (*In Praise* 82). The misalignments, of depth cues and graphic matches and intentionalities, matter, but the slippage between consciousnesses in this scene is only partial. Roemer's editing hides and reveals, and so do Duff and Josie. Duff does not answer Josie's question, "What happened?" (as if his meeting with his son would explain the marriage proposal), and Josie does not ask again: silence responds to silence as an accepting gesture. Duff accuses Josie of needing a theatrical display ("I guess you want a big scene") and she disagrees but agrees, modifying his claim ("No—but a small one."). Roemer alternates points of view as Josie and Duff negotiate their intimacies without achieving a single-threaded story or a transcendental union of subjectivities. Nonetheless, they achieve a significant closeness, partly through the acceptance of silence in the other. Duff indeed does not answer Josie's question, "What happened?" But his silence acknowledges that *some*thing happened, and that in some way it at the least nudged forward his proposal of marriage. And Josie's abdication—not asking the question again—acknowledges

Duff's acknowledgement and tells him she is at peace with it, at least for the moment.

Let me sketch briefly here an outline of how the traditional suture theorist might read this scene, in order to clarify what is different in my account. Of course the challenge in such an outline is to be fair to an approach that I am seeking to criticize and repurpose. It would be appropriate to focus on Dayan and Silverman, since *Nothing But a Man* would seem to ask for the ideological readings they offer: its gaps, both inside and outside the diegesis, would in their thinking provoke in response a fake plenitude that seduces both the flesh-and-blood viewer and the authorial or implied viewer. To put their view simply, the power of this love story personalizes the social and racial conflicts in the tale and lets viewers off the hook; otherwise, they might ask difficult questions about their own subjectivity and its ideological contexts. Silverman summarizes these views nicely: "[suture] is inherent in all the operations which constitute narrativity" and which are examples of "the disembodied cultural voices which speak not only the books we read and the films we view, but our own subjectivity and the world in which we live." Shot / reverse shot strategies "provide the agency whereby the subject emerges within discourse, and (at least ideally) takes up a position congruent with the existing cultural order," but its smooth operation seeks "to conceal all signs of [its] actual production" (236).

In such a reading of this scene, then, the operations of discourse, the conventions of continuity editing, obscure their role in narrative construction; no jarring intervention draws attention to the extra-diegetic role of camera, film editor, or screenplay choices. The alternating shots of Josie and Duff, for example, are examples of the strategy of obliqueness, confessing to the viewer's need for evasion (a topic I will develop more fully in section iv of this chapter), but the close-ups serve to obscure the oblique angles and the agency that manages them, avoiding the question, whose gaze hovers over each character's shoulder? Instead, the role of eavesdropper for the authorial viewer provides a comforting position as voyeur, to listen from behind the arras, with no risk that someone will break the fourth wall (to change the image) and address us (as, say, Ferris Bueller does on his famous day off). The charismatic faces of the actors draw us into their conflict, so that from one shot to the next, we ask, will Josie accept Duff's story? Will the little boy, Duff's son, or the boy's mother, be a barrier between Josie and Duff? How deep are the differences in these life patterns and expectations? Differences that are clearly class markers (pregnancy outside marriage; speech conventions ["I ain't exactly housebroken"]) become specific emotions in faces, and translate into looks responding to looks. Ideology becomes bodies; it is sutured into story and so masked. The masking, in this account, occurs partly because of the impetus of shot / reverse shot conventions: as Dayan says, "The meaning of a shot depends on the next shot" (30). The narrative drives forward, and viewers immerse themselves inside the diegesis. Dayan describes the process: "to *see* the film is *not* to perceive the frame, the camera angle and distance, etc." (29; emphasis in original). Without some defamiliarizing move, story and plenitude triumph. What matters to us is the question, what will happen to the relationship between these people we really like? We chuckle at Duff's emphasis, delivered with a small smile, "Baby, I'm asking you to *marry* me." The implied viewer enters into his story, understanding what a leap this proposal is for him. We have left the production of subjectivity far behind. The authorial audience is passive, hobbled by its own blindness and absence of agency, and so are the film's characters inside the narrative.

My own reading of this scene emphasizes agency and presence, not passivity and lack, in both authorial audience and inside the diegesis, in its characters and their story-world. Part of the argument for agency is an argument for the subtle deployment of conventions. For example, inside the frame the dialogue draws attention to the gaze and issues of theatricality. As I said above, Duff and Josie both know they are always subject to supervision, to the gaze of others, as Duff warns her, in a line whose bleak humor (Duff chuckles) points to something deep at stake, "Don't look so scared." Josie's later reply about the need to keep the scene small is in part her admission that they cannot afford to "make a scene" here. The fear she confesses emerges, yes, in a more general, diffuse way from her role as middle-class, educated African-American woman (no inappropriate public displays). These characters are deeply aware of the politics of the gaze in 1960s Alabama. But her fear also has an immediate, specific source (even if she is not directly conscious of it): that middle-class white man (in suit and tie) that every third shot places between Duff and her.

Also, rather than hiding a gap, the editing patterns here alert a thoughtful authorial audience to the power of the gaze of others and to the dynamics of "scene" construction. Dayan claims that seeing the film means *not* seeing the frame, but what would be his supporting evidence? Surveys of flesh-and-blood viewers (which of course he does not provide)? I believe there is a signal inside the text to its ideal audience about its frame construction, about deep space in this particular mise-en-scène. Here are two African-American characters in a public space—a bus station in Birmingham, Alabama—discussing how one *looks* to people *looking,* and discussing the choice to make either a big scene or a small scene, and throughout they are overseen by an apparently indifferent but nonetheless privileged voyeur, who might become less indifferent at any moment. Neither form nor content seems designed here to hide what is missing (or indeed what is present, lurking in the background), or to lull a passive audience into formulas about passive characters. The progression from shot to shot in this sequence requires the astute attention of its competent viewer, and this attention mirrors the careful, anxious mindfulness of Duff and Josie in the face (literally) of the supervision they live with, and the scenic composition they could (and will eventually) disrupt.

Josie and Duff are still two deeply separate subjects, with different narratives and experiences of fear and even different grammatical conventions. The act of hope in this film is to position these two characters on either side of that white man; they have lived enormously different experiences of gender and race, and yet their film suggests a threading across the gap, a chiasmus of gazes and stories. This sequence could have offered, as it were, in microcosm, the distrust and fear between the Prince and the Princess from *The Golden Bowl,* Dewey Dell and Darl from *As I Lay Dying,* or Nicole and Mitch Stephens in *The Sweet Hereafter* (Russell Banks's or Atom Egoyan's), but Josie and Duff build their wall, to cite Merleau-Ponty's image again, with greater mutual understanding, each putting their stone in the niche left by the other.

The design of this sequence is chiasmatic in more ways than I have claimed so far, because it weaves together representations of not only Josie's and Duff's intentionalities but also of an editing—a suturing—consciousness. With three threads in the tapestry of intersubjectivity here, we have moved even further away from Oudart's absence. This claim for three consciousnesses works for Roemer's film if one takes the position on film narration, as I do, that all shots imply a narrating agency or consciousness (call it the extradiegetic narrator or the enunciator, for example), and that each shot and suture in this sequence not only represents Josie and Duff's perspective but also expresses a third perspective, *about* Josie and Duff and their world. The best example of this third perspective is a feature of the text that I have already discussed: the choice of timing to place and replace that master two-shot of Jose and Duff in the bus station, with the third figure between them in deep space, between the intimate shot / reverse shots of the couple struggling with Duff's proposal of marriage. The structure of each frame's mise-en-scène and their interrelationships as edited together constitute another kind of discourse about power and space in a story. I see several layers of consciousnesses in this scene, including a narrating agency's further consciousness and implied commentary.[14]

The third consciousness, the enunciator in Roemer or the narrating subjectivity in a Henry James novel, for example, adds a second twist to the chiasmus, as if the figure of the crisscross were crisscrossed again. An example from Henry James's *What Maisie Knew* will be useful to illustrate how an invisible hand (or perhaps not so invisible) arranges a series of mirrors to reveal consciousnesses responding to each other, as James's storyteller frames Maisie's framing of Beale's framing of her (the example occurs in the scene in the Countess's elegant rooms, where Beale has taken Maisie after snatching her away at the Earls Court Exhibition): "while they sat together, there was an extraordinary mute passage between her vision of this vision of his, his vision of her vision, and her vision of his vision of her vision" (150). The authority in the words "there was an extraordinary mute passage" makes explicit what is implicit between Maisie and her father, articulates what was "mute," sees the acts of seeing and of seeing others see oneself see. This agency is powerful and enabling, and in one sense, once we see it seeing, not invisible at all. I will return to this argument in chapter 3.

---

14. For a review of the debate over implied narrators in film, see Stam, Burgoyne, and Flitterman-Lewis 103–13. My position is similar to Nick Browne's in "The Spectator-in-the-Text" on the authority that narrates: "Certain formal features of the imagery—framing, sequencing, the prohibition and 'invisibility' of the narrator—I have suggested, can be explained as the ensemble of ways authority implicitly positions the spectator/reader" (38). I also find Seymour Chatman's considered response to David Bordwell persuasive: " My only real criticism [of Bordwell's theory of film narration] is that is goes too far in arguing that film has no agency corresponding to the narrator and that film narrative is best considered as a kind of work wholly performed by the spectator. Bordwell allows for film a 'narration' but not a narrator" (*Coming to Terms* 124–25). Chatman then argues for some "authority" (using Browne's word) as an origin for film narrative, though it need not be conceived as a person; personification for film narration is a heuristic move that Bordwell continues to critique in *Making Meaning* as another "trick of the interpretive trade" (168). In the context of literary narrative, as I wrote in chapter 1, Daniel Gunn makes an argument similar to Chatman's about free indirect discourse, a strategy that some narratologists see as "autonomous" or "impersonal," but for Gunn is in fact an expression of "narratorial subjectivity" (36–37). A recent critic, Jeremy Hawthorn, writes extensively about this issue, and agrees with Chatman that some "consciousness" controls film narration, but suggests that such a narrator, "if his or her existence is accepted, is a far more ghostly and fragmented presence than a typical literary narrator." Hawthorn also argues that this film enunciator (my word) may function for an especially complicated text like *Rear Window* in ontologically confusing ways, sometimes possibly as "a personified and intradiegetic viewpoint," at other times "an extradiegetic narrative authority" (138).

The linkage in this book, between suture in film and suture in print narrative, depends on common strategies of indirection and obliqueness that we see in both James and Roemer and that are enabled by these narrating agencies. In Roemer each close-up in our sequence works to expose consciousnesses, but as it were from behind a screen, as subjects respond in a network of gestures to each other. Roemer's second close-up (figure 2.3) frames Josie at the edge of the mise-en-scène as she concentrates on the middle distance while Duff makes his marriage proposal; the camera's implied viewers concentrate too, not as if they were Josie, but in alignment with her, like James's reader aligned with Maisie but sheltered behind the "she" of James's indirect narration. Earlier (in figure 2.2), Roemer's viewer filtered Duff's desire through Josie's startled glance; now her posture, angled partly away from the camera's gaze, casts her as a safely surrogate receiver, so that the scene's audience gets to watch Duff watch her without encountering his look directly, without risking *her* risk (that direct encounter with his gaze). In the same way that James's audience participates intimately with Maisie's feelings from a safe distance, the oblique shot / reverse shot sequence allows the camera to be both inside and outside a character's subjectivity at the same time (the sequence also allows the camera to be inside and outside the observing consciousness). The camera can do so because the shot is framed at the edge by the observer's body, which is illogically included inside the shot that seems to represent the field of vision of that observer (as well as the vision of the observer of the observer).

In this plenitude that it articulates and yet partially evades may lie some of the magic of the oblique shot / reverse shot posture for the film's authorial audience: it eavesdrops, watches, but asymmetrically, *not* targeted by a 180-degree reverse shot that would implicate that audience because *it* would have to look Duff in the eye, and even behind the fourth wall the audience might tremble a little.[15] The pleasure the shot offers comes from watching the reciprocity to reciprocity, the response to a response to a yet earlier response between Josie and Duff, in the narrative construction of a deep intersubjectivity that the narrative's audience can watch safely, protected by that 30-degree camera angle. I will return to the subject of this strange angle in section iv of this chapter.

---

15. This shot, in which the observed subject who returns the observer's look also looks into the camera's eye and the cinema audience's, is quite rare because it is so powerfully confrontational. I will discuss the famous example of this dynamic in the moment Thorwald sees Jess watching him across the courtyard at the end of *Rear Window* in the next section of this chapter.

The architecture of this chiasmus is indeed yet one further gesture by the film's "narratorial subjectivity," in a move to interpret, to proffer its narration as a *version,* a commentary. As James's enunciator selects when to shift consciousnesses and colors his world with imagery and rhetorical choices, suture in *Nothing But a Man* embodies a rhetoric too. That narrating subjectivity I proposed above is always at work, however "figural" or "objective" the narrative seems to be. That suturing consciousness frames the framing inside which Josie and Duff try to weave their own interworld. The mise-en-scène here explores how intimacy and supervision collide; racial violence gets braided with family and sexual energies, in ways the film's formal design explores. For example, the film's editing frames these moments of intimate struggle (figures 2.2 and 2.3) with the master shot (figure 2.1), reminding the audience of that white man separating Josie and Duff. Or when Duff admits that he's hardly "housebroken yet," in the master shot (figure 2.1) and Josie returns to her wound, "What about that girl?" (the mother of Duff's child), Duff's look is hidden from us, in the out-of-focus face at the edge of the reverse shot (figure 2.2). Roemer chooses to let his viewer see Josie's pride (for once she doesn't look down) and lets Duff compose his reply without an embarrassing reverse shot. What is Duff's self-definition ("housebroken" usually applies to pets)? How does dignity compose itself in this Alabama bus station? Yet another example of the architecture-as-commentary is the timing of the final shot (1 again), inserted two beats after Josie's quip about the "small scene" that lets both of them off some kind of hook. That spacing is the enunciator's comment on this process of negotiation over commitment and boundaries: the film breathes deeply, steps back a little, takes heart, and then returns to the frame shot to notice Josie's anxious look at Duff; the resolution is only temporary, and that white guy with the tie still lurks in the background between them.

Deep suture explores the threads of the chiasmus that crisscross inside and between frames, in complex patterns of subjectivities and their narratives. Unlike the first example, my second scene from *Nothing But a Man* is one long painful shot of Josie and Duff, late in the film, immediately after Duff's confrontation with Josie's father (the minister), who has just said he knew the marriage would fail, and Duff has replied, "Well, at least she ain't married to no white man's nigger. You been stoopin' so long Reveren' you don't even know how to stand straight no mo'. You're just half a man" (1:08:00–10). In this following scene, Josie and Duff are both visible in the frame for the entire shot, so that there is no escape for the audience from the torment they experience together. The scene confirms

FIGURE 2.4. *Nothing But a Man* (1:09:42): "They can reach right in with their damn white hands and turn you off and on."

the nature of intersubjectivity as chiasmus precisely in the absence of suture—that is, in this case, the sewing together of shot / reverse shots. The edges are all inside the frame, as Roemer recalls here Duff's anger, Josie's fear, and their vulnerability to humiliation and violence.

> DUFF: How come you don't hate their guts?
> JOSIE: I don't know. (Pause.) I guess I'm not afraid of them.
> DUFF: You were plenty scared that night in the car.
> JOSIE: Just of getting hurt. They can't touch me inside.
> DUFF: Like hell they can't. They can reach right in (stands up: fig. 2.4) with their damn white hands and turn you off and on.
> JOSIE: Not if you see them for what they are, Duff.
> DUFF: Jesus, baby, you so full of talk. But you ain't never really been a nigger, have you, living like that in your father's house? So just shut your mouth.
>
> (Turns his back to Josie.)
> (1:08.55–1:10.05)

Our vocabulary of chiasmus allows us to say something about the absence of suture and its consequences. In this extraordinary scene, the threads of power and violation spread out before the viewer, with no evasion, no faces hidden, no obliquely angled reaction shot to serve as a screen. Nor do Josie and Duff find any release from their frame together; their response is resolutely to avoid seeing each other see the other. Once again Josie is afraid, but now she is deeply alone, even by Duff's side (or back, as he moves away). The force of that white man in the interstices of our earlier frame shot now surfaces, as *Nothing But a Man* studies the interiorities of racism. A narrative of embodied consciousnesses will trace the body through the matrices of class, gender, and race, but especially race, as Duff well understands (remember, Ivan Dixon was refused service in white restaurants while making this film). Josie claims not to be afraid, deep inside; Duff doesn't buy that claim for a moment: "They can reach right in with their damn white hands and turn you off and on." For Duff, her body-blindness is a product of a different class experience: "But you ain't really never been a nigger, have you, living like that in your father's house."

One undertone of this scene with no cuts to be sutured is the closeness of bodies to each other inside a film frame, a closeness that terrifies and promises, sometimes (as here) at the same time. When Duff turns away from Josie, his angry words hanging ominously in the air ("So just shut your mouth"), there is no sense in which the space between their backs is empty. We remember that Merleau-Ponty observed, in his film essay, "The objects behind my back are likewise not presented to me by some operation of memory of judgment: they are present, they *count* for me" ("Film" 51). In the absence of a sutured montage, the space between Josie and Duff counts with such intensity because a blow would bridge it so easily, and the film's audience remembers that Duff hit Josie once before.

Shot / reverse shot sequences are full of intentionalities and subjectiv*ities,* I have argued, and they also help us understand the narration of consciousnesses in a scene where suture is visibly absent. These two brief sequences from *Nothing But a Man* can be taken to offer representative strategies by which suture narrates subjectivities—that is, intersubjectivity—as presences, not absences. Such narrative sequences in film share some common ground with intersubjective narratives in other forms, and suture in film stories is not uniquely different from sutured consciousnesses in prose fiction, for example: hence my comparison of oblique angles in shot / reverse shot chains and free indirect narration in *Nothing But a Man* and *What Maisie Knew*. There is a scale to intersubjectivities, from simpler to more complex, just as there is a scale to the depths (and number) of consciousnesses narrated in free indirect discourse. These examples, like most of those in this book, come from the deep end of the scale. In these cases, the webs of sutured shot / reverse shots in film, like the webs of free indirect discourse in print fiction, are not only not about emptiness, and not only represent subjectivity, but represent subjectivity squared and cubed in intricate Mobius strips of interconnecting consciousnesses (that is, deep intersubjectivity).

iv. THE MYSTERY OF THE OBLIQUE ANGLE AND *THE SILENCE OF THE LAMBS*

That oblique angle of the reverse shots in film narrative's shot / reverse shot sequences is one of the oddest features of suture as chiasmus, one whose mysteries suggest profound implications for suture and the narration of deep intersubjectivity. This strange feature of almost all narrative film practice is widely noted and widely normalized. Most narrative films shoot and edit shot / reverse shot sequences between two or more people at oblique angles—but the degree of obliqueness varies greatly. Everyone who has worked on this topic—Jean-Pierre Oudart, Daniel Dayan, Kaja Silverman, David Bordwell, Barry Salt—acknowledges these sequences do not consist of point-of-view shots that swivel exactly 180 degrees from each other; if they did so, the film's editing would cut between speakers not only on eyeline matches, but along a line one could draw from eye to eye. Point-of-view (POV) shot would turn directly to the previous POV shot. But these sequences are not so edited, and yet they almost always suggest the successive points of view, if you will the consciousnesses, of its film's speakers and listeners, attending to and responding to previous responses, in a complex chain of reciprocation (or sometimes not; bad faith and misleading performance of espousal occur as well: think of the opening conversation between Sam Spade and Bridget in *The Maltese Falcon*). After acknowledging the anomaly here, most critics simply dismiss it. Kaja Silverman's reasoning (or nonreasoning) is typical. She observes the illogicality of the angle: "Often we are shown the shoulders or head of the character through whose eyes we are ostensibly looking" (202). Silverman then notes that "a loose application" of the convention is, however, more "successful" in its "approximation of 'reality'" than a strict application, and then, without offering any explanation of what "success" or "reality" might mean here, she, like everyone else, moves on.

The mystery of the oblique angle in film narrative's representation of human subjects echoes the oddities of free indirect discourse and points to a profound issue in the narration of intersubjectivities, an issue that I will track through various examples, but *The Silence of the Lambs* will be the dominant one. This mystery suggests a poignant and troubled relationship between the shot's implied narrating agency and its implied audience. The frequency of illogical framing and oblique angles in the shot / reverse shot chain strikes me as the fundamentally important feature of this practice in several ways. Like free indirect discourse, it allows the authorial audience to be closer to a character's interiority, but also distanced, inside a character's perspective but also outside it, just over her shoulder. The important point here is not the *content* of free indirect narration, whether inner speech, discourse, thought, consciousness, unconsciousness, or "perspective." I want to draw attention to the stance of narration, to this "over the shoulder" position of the narrative voice (or eye), shielded by the indirection of "free/indirect" narrative masks, or the oblique shot / reverse shot convention. This intimate distance from character consciousness defines a safe niche for the tale's audience, removed at least one degree from the anger and violence and passion in a story. The framing of shoulders and the oblique angles also announce the presence of multiple consciousnesses: the character observing, the character observing the observing, and the narrating agency that frames so artificially all that seeing. (Some examples of free indirect discourse offer only two layers of consciousness, when the observing character is not the object of another observer inside the diegesis. In these instances, the stance of the oblique angle still provides a curiously intimate distance between observer and enunciator and the world observed.)

Normalizing the oblique angle in film narration has seemed easy to do. Silverman said, as I quoted her above, that the oblique angle is more "successful" at approximating "reality," though avoiding characters' gazes seems an odd definition of success, and "reality" is a little vague. Barry Salt also dismisses the problem succinctly: since "this device is an obvious way of securing audience involvement" with character, it "is really in need of no further explanation" (50–51). This logic fails on a couple of counts: Which audience does Salt mean? If a flesh-and-blood audience, which one? (French taxi drivers in the 1950s? American community college students in California in 1985? Contemporary graduate students in 2015 in a film theory class?) Furthermore, why would the oblique angle "secure" involvement, more than, say, unmediated (or less mediated) point-of-view shots? Adam Gopnik offered another approach recently in *The New Yorker*:

> In every art the Too Perfect theory helps explain why people are more convinced by an imperfect, 'distressed' illusion than by a perfectly realized one.... The theory explains the force of the off-slant scene in a film, the power of elliptical dialogue in the theatre.... Illusion affects us only when it is incomplete. (67)

Again, of course, we do not know which "people" feel this way. Furthermore, why is an "off-slant scene in a film" either "imperfect" or "incomplete" (these are not the same idea), and why is either a more affecting effect? (What would "affecting" or "effect" mean?)

David Bordwell's normalizing is more substantial than these other efforts in its evasion of the key issue. First, he claims that Oudart is wrong to say shot / reverse shots represent points of view, since each shot "does *not* represent either character from the other's optical standpoint" (*Narration* 110). Of course, Bordwell is correct at the literal visual level. (He also says other theorists miss this fact, but although Dayan does, Silverman does not, as we saw above, nor does Nick Browne, who struggles at some length with the "obliquity" in the angles of these shots [37]). But what *is* the function of the oblique angle, then? Bordwell gets somewhat distracted by his effort to block any plan to resurrect "the phantom narrator" or "the ideal observer"—issues I discussed earlier—by means of this phenomenon of obliqueness (*Narration* 111, 113). Bordwell's answer finally seems to see in shot / reverse shots a series of cues to the spectator (flesh and blood) about construction of narrative space: "'suture' furnishes redundant cues, confirming our construction of a space that we have seen or will see in a more comprehensive view," and Bordwell is correct to emphasize the function of establishing shots for such sequences (*Narration* 113). Still, why the oblique angle? Again, Bordwell's only reply is to emphasize their "redundant cues: the shoulders in the foregrounds present strong landmarks, while complementary body positions and eyelines enable the spectator to assume that an imaginary axis of action, or 180-degree line, connects the characters" (*Narration* 112). Bordwell cites appropriately the confusion of space in films where the shot / reverse shot conventions get sabotaged (his example comes from Bertolucci's *The Spider's Stratagem*), and certainly viewers (flesh and blood and implied) interpret shot / reverse shot sequences according to conventional schemata. But whence this particular, and quite odd, convention, even if its purpose is to provide redundant visual cues for a film's viewer?

Nick Browne also recognizes the convention and its oddity, and offers a different account for its purpose, as rhetoric and as defamiliarization.

For Browne, the text constructs a "prohibition against the 'meeting,' though no such act is literally possible, of the actor's and the spectator's glances" (36). This prohibition "establishes a boundary at the screen" that "places [the spectator] irretrievably outside the action," even though this "narrative system" also "introduc[es] the spectator imaginatively into it" (37). In Browne's argument, this "obliquity" defamiliarizes the diegesis for the skilled viewer and marks the rhetorical stance of the narrator (two presences in a film that of course Bordwell rejects). Browne in effect sees the oblique angle as a kind of visual pun: as an example of "the narrator's construction of a commentary on the story and ... placing the spectator at a certain 'angle' to it" (37). In other words, the angle of the reverse shots is symptomatic of the interpretive stance the viewer is invited to take *on* characters. Browne is right that these shot conventions articulate a rhetoric, a marking of an attitude toward and an evaluation of the story's actors and actions. But the oddity of the oblique angle exceeds this rhetorical structure; that is, it is more than defamiliarization, more than a marking of the text's narration's view (in several senses). The angle does serve those purposes, but it does more. After all, the enunciator announces its presence (and its rhetoric) in many ways, as a careful study of narrative form in film makes clear (camera movement, manipulation of nondiegetic music, manipulation of diegetic music, three-point lighting, the absence of three-point lighting, just to name a few examples).

A deeper anxiety lies behind the shot / reverse shot convention, I believe. Oudart pointed in the right direction, and Bordwell noted Oudart's hint about the spectator's "unease" (*Narration* 111 [46]). Then both failed to pursue the notion of risk, of something fraught in the eyes-on-eyes shot. Oudart suggests that a nonoblique shot is somehow disturbing to the viewer (I'd say either implied or real, but Oudart's emphasis is on the flesh-and-blood spectator) but never exactly clarifies the nature of that dis-ease. Oudart keeps returning to the oblique angle as something *necessary* in film narration. It positions the viewer in a safe place between complete alignment with the character inside the diegesis and complete separation.[16] In Oudart's view, "'subjective' cinema"—that is, film's representation of subjective experience—can only work "obliquely" (37). One explanation is formal, but oddly counterintuitive: Oudart believes the subjective camera shot will lead spectators to "denounce its fiction," since

---

16. The "other" space the spectator needs to avoid belongs to the Absent One, in Oudart's scheme. I addressed that part of Oudart's thinking earlier, and will not include it here, since it does not add much to Oudart's theory about the role of the oblique angle as I am using it now.

they do not live inside the diegesis (37). The subjective shot paradoxically defamiliarizes the cinematic apparatus, rather than pulling the spectator into a naive identification with the character of film narrative. The camera's "obliqueness indicates the spectator's own position" (45). The spectator will "fulfill the role of imaginary subject of the cinematic discourse" only from a "displaced" position (37), a "position out of alignment" that confesses a separation from that subject (45). This displacement/fulfillment occurs, of course, in a range of degrees of obliqueness.

In the films of Robert Bresson, especially *The Trial of Joan of Arc* (1962), Oudart discerns a study of "the camera's obliqueness, at last openly admitted and established as a system," a study that includes "the need to search for the right angle, the right margin of obliqueness for the camera" (37). Indeed, Bresson investigates "infinite modulations of shooting angles: the characters may either be almost face-on (the judge) or in three-quarter view (Joan)" (45). Bresson's "variation of this angle of attack" supports Oudart's claim that "only during the intervals of such borderline moments is the spectator's imaginary able to function freely" (45). Narration delivers an "attack" in moments of shot / reverse shot editing, one whose threat is serious enough to require some kinds of "displacement" that need experimentation across "infinite modulations of shooting angles" to discover a range—if you will, a ratio of safety to risk. This range of angles allows various degrees of participation in the life of the characters, since the spectator is free to imagine only when separated by smaller or larger margins from the character's line of sight. The freedom part is limited by the attack, the anxiety about which the oblique angle avoids or neutralizes. But what is this anxiety?

The origin of that anxiety lies in the geometrically and ontologically confrontational 180-degree reverse shot that spears the viewer, both implied and flesh and blood. The shot unmasks the voyeur when remaining inside the character perspective (often a comfortable place to be) becomes too risky. A pair of frames from Hitchcock's *Rear Window,* only the first of which is well known, may serve as an introduction to these questions. The first, the famous image, pictures the moment the murderer Lars Thorwald sees the eye that sees him from the other side of the courtyard. The iris mask on Hitchcock's frame emphasizes the fact that Jeff is looking through his camera: this is a point-of-view shot with a vengeance. The iris (hard to see in this frame capture) emphasizes the confrontation of eye to eye, since Jeff's camera's images are themselves in fact (or in the diegesis) rectangular, not circular (remember the shots of the rosebush) (figure 2.5).

FIGURE 2.5. *Rear Window* (1:41:53)

In this moment, Thorwald confronts (and threatens) both Jeff and the film's authorial audience that participates in the point-of-view shot. The next image is, however, the more interesting one in its choices: it retreats to obliquity, as it photographs Jeff from the side, his camera inscribing a dramatic diagonal across the screen (figure 2.6). This frame contains no iris, in contrast to the previous frame. Is this diagonal some kind of response by the enunciator to the assault of the prior shot on Jeff, but also on the implied viewer, who has also been threatened? We see Jeff recoil, but to some extent the implied viewer pulls back too, certainly to observe Jeff, but also to avoid Thorwald's eye. The enunciator chose to drop the oblique angle's defensive power at that key moment, in the previous shot, and so exposed the audience to an unfiltered version of Jeff's experience.

It is useful to remember Peter Rabinowitz's subdivision of implied audiences (viewers here, of course, not readers) into the authorial and the narrative, and to note some of the ways it allows us to advance Oudart's thought. The authorial audience knows it observes a film, with specific editing and cinematographic choices, and seeks to align itself with the film's story-world, pretending if necessary to understand allusions and historical background. The narrative audience believes the story-world is real, and might look up Lars's phone number in the 1954 Manhattan telephone book if it had one handy. Competent real audiences play both roles, and as Rabinowitz says, an author (and presumably a filmmaker)

FIGURE 2.6. *Rear Window* (1:41:55)

"rejoices" in the difference between them and "expects his or her actual audience to rejoice as well. For it is this difference that makes fiction fiction and makes the double-leveled aesthetic experience possible" (*Before* 98–99). So the oblique angle, to extend Oudart's paradigm, protects *both* audiences, or viewers playing both roles. Jeremy Hawthorn's recent study, *The Reader as Peeping Tom,* extends the meaning of Oudart's anxiety even further, especially in films like *Rear Window,* where looking becomes spying. In Hitchcock, for example, repeated acts of surveillance place observers both inside the diegesis and those watching it (whether flesh-and-blood viewers or the authorial/narrative audience) in a serious moral dilemma that is personal and political: "Like America, Jeff is portrayed as one who believes in the sanctity of individual privacy, but who feels a compulsion to violate it" (173). Unauthorized, "non-reciprocal" (in Hawthorn's phrase) peeping is a particularly troubling version of the over-the-shoulder gaze, of the oblique angle that can provide a screen for both sympathetic and invasive looking.

    I want to propose two alternative lines of thought about these oblique angles: one line emphasizes meta-diegetic implications, and the other returns inside the text to untangle threads of consciousnesses inside the story-world. Both avenues of thought point toward a comparison of the oblique angle in film's narration of these shot sequences and the special features of free indirect discourse in print narrative, a topic I will pursue further in my chapters on Henry James and on the Peter Pan stories.

FIGURE 2.7. *The Silence of the Lambs* (12:34)

I think obliqueness has similar structural and thematic effects in both narrative practices.

To pursue the meta-textual line first, the oblique angle's "over-the-shoulder" narrative stance occurs in both film's shot / reverse shot sequences and in print fiction's free indirect discourse, and this obliqueness emphasizes the positionality of the story's enunciator. This argument takes as resolved the question of a narrator's presence within or behind both free indirect discourse and film narration—topics I discussed in chapter 1, which are still contentious. As I wrote there, I find Daniel Gunn's ideas persuasive when he argues that not only is there a narrator's "continuing presence" in free indirect discourse, evidenced in the consistent imitation and "mimicry" by the narrating agency of figural thought or speech, but that this imitation and mimicry are intensely active, offering the "energetic play" of wit and commentary for the authorial audience's pleasure (37, 48). Nick Browne offered a similar approach to film's oblique angle in the essay cited above, where he explained: "An obliquity between our angle of viewing and that of the characters... works to make a difference of angle and scale readable as representation of different points of view" (37). In other words, a gap between character and enunciator's angle of focus functions to alert the authorial audience to the difference between them, and to the presence of a mediating agency. This gap sounds a kind of warning bell that reminds the audience there is a way out when the gaze threatens too deeply, while in the meantime allowing for clever commentary.

FIGURE 2.8. *The Silence of the Lambs* (12:36)

A profound example of this threat and how this gap works occurs in figures 2.7 and 2.8, from *The Silence of the Lambs*. In both frames, the eavesdropper position is blocked in fully half of the frame by the listening head (first Hannibal Lecter's, and then Clarice Starling's). This blockage is an unusual frame design that draws attention to the audience's need to peer around a large intervening figure to see the speaker, whose reduced size in the frame places the implied viewer in a conspiratorial relation with the listener in each frame. One of the brilliant thematic effects of these shot / reverse shot sequences in this first encounter between Hannibal and Clarice is to isolate each frame's viewer into one, and then into a different alliance (with the other listener). The alliances are ambiguous from the first, because in each frame the body of Hannibal and then Clarice functions as both barrier and shield; the viewer needs to see around the figure, while using it as a kind of protective screen. To play these roles behind these very different bodies (and power positions) introduces Demme's viewer to the labyrinth of gender and the gaze in this film. The agency that leads us into this labyrinth is the enunciator of these two shots, which announce in their framing an unconventional, witty, even perverse use of shot / reverse shot conventions.

Daniel Gunn sees this same witty, playful positioning throughout Jane Austen's *Emma,* as, for example, in the moment when Emma's thoughts about Frank Churchill are re-presented by Austen's narrator and mimicked for the delight of the knowing audience: "He looked at her as if wanting to read her thoughts. She hardly knew what to say. It seemed like the forerunner of something absolutely serious.... He was more in love with her than Emma had supposed; and who can say how it might have ended if his father had not made his appearance?" (177; II/12) This example, which is not one of Gunn's, nonetheless illustrates his principle of mimicry and enunciator commentary: "The comedy involves the narrator imitating figural language for our amusement.... This is energetic play, *presented* to us by the narrator, as is most of Austen's FID" (Gunn 48). Listening first with Hannibal, and then with Clarice, is a witty, slightly tongue-in-cheek enunciator choice. The two frames also establish gender-bending graphic matches—the looming Lecter of the first frame takes Clarice's reduced position in the second, and she occupies his position of power, shifted from the more ominous left side of the frame to the right side. Editing and mise-en-scène are the enunciator's language for representing gender positions, and then framing and commenting on these positions.

In the second line of thinking about oblique angles, I would suggest that obliqueness is not only a significant gesture in this pantomime of defamiliarization but also a key strategy in suturing consciousnesses inside film's story-world and in fiction's free indirect discourse. Critics have long noted obliqueness as a feature of the narration of consciousness in free indirect discourse. Even Dorrit Cohn—who thirty years ago did not see in what she called "narrated monologue" an enunciating agency that was playful, witty, or audible while mimicking its subject—even Cohn used a telling peek-a-boo imagery for this narration. She wrote, "[The narrated monologue's] dubious attribution of language to the figural mind and its fusion of narratorial and figural language charge it with ambiguity, give it a quality of now-you-see-it, now-you-don't that exerts a special fascination" (Cohn 107). The over-the-shoulder stance of my earlier Austen quotation illustrates this obliqueness ("He looked at her as if wanting to read her thoughts. She hardly knew what to say"). The implied reader or viewer who listens over the shoulder may take on a voyeurist's role, as J. Hillis Miller suggests, "possess[ing] from within the mind of another without that other's knowledge. The reader enjoys the pleasure of knowing without being known" (*Versions* 40). James Barrie calls this illicit participation "a form of eavesdropping," one which may be troubling "if our hands are not clean enough to turn the pages of" (in this case) "a young girl's thoughts" (see chapter 4; this language comes from *Alice Sit-By-The-Fire*, the play Barrie wrote immediately after *Peter Pan*). But then Barrie concludes, with a characteristically destabilizing irony, "It cannot be that, because the novelists do it" (Barrie, *Alice* 2). The oblique stance

FIGURE 2.9. *Citizen Kane* (30:18)

of film's shot / reverse shot editing and of fiction's free indirect discourse here suggests complex themes of power, voyeurism, gender positions, and also the role of narrating agencies as observers of their own observation.

A series of film shots will clarify the conventions of shot / reverse shot sequences by staking extremes on either side of the conventional practice. In all of these examples, an enunciating force plays with watching watching—the fundamental intersubjective premise of shot / reverse shots—in a witty, now-you-see-it, now-you-don't way. These limit cases will help define the peek-a-boo, over-the-shoulder quality of these core moments in sutured narrative. In the first example, *Citizen Kane* refuses to let its audience observe the observing interviewer from the point of view (or shoulder) of the interviewee. Thompson talks to Bernstein, but we never see back over Bernstein's shoulder (or over the shoulder of anyone else Thompson interviews in the film). (See figure 2.9.) In this example, which is perhaps more clever than witty, the film denies the peek-a-boo impulse. We never see who Bernstein is talking to (except as a shadowy figure on the side of a few frames), never see Thompson's response to Bernstein's gaze. Despite the solitude in his big office and the elegant slow camera work (the three-minute sequence is a single long shot), the scene with Bernstein is not intimate. Bernstein is only lonely, or alone in the frame. His position is emphasized by his melancholy memory of the girl in the white dress with the white parasol that he glimpsed, in a brief searing

FIGURE 2.10. *The Silence of the Lambs* (56:46)

moment, on the Jersey ferry fifty years ago: "I only saw her for one second. She didn't see me at all." But "a month hasn't gone by since that I haven't thought of that girl" (30:50). The absence of a reverse shot is thematically right here as it concentrates the sadness in Bernstein's story.

On the other end of the scale, a later scene from *The Silence of the Lambs* (but one that rhymes with our previous scene) contrives to collapse shot / reverse shot choices onto the same plane, eerily reminding the viewer of our need for a boundary (as well as the characters' need), a glass wall, say, between Clarice and Lecter. Again, my example here is not a pair of shots, but one shot that combines shot / reverse shot frames, as Lecter looms over and behind Clarice (even more of a ghostly echo in this frame capture). (See figure 2.10.) This image works as a chiasmus, a visual loop, in several stunning ways. First, one structural irony lies in the fact that in the diegesis of this scene, Lecter appears behind Clarice only to the frame's authorial viewer, since of course the camera, inside Lecter's cell, sees his reflection on the window, but Clarice cannot, and the reflection that seems to place Lecter behind her is in fact on the window in front of her. This dazzling tromp l'oeil both deceives and alerts that viewer, unmasking a labyrinth of gazing and power in the deceptive screen of the prison window. Second, this frame echoes the earlier scene from *The Silence of the Lambs* that I discussed above, in which the over-the-shoulder convention of shot / reverse shots dominated the frames, in a way that I argued was defamiliarizing. Lecter takes now the behind-the-shoulder position of the camera in the classic reverse shot, which is also the privileged position of the film's watcher. Lecter's assumption of our place is almost as disorienting as Thorwald's penetrating gaze into Jeff's (and our) lens in the pair of shots from *Rear Window* that we also looked at above (Jeremy Hawthorn questions whether Thorwald's gaze truly breaks the fourth wall or is instead directed "slightly to one side of the camera"; I don't think it is, for reasons I will discuss below) (171).

In an eerie way, Lecter might be a reflection of *us,* peering over Clarice's shoulder also, as if the film screen suddenly turned into a mirror and revealed us stooping, so to speak, at the keyhole. (The image is Sartre's for the shame always lurking for those who look at the other, because at some embarrassing moment another other may surprise us from behind, exposing our voyeurism by turning on the light in a dark room [347, 349].) But most important in this frame is the sense of danger to people who look at looking, and the recognition (in the authorial audience, at least) that peek-a-boo looking is not safe either. This frame identifies the drive behind the film convention of oblique angles (safety) and unmasks the network of gazes at gazes gazing that the convention typically obscures. This shot begs for an evasion, for a recuperation of obliqueness, like the recuperation (one could argue) that occurs in that second shot in our Hitchcock example that we discussed above, as the film's editor cuts from Thorwald's burning look to a sideways shot of Jeff, his heavy camera slanting down across the frame, the voyeur unmasked, the spy espied, as Hawthorn emphasizes.

Yet another witty variation, another kind of limit case, is a pair of shots from Alain Resnais's *Last Year at Marienbad,* in which the second, reverse shot dismantles convention in multiple ways. The sound recording that connects these two shots, which are exactly sequential, is the male character's word, "Please." (See figures 2.11 and 2.12.) Resnais's staging sabotages (perhaps almost too neatly) the elements of continuity editing: the setting changes from day to night, from outside to inside, from open to closed space, from casual to formal dress, and he violates the 180-degree rule by switching the characters' positions on either side of the frame. Technically, of course, these shots are not oblique points of view. Instead, they enact a clever literalization of shot / reverse shot logic. Rather than reversing camera angles, the film reverses the lovers' figures, but instead of reciprocity, there is no mutual acknowledgement, no chiasmus of response and counterresponse. Furthermore, in the first frame the stone couple in the upper left mirrors (or doesn't mirror) the human

64 | CHAPTER 2

FIGURE 2.11. *Last Year at Marienbad* (27:04)
FIGURE 2.12. *Last Year at Marienbad* (27:07)

couple, but in the second frame no doubling figures appear. The first frame is primarily horizontal in line, and the second is heavily vertical, with the staircase and curtains rising behind the couple in the foreground. These binaries lead to no suturing across these gaps. There is no answer to the man's spoken plea, "Please" (as there is no answer in the rest of the film). The putative lover's yearning across the cut from one shot to its reverse leads nowhere. The narrative arc almost universally implied in this editing convention ends in midair. There is no connection, only misdirection and loss.

But let's return to *The Silence of the Lambs* to look at the way these narrative conventions of the over-the-shoulder gaze, brought into focus by the oddity of the oblique angle, deepen the intricate webs of consciousnesses that get sutured together. Let's look closely at that first interview between Clarice Starling and Hannibal Lecter as an exercise to test the

FIGURE 2.13. *The Silence of the Lambs* (12:23)
FIGURE 2.14. *The Silence of the Lambs* (12:36)

proposition that one mystery of the oblique angle is its power to construct deep intersubjectivity in a particularly disturbing way. The first point to make about this sequence is how it emphasizes the importance and difficulty of seeing clearly. My next frame shows Clarice straining to see around the edge of her frame and the frame of Lecter's cell (see figure 2.13); the following frame concludes a point-of-view tracking shot that brings Clarice and the implied viewer abruptly face-to-face with Lecter, with his direct, unblinking gaze (see figure 2.14). Not seeing and struggling to see suddenly encounter clear seeing, and more menacingly, being seen trying to see. Throughout this sequence, looking continues

66 | CHAPTER 2

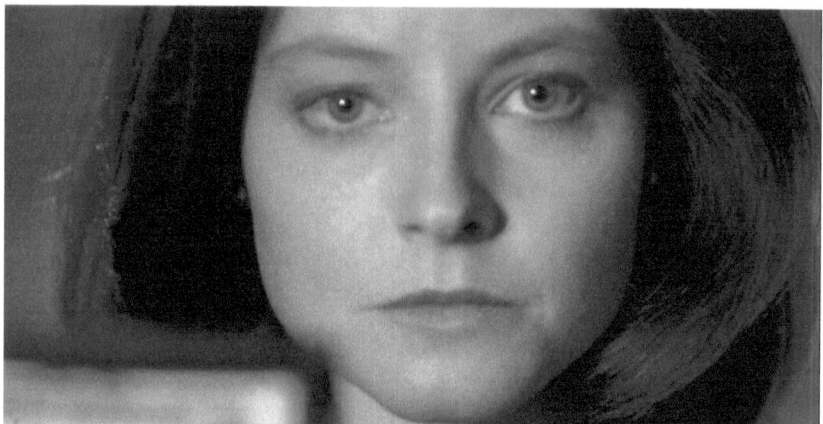

FIGURE 2.15. *The Silence of the Lambs* (13:12)

to be peek-a-boo looking, around corners, frames, edges, and heads blocking the view. This scene provides an especially threatening version of Merleau-Ponty's chiasmus—indeed, it's more like one designed with Sartre's shamed eavesdropper in mind, one in which Lecter not only surprises Clarice by watching her watch him, but enjoys her struggle with the fear produced when she sees him seeing her see him. The web of deep intersubjectivity in this case threatens to tighten into a noose. Peek-a-boo is exposed as providing only an illusion of safety.

My final pair of frames provides a deeply ambiguous fulfillment of the desire to see safely and also transparently: these close-ups almost evade the blocking shapes, though Clarice's frame includes the edge of her plastic identity card, held up in what is still the trace of a defensive gesture, and the camera abandons its over-the-shoulder evasions (see figures 2.15 and 2.16). The starkness of these two images grows partly out of the deeply minimized obliquity: only with care do the implied viewers notice that Lecter and Clarice, unlike Thorwald and Jeff in *Rear Window,* are really *not* threatening to cross the fourth wall with a gaze that endangers the film's audience. Instead, protected by a very small oblique angle, the shot's implied audience watches each character respond more and more intricately to the other's construction of him or her. Lecter is offended by the crudity of the questionnaire that Claire has brought (from Crawford), and she performs yet another identity in response to his decoding of her accent, class ambitions, and fashion accessories. The glass panel that separates them is deceivingly transparent. Seeing them see each other,

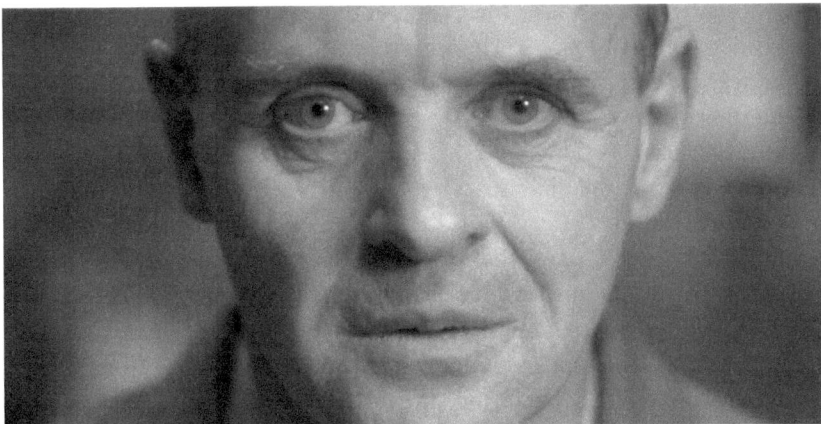

FIGURE 2.16. *The Silence of the Lambs* (13:10)

but still just at an angle, is a way of measuring their evasive yet partial acknowledgement each of the other's projected perception of them.

One small nagging question hovers over the issue of obliqueness: when evaluating the angle, one might ask, can small be too small? Inside the story-world there are usually good spatial and verbal cues to let us know the observer has been observed watching. But when does a film confirm an eyeline match between a character and the authorial viewer? Or not confirm? And how small can the oblique angle become and still provide a screen for the audience? In some cases, real viewers will see very narrow oblique angles differently. Some may reverse my examples above, perhaps seeing no protection for the viewer from the gaze of Clarice and Lecter in this pair of shots, but agreeing with Jeremy Hawthorn that Thorwald does *not* return the camera's gaze directly in that climactic shot in *Rear Window*. In each case, context from the immediate scene might support an argument one way or the other—in Jeff's situation, for example, Thorwald's discovery of Jeff's Peeping Tom gaze is terrifying to Jeff, and it might make thematic sense if the implied viewer is afraid too. Even if Thorwald is looking slightly to the side of Jeff's eye (marked by that iris around the frame), he has detected the presence of the hidden spy and perhaps those spying with him. In contrast, there is no particular dramatic logic to threatening the implied viewer in the *Silence of the Lambs* scene, though Lecter might need no logic to enjoy terrifying someone. But clearly some oblique angles are so subtle as to seem to ask for differing readings. Perhaps these uncertainties actually confirm the thematic issues here: observers need to hide their gaze, and the narrower the hiding place, the riskier the surveillance. The uncertainty magnifies the risk, and this magnification emphasizes the reasons—psychological and political—for taking the risk.

Oudart himself addressed this topic when he referred to "the variations of angle that the obliqueness of the camera with regard to the place of the subject allows" (39). In a different context, I cited Oudart earlier on Bresson's *Joan of Arc,* the film in which "the camera's obliqueness [is] at last openly admitted and established as a system" (37). Bresson "introduc[ed] infinite modulations of shooting angles: the characters may either be almost face-on (the judge) or in three-quarter view (Joan)," and Oudart celebrates the "variation of this angle of attack" (45). "Almost face-on" or not, the position of the implied viewer achieves a similar effect: the possibility of confrontation between gazes, which Oudart indeed bluntly phrases as an "attack," one which is deeply disturbing to the attending viewers. Oudart was primarily interested in the "unease" that flesh-and-blood viewers experienced before the ontologically confrontational 180-degree reverse shot, but the same "unease" applies to the narrative's authorial viewer. It applies even more fearfully to the narrative viewer, who believes Thorwald really lived in Greenwich Village. But there is no standard measure for the degree of that reverse shot's reversal. And, more importantly, wider or narrower oblique angles only dramatize the range of risks. Subtle gradations of fear may only accentuate what is at stake here.

But we need to extend Oudart's insight. The possibility of ontological fear, perhaps terror, also occurs *within* the story, within the frame, as I wrote above, and the edging in and out of that confrontation is a part of the way narrative discourse investigates intersubjectivity. For example, in the larger arc of the narrative of *The Silence of the Lambs,* Clarice's relation to Lecter is deeply unstable: Is she pursuer or pursued, predator or prey, collaborator or betrayer, daughter or beloved? Which role is Lecter's? Viewers of the film will remember that immediately after that first interview, on returning to her car outside the Baltimore state hospital, Clarice has the film's first memory sequence about her father who dies such a painful death. The timing of the memory links Clarice's father to Lecter, but what is the nature of the link? Is Lecter a strange version of or parody of the protective father, in contrast to those fumbling lovers that *he* (Lecter) imagines? Or is he a murky variation of that other serial killer, Buffalo Bill?

These possibilities lurk in the stark moments of mutual gazing that you have before you, as Clarice watches Lecter watch her watching him. The ontological confrontation is deep and disturbing—to Clarice, and to Lecter also, I think we come to know—whether the confrontation leads to loss of or access to some kinds of mutual recognition of recognition, even if partial and partially mistaken ("Look deep into Yourself/Urself": which self, which dark storage chamber?). These shots that I have reproduced from that interview encapsulate issues of knowledges between people that I argue shot / reverse shots and free indirect discourse raise, and obliqueness is fundamental to this study of intersubjective knowledge as both transparent and opaque. Henry James, in chapter 3, will provide equally rich examples of representing in multiple consciousnesses the troubling experiences of oblique intimacy.

v. THE POLITICS OF SUTURE, AGAIN

These close readings of paradigmatic moments of narrative suture, especially deep suture, in those moments of oblique intimacy in *The Silence of the Lambs* and *Nothing But a Man* may seem to concentrate in an austere way on narrative strategy. But suture includes the content as well as the form of human experience. The weight of "race," gender, and the promise of violence in these stories challenges a phenomenology of narrative to work out the political and ideological implications of that phenomenology, to avoid the predilection of some phenomenologists, including some students of narrative, for the transcendental and ahistorical.[17] Laura Doyle pointed us in this direction, in that call to understand our "involuted resistance to and with ourselves and others, a knowing of, against and through others" (Doyle xxv). Doyle's language already images political life as chiasmus ("of, against and through others"), and so it is not a large step to claim a significant politics for chiasmus and suture in narrative. The threads of Merleau-Ponty's chiasmus also trace the matrices of power. Some observers, like Raymond Aron, have argued that Merleau-Ponty's existential phenomenology recommits the sins of his philosophical tradition—individualism, transcendentalism, essentialism—and so rules

---

17. See note 9 in this chapter for this context. A recent student of phenomenology discusses, for example, the elements of his work that provide "the basis of the feminist invocation and feminist critique of Merleau-Ponty" (Olkowski 4).

out a truly radical politics, and even an adequate attention to the weight of history.[18] If Aron was right, then phenomenological narrative theory also risks an ahistorical recourse to transcendental notions of universal subjectivity, intersubjectivity, and suture. But despite some strands of idealism that threaten to erase the specific marks of class or gender, Merleau-Ponty's work sought to locate bodies in specific space and time to avoid idealizing universals. A narrative theory grounded in Merleau-Ponty will seek to explore the politics implicit in the practice of suture. Those politics will range across the variety of human arrangements; the point here is simply that because suture is embedded in the social life represented in a narrative, it will carry political implications.

For Merleau-Ponty history and political experience are loops of experience that touch in a chiasmus and yet may be isolated. This imagery recurs insistently in his account of the weight of history in his experience in *Humanism and Terror* (1947), when he describes his difficult situation, torn between the betrayals of the Moscow trials of the late 1930s and American imperialism:

> Thus we find ourselves in an inextricable situation. The Marxist critique of capitalism is still valid.... On the other hand, the Revolution has come to a halt: it maintains and aggravates the dictatorial apparatus while... abandoning the humane control of the State. It is impossible to be an anti-Communist and it is not possible to be a Communist. (xxi)

On the one hand, and on the other: it is impossible to be this, or that; the self is split but is embedded in this moment: there is no extrication, no espousal across the gaps. Yet *Humanism and Terror* also offers one of Merleau-Ponty's most hopeful explorations of politics as deep intersubjectivity:

> Doubt and disagreement are facts, but so is the strange pretension we all have of thinking the truth, our capacity for taking the other's position to judge ourselves, our need to have our opinions recognized by him—in short the experience of the other person as an *alter ego* in the very course of discussion. The human world is an open and unfinished system, and the same radical contingency which threatens it with discord also

---

18. See Laurie Spurling, *Phenomenology and the Social World*, chapter 4, where she cites Aron and argues that Merleau-Ponty's notion of agency is fully consistent with Marxist activism.

rescues it from the inevitability of disorder and prevents us from despairing of it. (188)

Human consciousnesses perceive each other perceiving each other: that is the loop of chiasmus and suture at their most constructive—"our capacity for taking the other's position to judge ourselves, our need to have our opinions recognized by him." Here, as elsewhere, Merleau-Ponty's hopefulness about the Other, as partner in this deep intersubjectivity, drives the politics of his phenomenology toward espousal, while, for example, Sartre's suspicion of the Other warns of shame and violation.

The politics of absence is an especially useful topic because absence was fundamental in the Lacanian paradigm for suture that has been so influential in narrative film theory. In this chapter, absence has become less empty, whether the absence within sutured film frames or within the *un*sutured film frame, because both are examples of Merleau-Ponty's interworld of intending bodies. Once again Merleau-Ponty and Sartre provide paradigmatic moments, in this instance for reconceiving absence in dramatically different, yet equally post-Lacanian terms. Merleau-Ponty's *Humanism and Terror* begins with the missing, those "friends whose names we would inscribe here were it permissible to make witnesses of the dead," including one who,

> after his men had been taken prisoner by the militiamen, went into the village to share their fate since he could do nothing more for them . . . : Then it will not seem strange if we, who have to speak about communism, search in darkness and mist for those faces that have gone from the earth. (xlvi–xlvii)

In contrast, when Sartre struggles to come to terms with the sudden death of Merleau-Ponty, he reviews their years of comradeship at *Les Temps Modernes,* the joint discovery of Husserl, the bitter disagreement over Stalin, and concludes without suture, in an astonishing image of pain and loss: "It was us, we two, who loved each other badly. There is nothing to be concluded from this except that this long friendship, neither done nor undone, obliterated when it was about to be reborn, or broken, remains inside me, an always open wound" (Cohen-Solal 439). For Merleau-Ponty, it is possible to place a stone in the niche vacated by the other; for Sartre, it is not. The open wound remains. Yet, despite their different notions of intersubjectivity, for neither Merleau-Ponty nor Sartre was emptiness empty.

Instead, absence is attachment and wound. The same doubleness—attachment and wound—fills the gaps in the chiasmatic frames that narrate Duff and Josie's difficult intersections in *Nothing But a Man*. African-American life in 1960s Alabama knits together visibly the personal and the political; both promote attachments that wound. This marriage bears the weight of many hopes and fears both personal and political, as Duff the lost son finds his son, and he and Josie refuse to abandon the South: they *will* make their lives here, together, all of them. The same link, between attachment and wound, haunts Gawande's account of cutting flesh with which I began. And the absence of attachment looms in Plath's poem, in which the wound is all. Suture as form and theme takes multiple forms, with versions of indirection as an enabling strategy. Next I look at my first example of such enabling strategies of indirection: free indirect discourse's over-the-shoulder narration, what in chapter 1 I called Obliqueness I, in some of the late novels of Henry James, and its respective form in some James films. This case study points toward my larger theme as well: that suture is one narrative strategy by which stories suggest what can be stitched together and what cannot, and what is at stake in either case.

CHAPTER 3

The Case of Henry James

Suture and Deep Intersubjectivity

"Yes, look, look," she seemed to see him hear her say even while her sounded words were other.
   —Henry James, *The Golden Bowl*

It is because there are these 2 doublings-up that are possible: the insertion of the world between the two leaves of my body / the insertion of my body between the 2 leaves of each thing and of the world
   —Maurice Merleau-Ponty, *The Visible and the Invisible*

There was an extraordinary mute passage between her vision of this vision of his, his vision of her vision, and her vision of his vision of her vision.
   —Henry James, *What Maisie Knew*

i. THEORY I: SUTURING CONSCIOUSNESSES

The labyrinths and obliquities of suture in narrative could have no better examples, serving perhaps as a kind of limit case, than the fiction, especially the late novels, of Henry James. Indeed, human consciousness functions in such intricate ways in Henry James's work that readers have commented on those intricacies from the first, from early reviews of *The Portrait of a Lady* and *The Golden Bowl* to F. R. Leavis, Dorothy Van Ghent, and Millicent Bell, who observes simply, "Subjectivity is his subject" (32). In 1882 W. C. Brownell wrote, of *The Portrait of a*

Lady, that James's "secretive natures are turned inside out for the reader's inspection," with such "microscopy" that, he concluded, "Mr James's powers of observation are not only remarkably keen, but sleepless as well" (664). Thinking in James—though consciousness is more than thinking—has been a significant topic, even a title, in James criticism. Conceiving with enough clarity just how consciousness gets represented has, however, been difficult. The sand keeps running through our fingers.

Various theoretical and methodological questions contribute to the difficulty beyond the apparently amorphous notion of "consciousness" itself: these representations raise issues of rhetoric, convention, genre and audience, just for starters, and then there are the narratological questions: what do we make of the Jamesian narrator/"historian"/observer? Who is this "we" in *The Wings of the Dove*: "Other things than those we have presented had come up before the close of his scene with Aunt Maud" (II, ii; 110)? And at a more implicit level, who or what orchestrates the fitful flashes of the lamplight into, say, Isabel Archer's thoughts? What narrative agency is in control of the Jamesian *syuzhet's* elegant arabesques across his tale's *fabula* (and its windows opening at carefully timed moments into one subjectivity or another)? Finally, to raise the topic of consciousness in James threatens to remind readers of the sins of some earlier phenomenological criticism, with its claims of transparent authorial intentions, transcendental reader participation in texts, and even transparent characters in what seemed to be unmediated narrative.[1] My approach to suture offers new ways to conceptualize James's narrative practices by tracing out the implications of the chiasmus and then by connecting them to conventions of free indirect discourse. This chapter assays a closer study of what in chapter 1 I called Oblique I. My final section will compare the kinds of indirections we have studied in James's novels with the kinds of indirections that are important in a few usefully comparable James films.

Critics return to phenomenology because something significant remains to explore in James's special constructions of human experience,

---

1. For a study of the Jamesian representations of consciousness as rhetorical strategies, see Sheila Teahan, *The Rhetorical Logic of Henry James*, which "investigat[es] the Jamesian reflective center as a rhetorical rather than a phenomenological, structure" (13). A good recent example of narratological reflection is J. Hillis Miller's *Literature as Conduct*, for instance his examination of James's excessive claims about not "going behind" as narrator in *The Awkward Age* (117–22). On the sins of mid-century phenomenological readings, see Frank Lentricchia, *After the New Criticism* 72ff. and Butte 8–17. Other references in these paragraphs: F. R. Leavis, *The Great Tradition*; Dorothy Van Ghent, *The English Novel: Form and Function*; Sharon Cameron, *Thinking in Henry James*.

because we have not said enough yet about "consciousness" in James. But Robert Weisbuch, a critic who celebrates James's complex studies of consciousness, shows how easy it is to overstep into that transcendental mode: "his characters respond with the utmost consequence to each other's verbal and physical nuances to the point where a kind of mystical telepathy without the mysticism gets created" (102). Two of the best phenomenological students of James, Paul Armstrong and Merle Williams, avoid the telepathy and concentrate on those bodies and words. Not surprising, therefore, is the importance of Merleau-Ponty's work for both Armstrong and Williams. Although at moments Merleau-Ponty's phenomenology of perception echoes an older idealism, his thought typically seeks to critique Husserlian hopes for entering the "essence" of the Other, especially in his later work, as in the meditations on the chiasm in *The Visible and the Invisible,* which are fundamental to Williams's thinking, and to this chapter. This is the Merleau-Ponty that Derrida, in the extended meditation on his thought in *On Touching—Jean-Luc Nancy,* refers to as "a *certain* Merleau-Ponty" (192) in whom, Derrida explains several pages later, "we can recognize an increasing insistence on self-inadequation, dehiscences, fissions, interruptions, incompletion, and the visible body openly gaping, as well as hiatuses, eclipses" (212). It is this poststructuralist Merleau-Ponty and his chiasm that offer a new way to understand James's representation of human consciousnesses in much of his fiction. And Merleau-Ponty's chiasm enables the embodied approach to suture that I'm tracing in this book.

The architecture of human relationships in James is intricately, explicitly, and expansively intersubjective. I want to look at this structure of human consciousness, which is a structure of consciousness*es*, by way of this notion of "deep intersubjectivity," which, as I argue in *I Know That You Know That I Know: Narrating Subjects from "Moll Flanders" to "Marnie,"* is a narrative practice that emerges about the time of Jane Austen, with perhaps some earlier examples, which Lisa Zunshine has seen in *Clarissa* (as I noted in chapter 1). In these stories, the mirrorings of subjectivities multiply, sometimes almost vertiginously. Deep intersubjectivity extends the narrative of consciousness of consciousness to the all-important third (and exponentially different) orbit in this solar system of subjectivities, to one's perception, or the belief that one perceives, in the other's body or language a trace of one's own previous and now appropriated gesture, and so on down the long corridor of attending consciousnesses that, however indolent or perhaps malevolent, perceive or misperceive embodiments in subjects that attend to each other. "Deep intersubjectivity" names this string of perceptions, in a series of nested narrations represented as inside or beside other consciousnesses.²

In this paradigm, as in Merleau-Ponty, neither transparency or transcendence is possible, yet the consequence of this limitation is not impenetrable epistemological darkness. There is a third alternative. In deeply intersubjective narrative, characters perceive their own initiating gestures to be mirrored in others' responding movement or enunciation. This trace of their consciousness's gesture embodied back to them from the other is, within the narrative's diegesis, *not* entirely an illusion, although the degree of error and deception varies enormously, especially in James's fiction, as gestures responding (in good faith or bad) to gestures multiply in dazzlingly labyrinthine sequences. As Merle Williams said of Merleau-Ponty's social ontology, which illuminates James's, there is no effort "to achieve a utopian coincidence of the self with the self in pure transparency," yet the individual is "a network of relationships," in fact a chiasm (172, 171).³ Merleau-Ponty sees this knotting of consciousnesses

---

2. This paradigm bears important structural similarities to models of embedded representations of human minds in Lisa Zunshine's work on narrative in *Why We Read Fiction: Theory of Mind and the Novel*. Zunshine approaches theory of mind in stories by way of contemporary cognitive science and identifies certain limits in human brain circuits on the number of boxes inside boxes that we can track. One of her trenchant examples is that episode of the television series *Friends* that I cited in chapter 1, in which Phoebe realizes that Chandler knows that Phoebe knows that Chandler has been dating Monica and so in revenge has pretended to flirt with him, but Phoebe determines to complete the plan: "They're trying to mess with *us*? They don't know that we know they know we know!" The result, Zunshine observes, is "a momentary cognitive vertigo induced by the multiple mind-embedment" (30–31). My essay stops mostly at the third orbit, and works with the enormously rich interweavings of multiple intentionalities across multiple scenarios inside that orbit that our minds *can* track more or less easily. Another writer interested in multiple embeddings, as part of a different narratological project, is Alan Palmer, in *Fictional Minds* (see "Doubly Embedded Narratives," 230–39). Palmer frames this subject in a different way in *Social Minds*, where he lays out an anatomy of different scales of "intermental cognitive systems" (that is, minds that work together as a kind of organism) that "are, to some extent, independent of the individual elements that go to make them up" (44). Intersubjectivity occurs in these "units, large, medium, or small," where sometimes "so much successful intermental thought takes place that they can plausibly be considered as group minds" (48). Palmer offers long-term couples as a good example of the small units. Of course, in James even long-term couples may not be very successful in thinking together.

3. Williams understands the complex relation in Merleau-Ponty between centripetal and centrifugal elements in that social ontology his work constructs. Williams does err on the centripetal side when she mis-cites Merleau-Ponty on the mirror phase in children and its "'de-realizing' function": as the quotes inside quotes indicate, Merleau-Ponty is here paraphrasing Lacan's argument, which he then criticizes in important language

as an epistemologically uncertain web that offers partial, imperfect shreds of knowledge, as he writes in those lecture notes I cited in chapter 2: "There is woven between us an 'exchange,' a 'chiasm between two "destinies" . . .' in which there are never quite two of us, and yet one is never alone" (*In Praise* 82). Earlier in his career, Merleau-Ponty veered closer to a transcendentalism, suggesting the possibility of transparency, as in his early work *The Phenomenology of Perception* (1944):

> Suppose that my friend Paul and I are looking at a landscape. What precisely happens? Must it be said that we have both private sensations, that we know things but cannot communicate them to each other . . . ? At no moment am I aware of being shut up within my own sensations. . . . I believe, on the contrary, that my gestures invade Paul's world and guide his gaze. (405)

Although the later Merleau-Ponty will reject radical solipsism with equal vigor, his thinking becomes more contradictory, as befits his increased use of the image of the chiasm. In 1960, in the introduction to *Signs*, he argues that people are both distant and close: "[Others] are not fictions with which I might people my desert—but my twins or flesh of my flesh. Certainly I do not live their lives; they are definitely absent from me and I from them. But that distance becomes a strange proximity" (*Signs* 15).

Suture in James works through a variety of strategies for crossing this distance to produce a "strange proximity." The close readings that follow unpack this distant closeness that is once again neither transcendental, transparent, nor entirely opaque, and a major choice in effecting this ambiguous state of consciousnesses is the over-the-shoulder oblique stance of free indirect discourse. When I argued at the end of chapter 2 that shot / reverse shot conventions in film resemble the conventions of free indirect discourse, I was thinking of this claim in Merleau-Ponty that consciousness of consciousness at its best produces not transcendental perception but a sense of others that retains its "distance" that "becomes a strange proximity." This notion of strange, distant closeness anticipates J. Hillis Miller's notion, which I take up in chapter 4, that free indirect discourse has something of the "uncanny" about it. This sequence of thought captures a major effort of this book, to move from the phenomenological to the narratological.

---

as inadequately attentive to a child's prior embodiment for and to itself. See Williams 91–92; Merleau-Ponty, "The Child's Relation" 136–40; and Butte 19–20.

Here indeed is a phenomenology of narrative for Henry James: renouncing the (apparent) idealism of Husserl, the transparencies of Georges Poulet, and the austere loneliness of Lacan or Levinas, it can track what is remarkable in James, the extended threadings of the chiasmus of subjectivities in various story rhetorics, from my notion of the "intersubjective failure of intersubjectivity" in *The Awkward Age* (Butte 163), across a range of narrative forms, including what J. Hillis Miller recently pondered (and rejected) as "a general phenomenology of the kiss" in *The Portrait of a Lady* (*Literature as Conduct* 81), to the rare moments of comedy that celebrate—in Merleau-Ponty's terms—espousal, however partial and fleeting (see Butte 32–34). *Espousal* is an essential notion for my approach to James, because such moments, however fragile and rare, do occur in his stories. *Espousal* is Merleau-Ponty's word for those encounters in which subjects never transcend their separateness, yet appropriate *for* each other in a sequence of gestures to responding gestures. On one hand, says Merleau-Ponty, there is always "a sort of wall between me and the other: a partition; henceforth it will prevent me from confusing myself with what the other thinks, and especially with what he thinks of me" ("The Child's Relation" 19–20). And yet when

> from the depths of my subjectivity I see another subjectivity . . . , I understand this behavior, the words of another; I espouse his thought because this other, born in the midst of my phenomena, appropriates them and treats them in accord with typical behaviors I myself have experienced. (*Primacy* 18)

But espousal, however partial or even mistaken, is only one narrative practice of deep intersubjectivity, one particular chiasmatic threading, its rarity a way to estimate the sadness of James's typical world of misunderstandings added to misunderstandings added to deceptions. Moments of relative clarity in the circle of perceptions perceived between people do occur in James—Isabel to Ralph in *A Portrait of a Lady,* Maisie to Beale in *What Maisie Knew*—but it is a sign of the darkness of the last novels on which I will be concentrating that these moments become fewer and fewer. In *The Golden Bowl,* for example, the strongest examples of espousal—extenuated, tangled—may occur between Fanny and Bob Assingham. These labyrinths of perceptions (and misperceptions) do make some sense finally because of the heterodiegetic narrative voice that traces their pathways for its competent reader—in this case, a very competent reader.

Chiasmus names the partial and ambiguous threadings of consciousnesses that are the substance of James's deeply intersubjective narratives. You may remember from chapter 1 that the chiasmus or chiasm is a trope of crisscrossing (a more whimsical example: "the corn was full of kernels, and the colonels were full of corn"), sort of X-shaped, and Merleau-Ponty's chiasm points to both knowing and unknowing, linkage and bondage, the thickness of each separate thread yet the closeness of each to the other. The famous image occurs in "The Intertwining—The Chiasm," from *The Visible and the Invisible*:

> The field is open for another Narcissus, for an "intercorporeity." If my left hand can touch my right hand . . . , can touch it touching, can turn its palpation back upon it, why, when touching the hand of another, would I not touch in it the same power to espouse the things that I have touched in my own? (141)

Here is espousal once more, now as a theory of bodies rather than a theory of minds. And bodies lie at the center of the process. Merleau-Ponty's language does in fact oscillate between more and less transcendental tones. For example, on the more transcendental side: "When one of my hands touches the other, the world of each opens upon that of the other because the operation is reversible at will, because they both belong (as we say) to one sole space of consciousness" (*Visible* 141). A reversibility "at will" within a "sole" common world of shared consciousnesses does sound positively premodern. On the other, less transcendental side: "There is no coinciding of the seer with the visible. But each borrows from the other . . . , is in chiasm with the other" (*Visible* 261). Or this image of thickness to remind us of the body and its space: "this 1) does not realize a surpassing, a dialectic in the Hegelian sense; 2) is realized on the spot, by encroachment, thickness, *spatiality*" (*Visible* 264).

In truth it has been difficult to remember the doubleness of Merleau-Ponty's chiasm, and readers have often emphasized either the intimacy and reversibility of the threads, or the space between them and the thickness of each strand. Proponents of the transcendental reading fall themselves into two groups: those proposing such a reading to discredit Merleau-Ponty, and those defending the transcendental. In the first group is Jean-Paul Sartre, for example, who rejected what he saw as the idealism lurking in Merleau-Ponty's "continuum," an "interworld" linking things and human consciousness, and accused him of the essentialism Merleau-Ponty so stringently critiqued: "Reading [Merleau-Ponty] at times, it would seem that being invents man in order to make itself manifest through him" (Dastur 33, 47–48). Levinas in a similar vein rejected the move toward reversibility of bodies in Merleau-Ponty's chiasmus: in James Hatley's words, for Levinas "the other's body provides no place at all for my own erring" (Hatley 242), and Levinas wrote, as I reported in chapter 2, about Merleau-Ponty's hands touching hands touching, that these are "two hands, which precisely do not belong to the same body, nor to a hypothetical or only metaphorical intercorporeality" (Levinas, "Intersubjectivity" 59). Others, however, have celebrated what seems to them the transcendental strains in Merleau-Ponty's thought: as Fred Evans and Leonard Lawlor put it, "the trace of the Other would be a verticality from which on high a command would come," and "the Good beyond being would put a break in totality" (14). Derrida typically criticizes this Merleau-Ponty, in contrast to the more persuasive, skeptical (in his view) Husserl or Nancy.

Fewer readers emphasize chiasmus as loss, but at least one, Luce Irigaray, characterizes Merleau-Ponty's thought (in Tina Chanter's words) as dominated by "closure and solipsism," by both a "lack of questioning and [a] failure to preserve otherness" (220). For Chanter, Irigaray's essay emphasizes Merleau-Ponty's notion of reversibility (in touching the hand touching the other's touching) as a closed system, blind especially to gender's "creative" elements: this "way of talking about the flesh . . . already cancels its most powerful components, those that are moreover creative in their power" (Irigaray 175, cited by Chanter 220). Chanter's own analysis is diplomatic: she finds in Merleau-Ponty both "a genuinely radical alternative to traditional categories" that is useful for feminist philosophy, and also an inability to "[go] far enough" in rethinking gender and the body (220). Because of its blindnesses, the promise of the chiasm becomes in Irigaray a threat: in her own words,

> According to Merleau-Ponty, energy plays itself out in the backward-and-forward motion of a loom. But weaving the visible and my look in this way . . . , the texture becomes increasingly tight, taking me into it, sheltering me there but imprisoning me as well. (183)

There is no exit from this chiasm, with all its ambiguity as shelter and prison. In a contrasting move, Derrida sees the chiasm in Merleau-Ponty as threads with a gap (his note on "a *certain* Merleau-Ponty," cited above); in Ian James's words, while connecting Merleau-Ponty to a "continuist and intuitionist . . . tradition," Derrida nonetheless "himself points out there is a degree to which Merleau-Ponty's discourse of touch also implies rupture or separation, whereby flesh, although a site of intertwining . . . , is also a site of discontinuity" (I. James 130).

In response to these complexities and possibilities in Merleau-Ponty's image of the chiasm, it may be useful to reflect on complexities it does *not* include. One of the most significant gaps in Merleau-Ponty's work is its consistent and serious blindness about gender. Almost all of its assumptions and examples (even to watching that landscape with Paul) are masculinist, and there is little that complicates these assumptions, or even suggests an awareness of that framework. This absence is all the sadder because the focus on embodiment, on lived experience, in Merleau-Ponty's work from its beginnings had such promise for feminist thought. One reflection of that promise is Simone de Beauvoir's early review of *The Phenomenology of Perception* in *Les Temps Modernes* in 1945, which affirms its core notion of the situated, embodied subject (Olkowski 3). Indeed, Dorothea Olkowski says that Merleau-Ponty gave de Beauvoir credit for laying "the foundations of existential phenomenology" in her 1943 novel *L'invitee* (4). The sometimes bitter criticisms of later feminists like Luce Irigaray and Judith Butler reflect the complexity of this inheritance. When Butler reads Irigary's reading of Merleau-Ponty, she traces layers of misreadings of misreadings, albeit sometimes only partially mistaken, especially as she (Butler) tracks the asymmetry of the chiasmus; what Butler calls the "noncoincident ontology of the flesh" may suggest a failure of the project to defeat solipsism (Olkowski 124). Or not. For Irigaray, the image of the chiasmus points to "two lips" (an image I will use in chapter 4 for the lips of the wound in suture), and Butler then comments, about *The Visible and the Invisible,*

> It will be this text from which Irigaray cites and derives her own notion of the 'two lips,' and which she mimes into a feminist usage that Merleau-Ponty could not have intended. Does this not signify a life of the text that exceeds whatever solipsism afflicts its inception? (Olkowski 125)

Laura Doyle, whose work I discussed in chapter 2, offers another example of the response by feminist phenomenologists to the complexity of the body in chiasmus here: writing about women in prison and the suffering in Toni Morrison's *The Bluest Eye,* Doyle says, "Merleau-Ponty can help us understand this paradoxical dynamic in which bodily vulnerability forms the ground of resistance," how "the body is a reserve as well as an inescapable site of torture—exactly both at once in its doubleness" (Olkowski 183, 188).

Another paradoxical text that reflects this contradictory inheritance is Sara Ahmed's *Queer Phenomenology,* which focuses on "orientation" (meant literally) of bodies in space and time and asks, "What does it mean to queer phenomenology?" Her response begins, "In Merleau-Ponty's *The Phenomenology of Perception* queer moments do happen—as moments where the world appears 'slantwise,'" and suggests how "a queer phenomenology might offer an approach to sexual orientation by rethinking the place of the object in sexual desire" (23). But the situated body in Merleau-Ponty's chiasm is still not classed, not sexed, not gendered, not marked by ethnic embodiment or culture, not queered. These absences are in a way the more remarkable because the social ontology of *Humanism and Terror,* Merleau-Ponty's anguished work of 1947, acknowledges history and culture in deep and profound ways. The idealist strains in *The Phenomenology of Perception,* published in Paris in 1945 and written and revised during the Nazi occupation, stand in strong contrast to the powerful acknowledgement of the contingencies of history and class in the book published two years later, about Stalinism and political choices in an imperfect world. I want to recognize these contradictions and flaws in Merleau-Ponty's work, and to balance their effects with recourse to other thinkers in the phenomenological tradition who can address embodiments that he did not. The gendering of the situated body will be an especially important topic in some of the readings that follow.

However compromised Merleau-Ponty's work may be by some echoes of ancient transcendentalisms, and by its blindness to assumptions about gender, class, and ethnicity, his image of the chiasm is manifestly complicated in ways that will help us conceptualize deep intersubjectivity and the role of suture in James's narratives. The registers of the intersubjective in James are multiple, but all presume a fundamental limit to human perception: as Paul Armstrong puts it, "perfect transcendence escapes us," and in James's fiction, a key question always is "How does James understand the opacity of the Other," since "intersubjective opacity" looms everywhere (*Phenomenology* 135, 16)? Armstrong writes in a more recent book that despite the often unresolvable tangle of differing interpretations of the world, "overcoming the distance that divides selves is perhaps our most crucial moral and existential aim" for James, but "transcendental communion" is still not possible (*Challenge* 103). However, intersubjective opacity is not only a threat. Certainly, as Armstrong wrote in his earlier James book, it "makes the lie possible" in *What Maisie Knew* (16), but it can also protect and shelter, in the chiasm that Merleau-Ponty believed we knit together:

> It is said that the colors, the tactile reliefs given to the other are for me an absolute mystery, forever inaccessible. This is not completely true; for me to have . . . an imminent [note: not immanent] experience of them, it suffices that I look at a landscape, that I speak of it with someone. (*Visible* 142)

Twenty years later, Merleau-Ponty is still echoing that moment with Paul from *The Phenomenology of Perception* and figuring out its ontology and its epistemology. But some kind and degree of espousal is one product of these loops. Conversely, intersubjective *clarity* can terrify and exploit, exponentially so when we consider the power of deep intersubjectivity's nested narrations of perceptions of perceptions perceived. The chiasm allows for subtle degrees of mutually imbricated transparency and opacity. These imbrications vary along subtle ranges of intentionalities and confusions within the consciousnesses that are reading and misreading their webs of embodiments in the receding series of perceptions that make up the labyrinths of deeply intersubjective narratives.[4] Suture theory mirrors these multiplicities in its range of models for connections between the pathways of the labyrinths: from the oblique editing of free indirect discourse that either obscures or confesses to its gaps, which can promise Kaja Silverman's castrating coherence, to forms of plenitude, however partial, that promote the promises as well as the risks of connecting to the other (or Other).

James's language in his preface to *What Maisie Knew* articulates a model that suggests similar multiplicities for connecting and suturing consciousnesses in storytelling:

> No themes are so human as those that reflect for us, out of the confusion of life, the close connexion of bliss and bale, of the things that help with the things that hurt, so dangling before us for ever that bright hard medal, of so strange an alloy, one face of which is somebody's right and ease and the other somebody's pain and wrong. To live with all intensity and perplexity and felicity in its terribly mixed little world would thus be the part of my interesting small mortal. (25)

James's medal is an image curiously similar to Merleau-Ponty's chiasm: it brings together two threads of experience, two hands with a history of touching or two faces backing up to each other; these strains of consciousness are intimately linked, and their relation as a sequence is easily reversible.

---

4. See Butte, chapter 1, for a discussion of promises and terrors across deep intersubjectivity's array of clarities and obscurities.

As I have argued elsewhere, Merleau-Ponty's hope is always for reversibility leading to espousal, though like his contemporary and sometime antagonist Sartre, he knew intimacy could produce fear, shame, betrayal, and violation (Butte 28–29). James emphasizes the strangeness of the alloy that brings his two faces back to back, and the closeness of ease to wrong, of help to hurt, of bliss to bale; intersubjectivity in James's paradigm is intimate but devious, multiple, wounding, sometimes clarifying, always "terribly mixed."

This extraordinary image for confusion's intimacy helps explain the range of deeply intersubjective alloys in James: from Isabel and Gilbert's construction not only of the other but of a version of the other's perception (at least partially distorted) of her or him and their initial gestures, so that the novel's sad tangle is in one sense not the result of either's bad faith; to Maisie's comic/hopeless hope in chapter 19 that recounting the Captain's claimed perception of her mother ("My dear Maisie, your mother's an angel!" [131]) might inspire in her father not jealousy but emulation; to Fanny Assingham's byzantine speculations, sifted with comic despair by Bob, about who knew or believed they knew what Amerigo thought Adam thought Charlotte believed (see *The Golden Bowl*, chapter 33, page 426, for example). Here, then, with a vengeance, is the closeness of help to hurt, of felicity to perplexity, of consciousness responding to other consciousnesses responding also (consensually or not) across the loops of the chiasmus, getting things perhaps a little right and a lot wrong and partly making it up as they go along (especially Fanny). With these images of the interlocking (chiasm, medal) in mind, perhaps we can now begin to outline the range and varieties of deep intersubjectivities in James, and then the range and variety of suture's strategies for linking (or not) the threads of the chiasmus, and finally to reflect on the themes these strategies most persuasively explore.

ii. PRACTICE: READING LOOKING

> It's the hobbies you pursue together,
> savings you accrue together,
> looks you misconstrue together,
> That make marriage a joy.
> —Stephen Sondheim, "The Little Things You Do Together," *Company*

A study of deep intersubjectivities and their interthreadings in James could have three organizing subjects: one, a study of the representation of specific behaviors (the gaze or look, embraces or the kiss, two people alone, two people amidst others, more than two people, for example); the second, a study of social, ideological, and thematic outcomes (from specific degrees of misunderstanding, confusion, and masquerade or clarity and espousal, to wider implications about social convention, agency, the nature of the self and community, and genre practices that may articulate these implications); and the third, a meditation on the narratological implications of Jamesian deep intersubjectivity for questions about narrative authority, for example, and free indirect discourse. My plan here is to follow those three steps in miniature: first, to study a typically Jamesian moment of deeply intersubjective behavior, then to point toward a range of thematic outcomes, and finally to conclude with an outline of significant narratological implications in these examples of deeply intersubjective practice. This section ranges across the first two topics, from examples and their structure to themes. The next, the third, section teases out narratological implications of these examples, and then we step back to look at the larger thematic significance of these strategies for James's project in our novels. Finally, I'll compare themes and narrative form in some appropriate examples from the large body of James films (including television works) made in the last fifty years.

The Jamesian moment I want to examine, a knot of behaviors so common especially in late James as to be archetypal, is looking at looking observed, examples for which Merleau-Ponty's chiasm provides a particularly useful paradigm. Some of the most complex and poignant moments of Jamesian deep intersubjectivity begin with the look: however, not only the look, but looking at looking, and indeed, as the chiasm turns, so to speak, looking at looking observed and construed or misconstrued alone, or with another, in the complicated webbing that the Sondheim line in my headnote to this section proposes. The gaze is such a good and typically Jamesian moment because it immediately suggests issues of masquerade and performance that become even more labyrinthine in their deeply intersubjective forms. A paradigmatic moment of looking at looking observed occurs in *The Wings of the Dove,* when Milly happens upon Densher and Kate in the National Gallery. This small drama begins when Milly overhears an American woman and her two daughters evaluating some object of their gaze as "Handsome... in the English style" (V, 7; 241). Milly turns to discover that object to be not a painting but Merton Densher, who is unaware of her presence. She gazes at him until she discovers Kate Croy is watching her watching. In the following moments, various negotiations occur among these three characters, who had just parted earlier in the morning with no mention of anyone's plans to visit the National Gallery, and then Milly invites Merton and Kate to her hotel for lunch. Here is the moment of collision, so to speak:

> For in the very act of judging the bared head with detachment she felt herself shaken by a knowledge of it. It was Merton Densher's own, and he was standing there, standing there long enough unconscious for her to fix him and then hesitate. These successions were swift, so that she could still ask herself in freedom if she had best let him see her. She could still reply to this that she shouldn't like him to catch her in the effort to prevent it; and she might further have decided that he was too preoccupied to see anything had not a perception intervened that surpassed the first in violence. She was unable to think afterwards how long she had looked at him before knowing herself as otherwise looked at.... The source of this latter shock was Kate Croy—Kate Croy who was suddenly also in the line of vision and whose eyes met her eyes at their next movement. (V, 7; 242)

This moment of crisis mirrors exactly the paradigmatic moment of exposure and shame that for Sartre is always implicit in the gaze. A man stoops at a keyhole, only to discover he is himself being watched: to gaze is always to open oneself to the rupture of the other's gaze, says Sartre (in contrast to Merleau-Ponty, for whom espousal is sometimes possible).[5] But humiliation and bad faith even in masquerade are generally the rule in James, as in Sartre: "'Being-seen-by-the-Other' is the *truth* of 'seeing-the-Other.'... He is that object in the world that determines an internal hemorrhage" (Sartre 345). With the orbits of deep intersubjectivity added, the gazer unmasked becomes a figure in a series of ploys, of gestures that seek

---

5. The contrast here, as in chapter 1, between shame and espousal, between Sartre and Merleau-Ponty (see Butte ch. 1, 24*ff.*) resembles the contrast that Paul Armstrong draws between Sartrean conflict and Heideggerian "care" as models for intersubjective relations (*Phenomenology* 138–39). Armstrong's book, like this essay, charts a course between epistemological and thematic extremes. It is my view, however, that deep intersubjectivity serves in James more to illuminate types of opacity and misperception than to dramatize clarity of perception of embodiments in what for Merleau-Ponty was an intercorporeal interworld. Intercorporealities—touching touching, seeing seeing—do occur in James, and give to some moments of opacity an intensely painful intimacy. Merle Williams also draws comparisons between Sartre and Merleau-Ponty, whose "approach to human phenomena" is less "warily distrustful" than Sartre's (135). I agree, and would add that Merleau-Ponty's chiasmus allows us also to measure the deep darkness in a writer like James.

to block, penetrate, circumvent, expose, shield. Above all the unmasked gazer seeks to hide the bleeding inside. James's language represents these multiple strategies as his characters experience the shame and violence lurking within their strings of perception.

One of Milly's strategies is to deflect the violence by encouraging a kind of masquerade: by allowing the violators to restage the moment of violence, and to promote the impression that the restaging has succeeded, an impression she is pleased to see acknowledged. Merton, on turning to Milly, flushes or blushes, and employs a strategy of renaming for containing the moment's fearful implications: "Why Miss Theale: what luck!" (V, 7; 243). But Milly knows what the moment was: it's a "predicament," marked in the way that, she believes, she sees Kate and Densher *not* look at each other: "distinctly, his companion had no more looked at him with a hint than he had looked at her with a question" (V, 7; 243). All three agree to the renaming, "despite the monstrous oddity of their turning up in such a place on the very heels of their having separated without allusion to it," to avoid more specific language: "the predicament of course wasn't definite or phraseable—and the way they let all phrasing pass was presently to occur to our young woman as a characteristic triumph of the civilized state" (V, 7; 243). Pretense works for this moment in a deeply intersubjective series of looks and words named and avoided, in a comic yet desperate improvisation of a story that will preserve appearances, while leaving unclear who really knows what about whose relation to whom.

Milly is so pleased with her escape because the power of the aggressors is palpable to her. Early in the scene, she worries that Densher might "catch her" watching him, or worse, catch her trying to avoid being seen seeing. Another kind of power, at least in Milly's perception, works its spell immediately after Kate's initial smile, which tells Milly that Kate knows Milly has observed Kate's grasp of Milly's observation of Densher. Only later does Milly in fact understand the complex negotiations buried in this moment:

> The beauty of the case was that to do it all she had only to appear to take Kate's hint. This had said in its fine first smile, "O yes, our look's queer—but give me time"; and the American girl could give time as nobody else could. (V, 7; 245)

And indeed Kate's entreaty betrays her weakness and confesses to Milly's power, as Milly later understands: "What Milly thus gave she therefore made them take—even if, as they might surmise, it was rather more than they wanted" (V, 7; 245). But at the moment of the collision, so to speak, Milly thinks,

> She ... knew herself handled and again, as she had been the night before, dealt with—absolutely even dealt with for her greater pleasure. A minute in fine hadn't elapsed before Kate had somehow made her provisionally take everything as natural.... The handsome girl was thus literally in control of the scene. (V, 7; 243)

Yet Milly's response to Kate's power is also grateful—an ambivalence about Kate's role in the drama that echoes throughout the novel: the opportunity to rescue Merton "was what had saved her most, what had made her, after the first few seconds, almost as brave for Kate as Kate was for her" (V, 7; 243). In this interlocking web of readings and misreadings of other readings themselves at least partially wrong lies much of James's wisdom about humiliation, how it is blocked, evaded, suffered, and passed on for others to suffer.

In this dazzling sequence of evasions proposed and accepted, Milly is also deeply active, as she improvises another performance in this masquerade. Her great "inspiration" is to play the American girl, "as spontaneous as possible and as American as it might conveniently appeal to Mr. Densher" in a performance cast specifically in deeply intersubjective terms: "[Milly] flattered herself that she struck him as saying [things] not in the tone of agitation, but in the tone of New York" (V, 7; 244). Milly perceives, or thinks she perceives, that Densher registers her presentation of a personhood ("as spontaneous as possible") that is itself a response to an earlier perception of what "might conveniently appeal" to Densher's needs. That is, Milly believes that Densher believes in her performance of self constructed to appeal to his belief. Furthermore, Milly intends her performance as an act of generosity, because she is more embarrassed by the possibility that Densher might be embarrassed than by the fact of having caught him with Kate ("Merton Densher was ready to exclaim with a high flush or vivid blush—one didn't distinguish the embarrassment from the joy"): "the one thing she could think of to do for him was to show him how she eased him off" (V, 7; 243). And so, "he was at the end of three minutes, without the least complicated reference, so smoothly '*their* friend'" (emphasis added). No one has asked why Kate is with Densher, or why an hour before none of them spoke of their plans for the National Gallery. Silence looms behind the script's words, lest the "smooth" desperation of "their" be confessed. Milly has joined the performance that displaces this silence and that renarrates the violent moment of rupture among the small Dutch pictures.

If this example illuminates kinds of performance and masquerade within a labyrinth of gazes, a different example of looking at looking observed suggests another kind of deeply intersubjective practice. Here the topic is not the mutually scripted masquerade in the National Gallery, but the angry melodrama of partial recognitions and misrecognitions of intimate deception. The moment, from *The Golden Bowl,* is Maggie's gaze at the Prince's gaze at Fanny's look upon his wonderfully coincidental entrance into the drawing room at Portland Place at the moment Fanny has smashed the golden bowl.[6] Here is the core of the knot, the chiasmus:

> What she had recognised in [the Prince's expression] was *his* recognition, the result of his having been forced, by the flush of their visitor's attitude and the unextinguished report of her words, to take account of the flagrant signs of the accident, the incident, on which he had unexpectedly dropped. (34/432)

Maggie sees the Prince see Fanny's flush. But the process of watching watching has already been gaining momentum, intensely, for several moments. First, the Prince on entering the room has looked at Fanny, with a "penetration" unmatched since the afternoon four years before of Charlotte's return to London, and long enough for Fanny to gaze into Amerigo's gaze:

> This rapid play of suppressed appeal and disguised response lasted long enough for more results than one—long enough for Mrs. Assingham to measure the feat of quick self-recovery, possibly therefore of recognition

---

6. Coincidences are one significant marker of melodrama's genre practice. Emotional excess, revelatory outbursts, and dramatic, apparently simple polarities (examples of which will occur below) are others. Coincidence and violent polarities are part of what Peter Brooks calls the "Jamesian vocabulary of melodramatic outburst" that "imag[es] melodrama as the breakthrough of the violent latent and suppressed content of the gathered persons' relations and consciousness" (194). The motif of outburst is an expression of "the desire to express all [that] seems a fundamental characteristic of the melodramatic mode" (Brooks 4), a desire that becomes all the more complex amidst the orbits of deep intersubjectivity. Stanley Cavell takes issue broadly with Brooks in *Contesting Tears,* and Christine Gledhill surveys the gendering of these practices of melodrama in her preface to *Home Is Where the Heart Is*.

still more immediate, accompanying Amerigo's vision and estimate of [the golden bowl]. She looked at him and looked at him. (33/431)

But—and this is the moment of the hemorrhage—the suppressed and disguised lookers' looks are themselves the object of a gaze: "But Maggie was looking too—and was moreover looking at them both" (33/431).

The interlocking threads in this melodrama of deception revealed tighten here ominously, partly because although Maggie, like Milly, wishes, for a moment, to let off the man she loves ("she knew once more the strangeness of her desire to spare him" [34/435]), she is much more than Milly deeply angry at the layers of deception around her. The threads of readings of readings extend of course beyond the three participants in this scene (Fanny, the Prince, and Maggie) to include Adam and Charlotte, so that the chiasmus of consciousnesses—who knew or thought they knew what Charlotte thought Adam believed Maggie knew about Charlotte—becomes exponentially more complicated, approaching almost comically Lisa Zunshine's *Friends* episode (see footnote 2 in this chapter). But James's deeply intersubjective melodrama explores with intense sadness the paradoxical nature of intimacy, for this has been the fundamental question, as Fanny phrased it. When Maggie says, of Charlotte and the Prince, repeating the cataclysmic claim, "They were intimate, you see. Intimate," Fanny replies, "There's always the question of what one considers—!" (33/416–17). Despite the close quarters of these marriages, and the pressure of gazes on gazes on faces watching faces, the fabric so woven contains deep gaps, isolated threads, and brief moments of insight. This interlocking weave embodies James's profound study of intimacy, or intimacies, achieved in partial degrees if at all by means of anger, betrayal, caretaking and, yes, sexual passion.[7]

One feature of deeply intersubjective intimacy underwrites this climactic sequence in *The Golden Bowl* and indicates how James explores the themes of deception and exposure that are characteristic of melodrama. Maggie perceives, constructs, believes in intimacy as "traceable." Intimacy thus conceived presumes that knowing Amerigo would mean knowing he knows that Maggie knows him, and being able to track these knowings.

---

7. I am grateful to an unpublished essay by Melanie Ross, "The Art of Feeling in Henry James," for reflections on the nature of intimacy in James. She meditates on that moment in *The Ambassadors* when Strether notes that "the deep, deep truth of intimacy" is "so much like lying" (XI, 4; 468). I see a broader range of intimacies in James than Ross does, incorporating different kinds and degrees of deception, but she poses important questions about the relation between the intimate ("inmost") and surfaces.

Maggie's deeply intersubjective assumptions about intimacy surface in her language for her wish to "ease" Amerigo's dilemma (to use Milly's words for Densher): "her glimpse of the precious truth that by her helping him, helping him to help himself, as it were, she should help him to help *her*. Hadn't she fairly got into the labyrinth with him?" (34/436). It is this, her further consciousness of their entanglement, as James's deep intersubjectivity gets deeper, that Maggie really wants Amerigo to perceive:

"Yes, look, look," she seemed to see him hear her say even while her sounded words were other—"look, look, both at the truth that still survives in that smashed evidence and at the even more remarkable appearance that I'm not such a fool as you supposed me." (34/436)

Maggie's dream of knowing another's knowing her knowing allows her to think she perceives Amerigo's perception of the *real* words beneath the words she speaks. As Maggie gazes at Amerigo gazing at the broken bowl, her assumptions take, however, an even more remarkable turn: "He went no nearer the damnatory pieces, but he eyed them, from where he stood, with a degree of recognition just visibly less to be dissimulated; all of which represented for her a traceable process" (34/437).

Traceability is a fundamental belief for Maggie, and an extraordinary mark of her idealism or naiveté, given the enormous difficulty of tracing perceptions of perceptions that James's narrative itself traces. James's language emphasizes Maggie's need to see Amerigo seeing her seeing, most remarkably in a moment that reveals her belief that Adam must serve as an almost paralyzing anxiety for Amerigo: "To name her father, on any such basis of anxiety, of compunction, would be to do the impossible thing, to do neither more nor less than give Charlotte away." Maggie's anxiety surfaces in the telling repetition that follows: "Visibly, palpably, traceably, [Amerigo] stood off from this, moved back from it as from an open chasm now suddenly perceived" (34/440). "Visibly, palpably, traceably": Maggie's insistence that she can *see* and thus *mark* Amerigo knowing her knowing of his anxieties has a poignancy to it. It is a dream of the kind of intercorporeality, however partial, that Merleau-Ponty's chiasm promises, and it illuminates Maggie's hope for an intimacy that is primarily hopeless. However tough-minded Maggie can be, she is also in part a believer, even an idealist.

The capacity for belief and idealism to mislead is a recurring theme in James, and the question of misleading will also open the door to our last topic, the nature of that authority that can see so clearly how characters perceive or misperceive, can distinguish leading from misleading, the flush from the blush (to return to *The Wings of the Dove* for a moment). Such a moment of clarity about the opacity of intimacy appears in a moment of sad comedy during our crisis. Maggie thinks she sees Amerigo seeing her seeing, and her confidence grows: "Before he committed himself, there occurred between them a kind of unprecedented moral exchange over which her superior lucidity presided" (34/438). But in the event the Prince's gesture—a specific question about their immediate moment—does not reflect an "unprecedented moral exchange," and dramatically subverts Maggie's sense of "superior lucidity": "It was not, however, that when he did commit himself the show was promptly portentous. 'But what in the world has Fanny Assingham to do with it?'" (34/438). Apparently the Prince was not paying attention during the "unprecedented" unspoken exchange over Maggie's wish to help him (especially if he understands what he will need to pay for that help). Instead, he just wants to know why Fanny was there, and why on earth she has smashed the golden bowl on the floor. The gap between Maggie's belief in a deeply intersubjective intimacy and the Prince's actual behavior lays bare the work of a narrating agency in the syuzhet of *The Golden Bowl* that is itself capable of threading the labyrinth of deep intersubjectivity (in Maggie's illusion), even if the Prince is not (or at least does not).[8] The work of this narrative voice in fact enables the novel's further insights into intimacy, marriage, humiliation, and misunderstanding. And so our first two threads of inquiry lead us now to the third, the narratological implications of a rhetoric of deep intersubjectivity.

iii. THEORY II: SUTURE AND FREE INDIRECT DISCOURSE

This next line of thought remarks on the shifting strategies of James's narrating agent in representing the phenomenological fabric, the chiasmus, of deep intersubjectivity woven among a novel's characters. Its particular enabling strategy is the suturing of consciousnesses in the intricate layering of free indirect discourse. To begin, note how that narrator guarantees a perception of perceptions perceived along a sliding scale of verifiability.

---

8. The examples of deep intersubjectivities I am offering lead back into the labyrinth of controversies about these characters: how manipulative, for example, is Maggie (M. Williams 195*ff.*), how responsible in and for her perjury (Miller, *Literature as Conduct* 252–58), how compromised by her "position of the Jamesian artist" (Teahan 141), how idealistic, how mercantile, how American?

On one end of the scale, perceived perceptions of prior gestures seem reliable. For example, in our scene from *The Wings of the Dove,* Kate and Milly have settled the fiction that "they" are in some symmetrical way hosting Densher at the National Gallery: "The flash in which he saw this was, for Milly, fairly inspiring" (V, 7; 244). "For Milly" names the consciousness that encloses the report on Densher's consciousness, "the flash in which he saw this," a report James's narrator relays with no subversion of syntax or context. Another example occurs at the moment of collision: "Kate was but two yards off—Mr. Densher wasn't alone. Kate's face specifically said so, for after a stare as blank at first as Milly's it broke into a far smile" (V, 7; 242). Slightly more unreliability creeps into this language, because the perception that "Kate's face specifically said so" (that Densher was not alone) arises from the movement of Kate's face, which is at first blank, and then "broke into a far smile." How "specific" is a "far smile"? Still, the speed of the unexpected confrontation prevents even Kate from effective masquerade at first: Kate knows that Milly will link Densher and herself in the very time that Kate requires to don her "far smile," and any denial of that linkage, Kate knows, will constitute a more embarrassing confession to Milly. Free indirect discourse is famously obscure about the ontological status of the voice it voices: does the language reflect the subjectivity of the character "directly," or is the character's consciousness filtered in some demonstrable way by a narrative agency?[9]

However thorny the theoretical problem is, James's texts show how to manage with specific strategies a range of guarantees of partially reliable intersubjective strings of perception. Such guarantees can offer an astonishing, sibylline guidance in the midst of confusion, as in this moment early in Book 8 of *The Wings of the Dove* when Densher, on reacquiring his old rooms in Venice, meditates on his position between Kate and Milly, as Milly proposes that he propose tea for her in those rooms.

> It was constantly Densher's view that, as between himself and Kate, things were understood without saying, so that he could catch in her, as she but too freely could in him, innumerable signs of it, the whole soft

---

9. Gerard Genette raised the key issue in the 1970s when he claimed that in the indirect style, "the narrator's presence is still too perceptible in the very syntax of the sentence for the speech to impose itself with the documentary autonomy of a quotation" (171). Daniel Gunn recently reviewed the debate over "the interplay between narrative and figural subjectivities" in free indirect discourse, and argues a position with which I agree, that "the narrative voice *incorporates* the figural voice and so remains simultaneously present during free indirect discourse" (52).

breath of consciousness meeting and promoting consciousness.... It fell in so perfectly with what she had desired and foretold that she was—and this was what most struck him—sufficiently gratified and blinded by it not to know, from the false quality of his response, from his tone and his very look, which for an instant instinctively sought her own, that he had answered inevitably, almost shamelessly, in a mere time-gaining sense. (364)

The guidance is sibylline because murky, narrow, and unexplained; nonetheless it occurs, with breathtaking confidence, without significant dramatic irony to sabotage it. The voice measures precisely what Densher thinks Kate perceives or doesn't perceive (his "false" tone in replying to Milly), how he understands the dance of "consciousness meeting and promoting consciousness," how he then corrects his interpretation ("she was after all capable of that, capable of guessing and yet of simultaneously hiding her guess" about his deeper feelings, that he doesn't want to invite Milly to tea), and then, after questioning his perception of perception "a turn or two further," how he decides that "whatever apprehension of his motive in shifting his abode might have brushed her with its wings, she at all events certainly didn't guess that he was giving their friend a hollow promise" (364–65). The narrative agent guides the alert reader through each turn in this labyrinth with a sure hand. Kate does not understand Densher's motive, not truly, while he sees her blindness clearly, and the narrator guarantees his perception and his perception (even if partial and somewhat misguided) of Kate's understanding. Transparency between human consciousnesses—a limited transparency, yes—is possible, but such clarity from the guiding agent in navigating this tangle may be the most remarkable affirmation of these novels. To take a reader through this labyrinth of readings of readings, and to evaluate so clearly how partially mistaken or partially reasonable each reading of the other's possibly and partially mistaken or pretended reading is, requires enormous authority in the narrative voice, and a responding trust from the skilled authorial reader.

In contrast to these instances of clarity from the narrative voice about an achieved (if partial) transparency, other moments define an intermediately probable interlocking, a chiasmus whose touching the narrator has the authority to say may not succeed, or may succeed only quite partially, or only among two of three watchers. A good example of this clarity about uncertainty occurs in *The Golden Bowl* when Maggie explains to Amerigo that she did believe in it (the bowl), and bought it "'as soon as

I saw it. Though I didn't know at all then,' she added, 'what I was taking *with* it,'" and the text continues, "The Prince paid her for an instant, visibly, the deference of trying to imagine what this might have been" (34/442). "Visibly" guarantees that the Prince's effort of consciousness surfaces in a way "traceable" for Maggie: the chiasmus works this far. But James's narrating voice makes no promises about the success of the Prince's imagination. He does not touch Maggie's thought, nor does she see him touching her thought, though she does see him trying to, or at least signaling a moment of deferring to her in being seen to try. A similar move of intermediate intersubjectivity occurs in our museum scene from *The Wings of the Dove*: "Miss Theale had meanwhile the sense that for him too, on Kate's part, something wonderful and unspoken was predominant" (V, 7; 243). The text offers here a representation of a perception of a *possible* perception of a state of yet another character's mind. The value of deep intersubjectivity as an interpretative notion lies in the way in this example it clarifies a degree of depth to uncertainty, the way it refines a condition of intermediate opacity. Milly's sense of Densher's sense of Kate's unspoken feeling renders Kate's consciousness as a reflection in a reflection, yes, but not entirely incorrectly, since Milly (and her narrator) are careful not to claim too much: after all, Milly does not know *what* Kate is feeling, only that it is "something wonderful." Nor does she claim to know that Densher knows what the feeling is, though of course he may (or may believe he does). Part of the intelligence of James's narration is the way it so meticulously tracks grades of confidence in perceptions of perceptions, along the way cementing its own claims to a larger authority.

Finally, partial obscurity can darken to what seems like complete darkness. In such moments, James's narrative guarantees that no touching hands actually touch other hands touching.

> She was to wonder in subsequent reflexion what in the world they had actually said, since they had made such a success of what they didn't say; the sweetness of the draught for the time, at any rate, was to feel success assured. What depended on this for Mr. Densher was all obscurity for her, and she perhaps but invented the image of his need as a short cut to accommodation. Whatever the facts, their perfect manners, all round, saw them through. (V, 7; 244)

Not only does the narrative know that Milly does not at all know what Densher needs from the success of their collective evasion, it knows that what she believes may be a self-deception. What is most curiously unstable here is the nature of Milly's self-evasion: James's narrator chooses not to say exactly if Milly "invented" her interpretation of Densher (her "image of his need"), although the narrator is clear that if she did, it was a "short cut," an exercise in avoidance, in order to reach an "accommodation" in her later meditations. She feels the "sweetness" of their success at *not* speaking the uncomfortable truths (no ambiguity about her character there), and now (later) must simply find a way to accept that success whose source she doesn't quite grasp. So James's narrator is clear about what Millie doesn't know about what Densher knew, but is not clear about why Millie doesn't know. (I agree that free indirect discourse does not *necessarily* entail interpretative instability, but in this case I think it does [Gunn 42]).[10] These nuances are a good example of my earlier point in chapter 2 that obscurity and failure to see the other seeing are still the subject matter for deeply intersubjective narrative: the failures to read the other's gestures that block or fail to espouse the perceiver's gestures are themselves, in their obscurity, still the product of perceptions of perceptions not perceived, or blocked. Indeed, these layers of obscurity are especially useful models of indirection, obliqueness, of the suturing of free indirect discourse, which here becomes a narrative strategy that suits its very Jamesian theme.

This is a good moment to consolidate what we have learned about free indirect discourse and suture as important factors in the narration of intersubjectivities. My focus in this last part of this chapter has been the authority with which James's narrator tracks various kinds of intersubjective transparencies or obscurities or both at the same time. The ranges of transparency and obscurity become even more extensive once free indirect discourse allows James to track partial understandings of partial misunderstandings of yet other characters' consciousness. Every example of consciousness of consciousness in this chapter is an example of free indirect discourse and its suturing of multiple perspectives. We saw in chapter 2 that suture in both film and print narrative allows for linkages among consciousnesses that outline or conceal gaps (Oudart and Silverman), or for linkages that both evoke and conceal the bodies that look (Merleau-Ponty and Butte). I used the over-the-shoulder stance of film's shot / reverse shot convention as an image for free indirect discourse's mode of narrating consciousness; in both kinds of narration, an oblique

---

10. I want to thank Jim Phelan for a wonderful discussion about this scene and James's language that helped clarify for me the way James illuminates what we don't know about what Millie doesn't know.

angle gets naturalized and also defamiliarized, and both raise, on reflection, complex questions about how stories narrate that characters know, or misknow, or partially know, other characters and in particular what those characters know or believe they know or don't know or know in part about yet others. My broader claim is that much knowing in narrative is really over-the-shoulder, and that many stories are stitched together from oblique angles. James's fiction, like this scene from *The Wings of the Dove*, simply provides particularly intricate (and hence clearer) examples.

The obliqueness of James's free indirect discourse only adds to the difficulties of seeing and believing in espousal, partly because the effect of free indirect discourse in deep intersubjectivity is a kind of oblique intimacy, to use a phrase from chapter 2. The over-the-shoulder stance of camera or narrating agent imitates a voyeur's posture, or an eavesdropper (James Barrie's image for this position that I will pursue in chapter 4): hence the intimacy and the distance. The barrier of the primary perceiver, that back of the head that looms to the side of the frame, serves to protect the reader or viewer (from Hannibal Lecter's gaze or Kate Croy's, as we have seen). The brilliance of James's achievement is the range of obscurities that he creates with a range of obliquenesses. Hannibal Lecter's head interferes, in subtly different degrees in different frames, with the viewer's perception of Clarice looking at Lecter looking at her. Similarly, as I discussed above, James increases or decreases the fogginess of those perceptions themselves that his competent reader encounters obliquely, over the shoulder of free indirect discourse's enunciator. In some cases, James outlines clearly how perception layers on perception, so that the obscurity lies in the content of the perception, as in the third headnote to this chapter, from *What Maisie Knew*, an example I repeat from chapter 2 because its achieved communion is so rare in late James: "There was an extraordinary mute passage between [Maisie's] vision of this vision of [Beale's], his vision of her vision, and her vision of his vision of her vision" (150). In other cases, the shoulder rises into the frame, and the obliqueness of the angle increases to problematize perception (and perception of perception), as in this moment that follows the previous quotation: "What, further, Beale finally laid hold of while he masked again, with his fine presence half the flounces of the fireplace was: 'Do you know, my dear, I shall soon be off to America?'" (150). Beale "mask[s]" both the fireplace and his feelings about Maisie's feelings about his life. The body intrudes, almost as if mandated by the screenplay or a director's storyboard for this moment, and its "fine presence" bares but then hides what exactly Beale "finally laid hold of."

Here the theoretical argument over voice in free indirect discourse takes its aim at a very specific textual moment. It matters significantly whether one reads this language by way of Anne Banfield's claim that no narrating agency's tones color these words, or by Dorrit Cohn's sense in *Transparent Minds* that the narrating voice fades in and out, sometimes to be overheard only, or through Daniel Gunn's argument that oblique as the narrator's presence may be, it encapsulates and controls its version, its "pervasive mimicry" of the characters' voices and implied subjectivities (43). Throughout our examples from fiction and film, the obliqueness will at times be deeply enough angled that this debate will continue, although to my ear this last approach seems almost always to be the most persuasive. The syntax is simply too balanced, too rhetorically sophisticated, too knowing of its binary: "What Beale finally laid hold of while he masked again." And in the earlier moment from this scene: "There was an extraordinary mute passage." "Extraordinary" is a strong judgment, the tone of an observing agent, nestled inside a classic instant of free indirect report. Narrating over the shoulder produces that "strange proximity" that Merleau-Ponty discerned in perceptions of perceptions perceived, indirect, sutured, and only in rare cases entirely disconnected from some originating gestures.

Millie's reflections, in our last example from *The Wings of the Dove*, on what she knows and doesn't know about what Densher needs or doesn't need are another example of the extraordinary care with which James's narrator meticulously tracks kinds of knowledge and obscurity in a deeply intersubjective way: how characters grasp or do not grasp someone's knowing or misknowing of yet another's, or their own, subjectivity. This narrating agency also tracks the intensity of anxiety here, which we can measure by how seriously Millie and Densher evade knowing, or admitting knowing, what is really at stake in this scene (but their perfect manners saw them through). How deeply into the distance, indeed, does the text's light about darkness penetrate? Deeply enough that the light outlines quite sharply the distinct ridgelines of some of the foothills; not knowing about not knowing is, in the hands of this narration, remarkably more knowable.

The fabric of deep intersubjectivities in these narratives opens up large implications, rhetorical and narratological, for James's suturing of subjectivities into complex systems. States of consciousnesses interpreting and reinterpreting and partially imagining each other circulate extensively in James's fiction, to a large degree *are* James's fiction, in ways we can now clarify better. Furthermore, representations of perceptions in cycles of comic or desperate misperceptions are not entirely erroneous at all times, as a subtly measuring narrative agency cues its readers. The narratological implications are clearer now: how a complex authority in James's stories guarantees a range of (mis)readings of (mis)readings, even when filtered through free indirect discourse. Merleau-Ponty's chiasmus is thus a profound image for these phenomenological patterns in James's deeply intersubjective narratives of consciousnesses that circle, shame, rupture, invade, espouse, and deceive, sometimes all at the same time.

These narrative effects—shame, rupture, deception, and rarely espousal—are fundamental to the larger project of these late novels. Suture works through the oblique, the indirect, the loops of the chiasmus, and James's core interests are the oblique and indirect relations among his characters. Given this almost universal condition of obliqueness in perception and community in James, the fundamental tension in both narrative style and content is the tension between Maggie's notion of traceability (the hope or belief that one can track threads through the labyrinth of consciousnesses) and the triumph of the mask. Form and content mirror each other so well because James's subject here—the indirections of intimacy and the difficulty of knowing others and what others know of us—finds its excellent expression in James's use of free indirect discourse and the oblique angle. Masquerade is part of the study of indirection, because it deflects our view of the other, as characters play roles in performances that others may or may not have the cue cards for. And the roles change *in media res* to confuse the audience, or even the performer, as Maggie thinks in *The Golden Bowl*:

> and she felt not unlike some young woman of the theatre who, engaged for a minor part in the play and having mastered her cues with anxious effort, should find herself suddenly promoted to leading lady and expected to appear in every act of the five. (35/449)

Anxiety about mastering roles, old and new, permeates these stories, as characters try to see what others see, or don't see, or believe they see, whether it's the Prince ("I know nothing but what you tell me"), Maggie ("Find out for yourself!"), or Fanny ("I've never been so awfully sure of what I may call knowing you") (34/448; 34/448; 30/380).

Despite the desire to glimpse a self behind the mask or inside a role, the search for intimations of others confounds almost everyone almost all the time in our novels. "Confusion" reigns, James writes, also because the distinctions are murky between "the things that help" and "the things that hurt"—"bliss and bale" in those words of the *Maisie* preface—in our "terribly mixed little world" (25). Marriage, family, love, friendship, intimacy, narrative insight: for James, now, in the novels of his last decade, all are deeply indirect, in form and content.

iv. THE OBLIQUE ANGLE AGAIN: JAMES IN FILM

> Her husband's tone somehow fitted Amerigo's look—the one that had, for her, so strangely, peeped, from behind, over the shoulder of the one in front.
> —James, *The Golden Bowl* (16)

> Among many matters thrown into relief by a refreshed acquaintance with *The Golden Bowl* what perhaps stands out for me is the marked inveteracy of a certain indirect and oblique view of my presented action.
> —James, "Preface," *The Golden Bowl*

Henry James's novels, especially the two late novels we have focused on, *The Wings of the Doves* and *The Golden Bowl,* use indirection, and especially the over-the-shoulder stance of free indirect discourse, to measure the difficult traceability of human connections, from moderate degrees of transparency and espousal between subjects to the murkiest mistaken and sometimes hostile forms of deep intersubjectivity. Indeed, James's own language from his preface to *The Golden Bowl* gives pride of place to the same images: indirection and obliqueness of "presentation." The remarkable claim that follows parallels the logic of most modern scholarly readings: the claim that "this mode of treatment . . . , any superficial appearance notwithstanding, [is] the very straightest and closest possible" (xli). Although there have always been nay-sayers to the late James style, the argument of this book is that obliqueness, in late James or *The Silence of the Lambs,* is indeed necessary to shape the complex ontology of intersubjectivities in these narrative worlds. Given the homology I have argued between film's oblique angle in shot / reverse shot continuity editing and print fiction's free indirect discourse, it is remarkable to see a confirming image in Fanny's specific comment that "peep[ing], from behind, over the shoulder of the one in front" is her mode of puzzling out the Prince's real understanding of Charlotte's understanding of their relationship to Maggie and her father. It would be illuminating to look at looking (and how it's framed and edited, over whose shoulders, so to speak) in at least a few of the many James films of the last fifty years (16/209). How do these movie texts interpret the oblique angles of the James stories, especially the particular examples we have been studying? How do they read reading? Fanny, in the moment cited above, has just been reading subtext in the visual ("Wasn't it simply what had been written in the Prince's own face *beneath* what he was saying?"[emphasis in original])—a mode that suits film narrative especially (16/209). Indeed, it may be the repeated claims, which I discussed previously, that the intersubjective is "visible" that make the recurring desire to transfer these novels into film less odd and doomed than it might seem (though of course the visible text of the self responding to other selves' visible text is usually a layer of misreadings upon misreadings, at least to some degree, in James, which may not be so "visible").

But what kind of "transfer" can we expect to discover in a film version of, say, the scenes we have discussed, where the web of tangled consciousnesses in these late novels is especially subtle? Or in other scenes that may also address these subtle tangles? My aim here is to think about kinds of narrative, especially narratives that study the stories of complex subjectivities, and the existence of print and film versions of these same stories is too convenient to ignore. However, let me say immediately, to broach a vexed question in adaptation theory, that I do not endorse a narrower aesthetic of fidelity (to what of course is the question) for its own sake in moving from novel to subsequent film. Bad films, even faithful bad films, can be made of great novels, just as great films can be made of mediocre or bad novels (look, for example, at most of the pretty weak source stories for those brilliant Hitchcock films that are not original screenplays, from *Rear Window* to *Marnie*). Yes, there is some boundary where "fidelity" matters: when Peter Brook assigned some language of Edmund's to Edgar, is the resulting film still quite accurately to be named *King Lear*? But even if the film should have had a different name, it might, even as an unfaithful version, still be a great film. Speaking for a formalist approach, Matthew Bolton has recently made an excellent case for form as rhetoric, and asks what are the effects of a new media's forms (say, narrator's voice, camera movement, editing of graphic matches) on the ethical consequences of a story (he's studying print and film versions of *Atonement*). Bolton also critiques the excesses of a poststructuralist emphasis on "the deceptively simple fact that all texts are intertexual," which thus "simply discarded" any usefulness to even a more subtle idea of "fidelity" to a source (24). My own interest in film form in an adaptation hews closely to Bolton's claim.

I want to steer a narrow path through the complex field of adaptation theory: the issue here is not a literal faithfulness to details of character or plot or narrative form, but the rhetoric and thematic payoff in stories with various kinds of suturing of human consciousnsesses. I *do* claim here, of course, and in *I Know That You Know That I Know* that narrative film can represent intersubjectivity, and even deep intersubjectivity, in its own ways. The question will be what kinds of suture in our James films embody what kinds of stories about characters entangled with each other, with the kinds of deception, misperception, manipulation, espousal, embrace, and aggression that we have already seen in our other examples so far.

Other critics take different positions on the matter of "fidelity aesthetics," like Dianne Sadoff, who seeks to recuperate fidelity as a criterion against a variety of criticisms by arguing that fidelity itself is a "malleable notion," and that a more flexible approach to both original and adaptation can help identify the important "cultural work" that each does (xviii–xix). Sadoff seeks to understand the ideological and cultural contexts for the original novels of the nineteenth century, and for different kinds of readings in different film adaptations then to be viewed by different real audiences (from, say, Jack Clayton's original audiences for *The Innocents* in 1962 to other audiences of that film between 1962 and now—whenever "now" is for my readers). Sadoff's multiple contexts provide a wide range of moving targets for study, most of which are outside the focus of this book.[11] Laurence Raw also wants to move beyond an "exclusively formalist approach to adaptation" in his consideration, like Sadoff, of institutional imperatives (say, the BBC's notion of its mission in those television serials of the 1960s and 1970s) and of various film industry economies, markets, conventions, and protocols (1). I will on occasion look at such contexts, as, for example, studio conventions and how star codes work (the choice of Uma Thurman for the role of Charlotte in *The Golden Bowl* of 2000 is overdetermined by a different set of forces than the choice of Gayle Hunnicutt in the 1972 BBC serial), or at other historical contexts, but the payoff in each case should be an understanding of narrative form and its thematics.

The important connection between novel and film here will be structural and thematic, and I will work from the examples in sections ii and iii

---

11. See Sadoff, chapter 2, for an extensive review of adaptation theory and her responses. Linda Hutcheon also offers a broad study of adaptation issues in *A Theory of Adaptation* (2006), in which she addresses question like what? (is the thing that is adapted?), who? (adapts the object of desire?), and why? Hutcheon stakes a middle ground on the new work, in which the old persists but also changes: "adaptation is how stories evolve and mutate to fit new times and different places" (176).

FIGURE 3.1. *The Wings of the Dove* (29:33)

of this chapter. Looking at looking, for example, is a significant motif in Iain Softley's 1997 film of *The Wings of the Dove* as well as in the novel, and the museum scene I discussed above foregrounds looking as well in the film. The film changes many details—the paintings exhibited are Gustav Klimt, not old Dutch masters; Milly stumbles accidentally into the gallery to escape rain; she has not previously met Densher; and there is no issue of a surprise meeting of the three characters that could be suspicious on various counts. But the scene's mise-en-scène and cinematography raise a number of the same issues as the scene we discussed above in the novel. Perhaps the most important choice is the use of the over-the-shoulder shot to suggest a kind of voyeurism, and the way it leads to an isolation of the gaze that precisely blocks responses and responses to responses. That is, shot / reverse shots need not be isolating. Indeed, throughout this version of *The Wings of the Dove,* looking is almost always one-way, or with very limited reciprocity, or reciprocity that reaches a cul-de-sac, a point of no return, as in the film's final sexual encounter. In the scene in the gallery (a space of display, after all), Milly spots Merton through an archway as simply an attractive man whom she follows with a small smile of pleasure, and the camera holds its shot over her shoulder as she watches Merton study a small drawing of a nude couple lying together in a close embrace (figure 3.1). The four figures (counting the lovers as one figure) in the frame occupy almost symmetrically equal spaces, two of them gazers (Merton and Milly) and two of them displayed images, the romantic couple and, between Milly and Merton and occupying the center of the film frame, a large painting of a nude, very pregnant woman whose belly points directly at Merton. The frame seems to foreground two women studying Merton studying the nude lovers, and the camera's position behind Milly looks at the scene peeping as it were from behind her. The film viewer's position is private, protected by Milly's elaborately costumed and behatted figure, and no one returns anyone's gaze. This frame is a wonderful example of the oblique gaze as distant and intimate, but without reciprocity it only measures an intersubjective opacity.

The power of the gaze in this moment belongs strictly to the women (the nude and Milly), and its screened privilege almost leads one to hope for some unusual, perhaps embarrassing movement from the male watcher that would reveal his intimate thoughts about the nude lovers. For the women's gazes to frame Merton's so thoroughly is a powerful reversal of the traditional paradigm, developed by Mary Ann Doane in "Film and the Masquerade: Theorising the Female Spectator," in which her example of how the female look gets disempowered is a still photograph taken in 1948 by Robert Doisneu, with the wonderfully appropriate title "*Un Regard Oblique.*" In this image, as Doane traces out its structure, obliqueness is a strategy for marginalizing the gazing woman's look, in all its "vulnerability." Doane writes, "The spectator's pleasure is produced through the framing/negation of the female gaze," so that the "terms of the photograph's address... once again insure a masculinization of the place of the spectator" (770). In contrast, our movie frame in this scene emphasizes the oblique look particularly of Milly (oblique because she's looking at Densher from an angle behind him) and even of the Klimt nude (whose face, turned toward Merton, is mostly blocked by Milly's hat). Indeed, the female look here celebrates a kind of voyeurism that is classically gendered male but now spies, so to speak, on a vulnerable male, whose response to a deeply erotic image threatens significant exposure. In Doane's terms, the implied viewer of this frame enjoys the power of the female gaze to see around and estimate Merton's absorption in the nude lovers, and so in one sense this viewer is "feminized." In these examples, the dynamics of obliqueness open up questions of gender in multiple forms.

All of the energy of this frame moves to the left, toward Merton studying the nudes and to the nudes themselves. So the sudden movement in the reverse direction in the following frames is even more dramatic when Kate's voice calls, from offscreen right, "Milly," and causes Merton as well as Milly to swivel sharply away from the nudes. Kate then takes Milly to "show her" something, which turns out to be another nude, one that the viewer in fact saw over Milly's shoulder when she first entered the gallery (29:14). In other words, Milly does not attend to this figure until Kate brings her to face it. Kate then withdraws from the frame to allow Merton and Milly to gaze at the nude as they occupy the shot in a somewhat awkward silence. From her invasive "Milly," Kate has directed this scene and pointed its gazes and chosen when to disappear from the frame. Her position of power in this network of gazes is very different from the positions outlined in Laura Mulvey's classic essay on the gaze in film, where men look and women signify "to-be-looked-at-ness" (25). In this film sequence, if the female figure is an object of the male gaze, that gaze is encompassed by and directed by the woman's look. So the museum sequence becomes a study in display and looking at display, and the gender of looking. What we do not find, so far, is the layering of consciousnesses that we found in James's novel, and the study of masquerades and performances responding to performances. But the *regard oblique* clarifies in this example how gender works in the narrative of even a limited intersubjectivity, as editing and camera angles expose the operations of looking as women, here, exercise the power of the gaze even in an environment of decorative and objectified female bodies.

However, shame and anxiety do loom, as in the novel, though for different reasons. This scene emphasizes exposure in its repeated contrast between nude and clothed bodies, and shows that looking at exposed bodies raises significant issues of power and position. Looking at looking is safer when the looker is solitary and removed (Milly in figure 3.1), while looking with another at an exposed figure can be embarrassing, so that the power of the voyeur is markedly compromised. Throughout this sequence, looking moves from a single-direction vector of power to a triad of looks awkwardly acknowledged or avoided by various members of the threesome. Once all three gazers move out of their private worlds into their shared conversation, the camera mostly frames them together, not often in shot / reverse shot combinations. The widescreen mise-en-scène brings into focus the movements and conflicts across the group of three, the best example of which is the shot facing the figures when they gaze at the large painting of the reclining nude (*The Danae*) that Kate has commanded the group to regard (figure 3.2). Kate conspicuously occupies the central position in the triad, and the film's viewer scans the wide frame watching these people watching the Klimt and also in an edgy way noting the person beside them out of the corner of their eyes. We are watching watching, in a tense moment that betrays considerable uncertainty and anxiety. In the following shot, the camera crosses the 180-degree line to frame the group from behind, and Kate departs, leaving the center of the frame occupied by Klimt's sleeping nude, to be examined by the two newly introduced characters (figure 3.3). Their body language expresses

FIGURE 3.2. *The Wings of the Dove* (29:55)

their discomfort with looking together at such an evocative image, and the discomfort becomes even clearer to the audience given our knowledge that each has some kind of erotic interest in the other (Milly because she picked out Merton from the beginning of the scene, Densher because of Kate's effort to link him to Milly).

Finally, after Merton has left, Kate returns to occupy the frame with Milly, and as they walk out of the gallery, Kate lies to Milly, speaking sideways to her and facing the camera directly: "It's not what you're thinking"; Merton is only "a family friend." The lie spoken obliquely to the other while facing the camera is a key element in this film (it happens after the masquerade, for example, at 1:03:13), and suggests with special irony the power of the oblique angle to reveal and deceive in the network of consciousnesses. In both of these moments, Kate looks clear-eyed to the side of the camera as she lies, in a posture that promises directness and visibility. The authorial audience of the frame of course recognizes the lie, and sees how the posture of directness is a pose. There is some response here to a perception, or at least suspicion, of the other's consciousness, when Kate comments, "It's not what you're thinking," after Milly has asked Densher, "What are you doing here, the two of you?" So we can claim a degree of at least intermediate intersubjectivity, two layers perhaps of response to the other's gesture. The film uses its widescreen mise-en-scène to display its characters across the screen, in a kind of line of dancers, so that the viewer can track gesture to gesture from figure to figure, in contrast to the opening example of the oblique gaze over Milly's shoulder into the depths of the frame. Editing and figure placement do explore some layers of performances responding to performances and how lies function in a world of display, themes the novel also explores.

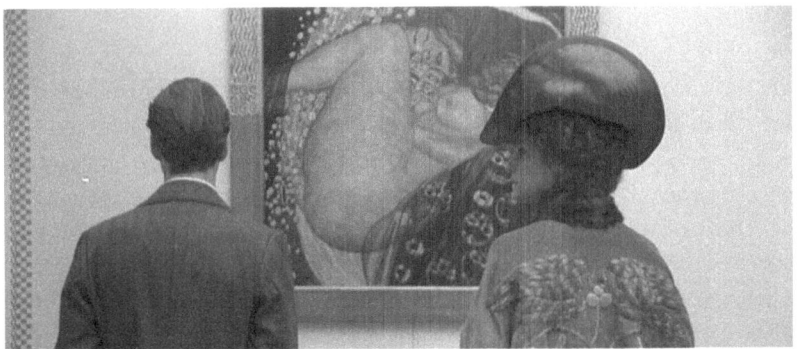

FIGURE 3.3. *The Wings of the Dove* (30:03)

The film, however, adds images of bodies clothed and unclothed, which are juxtaposed in curious combinations throughout this scene, promising pleasure but also embarrassment and even humiliation. So display and exposure carry extra ironies in the film.

Humiliation, and sorrow, are good words for the underlying threat here, because the final love-making scene in the film specifically recalls particularly the nude the three characters have regarded (see 1:31:29; figure 3.3). Diane Sadoff makes this same connection, in her thoughtful close readings of both scenes (in the museum, and finally in Merton's London flat), which are similar to mine, but she reasons further than I do. Yes, perhaps the soft-core porn conventions are a ploy by the filmmakers to address (and arouse) a certain kind of middlebrow audience in the late 1990s (Sadoff 180). But it's difficult to know which segments of which real audiences would have been educated enough not only in soft-core, but in hard-core pornography to know what a "money" shot was (a term circulated by Linda Williams's influential study *Hard Core*, published in 1989), or to have seen one (a close-up of a male ejaculation, a shot that, as Williams emphasizes, makes orgasm "visible"), or to expect such a shot in this scene, even with the recurrence of the word and topic "money" in Kate and Merton's conversation. Sex has sold movies (and books) for a long time, so how deep is the influence of this economic context in this case? Of course, texts can have it both ways: they can titillate and subvert, addressing different implied audiences at the same time. It may be more important to look at the internal logic and structure of this scene to estimate its ironies and complicities. The contrast between the undressed body of Klimt's woman and of Kate (or even of Helena Bonham Carter, to acknowledge that the star code does function here) highlights the death of eros at the end of the film, the loss of the energy and hope and color (this final scene is all greys) in the Klimt image. The key frames with Kate and Merton together (1:33:36, for example) are moments of effort to reach to the other (both say "I love you"), to touch and respond to the other's wish; they both want so much to have successful sex and to comfort the other. But too much—memory, loss, guilt—intervenes, and the final shots of the scene isolate each face; there are no exchanged looks in shot / reverse shot sequences now, no frames including both characters.

Maybe the film's final scene, following this one, trivializes these issues, as Marcia Ian argues, by means of the concluding voice-over, with Milly's sloppy and sentimental language (James deeply disliked the "slobbery" speech of young American women, in language Ian cites); she transcribes Milly's lines, a voice-over with words from earlier in the movie, echoing as Densher arrives at the end of the movie back in Venice: "I believe in you. I just do. I have a good feeling. I think everything's gonna happen for you, Merton, sooner than you think. Ther're certain people I know" (232). (In fact, on the film soundtrack Alison Elliott clearly enunciates "going," not "gonna," and at the end, there is no slur, only "Certain people I know" [1:37:33–52]; Ian exaggerates the sloppiness). Still, the film screenplay's language is not Henry James's, and it may be difficult to know how the authorial audience is to hear this modern colloquialism. Nonetheless, the prior love-making scene is still a bookend to the museum scene, and together they demonstrate how several kinds of looking get represented in the film: looking at looking unsuspected (Milly at Densher), looking at looking acknowledged and in some contested way performed together (the threesome before *The Danae*), and looking beside another looking, where both are profoundly separated and alone (at the end of the love scene in Densher's flat).

The melancholy in this concluding example is not superficial, I think. Novel and film both make use of the oblique angle of perspective and of an over-the-shoulder gaze to embody the difficulty of encountering the other, and of responding to the other's response to the observing subject: that is, the difficulty of deeper intersubjectivity, and the likelihood of misunderstanding, anxiety, and exposure to violation. In both novel and film, James's definition of technique applies: the "indirect and oblique view" is in fact "the very straightest possible." Softley's movie has been the target of different scholarly evaluations, some strongly negative. Alan Nadel writes that "the film opts to stabilize and literalize," and that Softley "reduces the problem of Milly Theale to simple melodrama" (202–3). Marcia Ian, in the essay cited above, argues that in the film "'the forces of looseness are in possession of the field'" (the words are James's) as the film ignores or reverses the novel's critique of gender and of the vulgar materialism of its dominant class values (Nadel agrees) (237). Sadoff analyzes the film's "fetishization of Milly—her fortune, her beauty, her magnificence," but it's not clear if she means the film promotes this view for a middlebrow audience, or satirizes it, or indeed does both (181). Laurence Raw agrees that the film offers a retrograde sexual politics, "neoconservative in the way it casts women as either angels or whores" (176). In contrast, Richard Kaye celebrates the film's "Lawrencian eros," its embrace of the "carnivalesque" (literally, in its Venice scenario) and its "willingness to tease out" the sexual triangles and the "bisexual implications of James's writing" (253, 257). My study of these bookend scenes cannot address all of the larger issues of the "cultural work" the film does, nor compare them to the work the novel does (or did). But I am convinced that the operation of the oblique gaze and the absence or minimal presence of reciprocal shot / reverse sequences in these scenes do not flatten James's nuanced exploration of power and gender. Indeed, they do the reverse. Yes, the intricacy of the intersubjective in Softley's film is intermediate, not deep, as in James's novel, but simpler layers of consciousness can still be complex and reveal melancholies (often gendered) of loss, betrayal, and the isolation of the gaze in a world of display.

How much is the elaborate display in elaborately produced heritage films itself the disease, or a diagnosis of the disease?[12] Display is part of the commodifying of people (not only women) in James and in these films. Does this particular film (and the even more elaborate production of *The Golden Bowl* in 2000) seek to seduce its audience with the pleasure of display, or does it problematize the commodifying? Marcia Ian quotes the director of *The Wings of the Dove,* Iain Softley, in a way that at first seems to tilt to the first answer: "I told the designer that I wanted people to want these costumes." It seems audiences should rush out to Bloomingdale's or Saks. But Softley's next line is a little more subtle: "If people say, 'I want to wear that!,' that's a long way on the road to understanding the characters" (215). Then the purpose of the display is to help the audience grasp the drive to present oneself in such a way, to play a role in the masquerade. Still, it's sometimes hard to tell the dancer from the dance, and the display of intricate, luxurious surfaces can seduce while one is looking the other way, confident of one's defenses. The strategies of the oblique,

---

12. For discussion of the heritage film, its cultural and aesthetic protocols and compromises, see Andrew Higson, *English Heritage,* and chapter 1 of Sadoff, *Victorian Vogue.*

which sutures consciousnesses together or into isolation, can provide one index of commentary, of rhetorical direction, but sometimes the index is complicated or ambiguous. Or maybe that is the comment of the indirect.

Films of *The Golden Bowl* might explore this set of problems too, with the story's elements of wealth, conspicuous display of objects collected, with parallels between people and those objects collected, and the study of how marriage and intimacy fare in such a setting. I will focus on two very different productions, the Merchant Ivory movie of 2000, and the BBC serial of 1972. Both in fact give a central role to display, as befits a story that I argued above is a kind of "angry melodrama." I use *melodrama* here, as before, as a word naming a complex, sophisticated narrative form, one that in the hands of critics like Peter Brooks, Christine Gledhill, and Stanley Cavell has become a mode of complex study of the externalized emotions of a self and selves. The novel is so famous an example of the oblique and of the dilemma of interpreting others because its characters must read others through the external, through their words and gestures and behaviors. Merleau-Ponty is such a good guide here because, as I argued in the first part of this chapter, this reading is not hopeless. But it is very difficult. Once again reading a character's reading of the other's prior reading of his or her own gestures almost defines the oblique gaze of shot / reverse shot conventions or the over-the-shoulder perspective. So difficulty—of intimacy, of knowing the other and the other's knowing of you—should in a sense be a natural topic for film narrative.

James Ivory's *The Golden Bowl* mostly does not represent that difficulty, even in a modest way. Gestures are transparent, and Adam Verver opens a door on the shameful couple; there is no real puzzle (1:48:40). But the problem is not transparency or display as such. The issue is how surfaces and performances function, and how they suggest what lies beneath (or not). The film tells its story with shot / reverse shots and some good oblique moments of surveillance (Adam spied through the balustrade of his palace immediately after he opens that door on the guilty pair [1:49:45]), but the technique does not illuminate obscurity, or ask about the nature of desire. Emotion is only the surface, and problems of interpretation (what did Fanny know when?) are only problems of gestures. Part of the difficulty may be miscasting, given the film's participation in the star system, in the ambiguous way of the heritage film that seeks both its "courageous" independent status and crossover mainstream success. Does Nick Nolte, for example, quite convey the reclusiveness of Adam? But Uma Thurman is not only miscast as Charlotte; her conception of the character, at least in Lee Clark Mitchell's sources, is problematic: "It's delightful to play someone who is kind of wicked, with no conscience, no guilt, no twentieth century psychology wrapping her up. She is quite free" (290). In the scene we discussed above, where Fanny breaks the golden bowl, the Prince and Maggie in this film mostly trade positions, on the right and left of the screen, and they shout at each other about what the Prince knew when and why he didn't tell Maggie. There is no real response to the other's reading of each other's words or gestures, or a suggestion of where such responses might come from. The film's notion of interiority is mostly simple gesture. A good example is the moment Adam, after accepting Charlotte's eager offer to come view those Turkish tiles with him, retires to look at Maggie's photo, and blinks back his tears (*The Golden Bowl* [2000] 25:21). What is the source of the tears? Guilt? Sorrow? Memories of their former life together? The viewer has no clue, because what matters in this moment is the performance of the emotion for the pleasure of that viewer. The strong, very masculine Adam Verver (or Nick Nolte) is weeping. A little. Display of emotion and display of great wealth and its collected artifacts work in a similar vein, without an analytic or thematic framework beyond the display.

Display is also a motif in James Cellan Jones's 1972 BBC version of *The Golden Bowl*. But display has a frame, a context, a more intricate rhetoric. A very good example occurs in the Lancashire House party scene, where Jones constructs a brilliant mise-en-scène to interpret issues of wealth and power as Fanny and the Prince discuss the ménage à quatre that revolves in their lives after Adam's marriage to Charlotte. Fanny looks at the extravagantly decorated young African serving woman as the Prince rests his white gloved hand on her shoulder and explains the freedom he and Charlotte have claimed (A 1:46:16).[13] Not only does this scene ask questions about whose freedom, on whose terms, as interpreted by whom, but it suggests an orientalist image for that freedom that resonates through the novel to the famous final description of Charlotte moving around Verver's collection on the leash, the "long silken halter," whose other end he holds (38/508). The specifics of Cellan Jones's frame develop the theme: The African girl's back is turned to the viewer and to the Prince and Fanny; she looks out of the frame to deep space on the right. What does she see? How free is her stance? In contrast, the Prince

---

13. Citations for the BBC version refer to the *Henry James Collection* (2009), disc 5. "A" refers to the first side, which contains the first four episodes, and "B" to the second side, which contains the last two.

and Fanny, elegantly costumed in evening attire, look inward as he tries to explain Charlotte and himself to Fanny: "Our boat is a good deal tied up in the dark. We can't help getting out now and then to stretch our legs or plunging in for a swim" (A 1:46:04–10). What movement within constraint is the Prince describing? What version of this choice does Fanny see as she looks at the African girl, across the Prince's earnest gaze? Cellan Jones's frame is both open and closed, glancing out to the right beyond the frame and closing in on the left. This paradoxical mise-en-scène triangulates two characters' conversation against the mute African figure and offers a powerful figure for their understanding of the absent ones (including Adam, but mostly Charlotte). This frame also identifies and I think comments on the situatedness especially of gender and class, on "orientation" to the world (to cite Sara Ahmed again and *Queer Phenomenology*) and the implications of positionality. Display of decoration and privilege in the film may genuinely suggest choices, or it may be only a masquerade for empire's control. Or maybe it can be both. This modest production, with a small aspect ratio, simple lighting, and modest stars, plumbs complexities of power and consciousness in more intricate ways than most other James versions so much more richly funded.

The scene in which Fanny breaks the golden bowl was important earlier in developing my claim for 'traceability" as a significant hope and motif in James. How subtle are the degrees of opacity in deeply intersubjective scenes, and in this scene particularly, in Cellan Jones's interpretation? How easily, how "visibly," can a character or the authorial viewer trace what characters know about what others know, or more to the point, what characters don't know, or only partially know, about what others don't know, or misknow, or know in part, about yet others? The disaster of the bowl scene works to develop these layers partly because Jack Pulman's screenplay includes language about these meditations, and Maggie and the Prince talk about what Charlotte knows or doesn't know, for example, and about what they know or what Adam knows. But the shot selection and lighting of this long conversation (after Fanny has left) shows how film narrative can develop these themes too. Like so many filmmaking choices in the BBC version, shots and editing seem simple. Maggie and the Prince talk. And we watch them talk. But in fact the way we watch and what we see are subtle and suggestive. For the first part of the conversation, Maggie is on our left and the Prince on the right, and the conversation is mostly over-the-shoulder in shot / reverse shot alternation, though the scene begins with a series of close-ups as Maggie tells the Prince the story of finding the golden bowl and Fanny's decision to break it. These close-ups establish a visual contrast that continues through the sequence: Maggie's face is brightly lit, with really no shadows, but the Prince's face is lit with strong side-lights to cast dark shadows over the right side of his face (B 40:52 vs. 41:11). A few minutes into the scene, Maggie and the Prince change positions, as he crosses in front of her, but Jones's lighting remains the same: now Maggie's face, on the right side of the screen, remains brightly lit, and the Prince's is mostly divided between light and shadow. This choice tends to make the Prince's figure more ominous (he's dressed in black, she in white), her figure more courageous in its bright confrontation of him.

But the scene's shot / reverse shots complicate this pattern. By alternating our over-the-shoulder positions, as the Prince faces Maggie's anger first, and then as Maggie faces his anxiety, we thread exactly Merleau-Ponty's chiasmus. At each moment the viewer watches two characters. The first we watch out of the corner of our eye while as voyeur we peep around that figure in front of us who occupies the side of the frame. The second is standing across the frame from us, the target of both our gaze and the character beside us. The viewer's eyes move across the frame, back and forth, threading responses together. When the camera shifts across the space to mirror the same positions in reverse, the same threading occurs, response to response to response, but with the complication that as voyeur we are now peeping around the character we saw across the room a moment before. This movement, repositioning closeness and distance, disorients the alert viewer, especially given the bitterness of this argument. The web becomes more intricate when the conversation mirrors this process, as when Maggie concludes that her purpose in this conversation was that "You should know that I know" (B 46:10).

But the balance between Maggie and the Prince is not symmetrical, the contrast not so simple as light and dark. Three close-ups change these patterns and complicate the viewer's allegiance. All three are extreme close-ups of the Prince's face, without shadows: In the first, when Maggie bitterly describes the couple's closeness in the antique shop, the Prince replies, "You've never been as sacred to me as you were then." In the second, when Maggie refers to "you" deep old Italians, the Prince replies, slowly, in the close-up, "It's you my dear who are deep." And lastly, Maggie drops her final bombshell, that she will never tell him anything else: "For the rest, find out yourself!" (B 46:41). Those words ring out from offscreen, as the Prince stares darkly into the camera (well, in oblique angle, slightly to the side). The camera denies the authorial viewer a simple place to stand, one consciousness to use as viewfinder.

Furthermore, each character seeks to read the other's face, as Maggie says earlier of the Prince, "You saw that I saw." But traceability, paradoxically, is more difficult in this visual narrative than in James's text, because people hide behind their faces (as was not the case in the James Ivory film; legibility was usually easy given the broad and impulsive acting styles).

When traceability occurs in the BBC version, its agent in Bob Assingham. Now we move into a fundamental narratological topic that we have pursued before, just as we confront perhaps the most remarkable innovation of the Cellan Jones film: its use of Bob to narrate the story, not only in voice-over, but often in direct address to the camera and to "you," the viewer. That fundamental topic is narrative agency: what architect manages the movement of free indirect discourse or the oblique angle of novel or film? Timing is all, and in this example Maggie's ringing challenge still rings, and the camera still lingers on the Prince's face as Bob's voice steps in to tell us about Maggie and what she really wanted (B 46:50). That is, Bob's voice begins several seconds before his face appears on screen. Such editing is not random, and signals a point of view. This choice is also very different from the novel's, where chapter 34 and part IV end with the cry, and the next chapter and part V open ten days later. But Bob is often eager to interpret and to place, and so his character, with its desires and foibles, plays a role that is a remarkable structural addition to the story. It is indeed a change, an interpretation, but perhaps one much in tune with the novel's concerns. Here is Bob's reflection on this scene:

> I told you once that Maggie was an extraordinary young woman. And I think now you'll see what I mean. For she was fighting, this you must remember, not simply to save her marriage, but fighting to prevent even a breath of what she knew from reaching her father. "Find out," she replied to her husband when he'd asked if anyone else knew, meaning of course her father. For she wasn't prepared to give him any help. And who can blame her? She must have believed then her father knew nothing. And that if he came to know, if would bring his own marriage to an end. And if *that* happened, her own could never again be repaired, bearing as it would such a weight of guilt. So she trod carefully. (B 46:50–47:30)

This language traces a range of motives, with interestingly varying degrees of certainty. Bob can vouch for Maggie's motives at the beginning—her "fight" especially to preserve her father's ignorance, and her refusal to help the Prince know more about what Adam knows. Also, she fears the effects of spreading what she knows on both her father's marriage and on her own. But then, Bob's confidence sometimes extends to knowing knowing—that is, to intersubjective exchanges: what Maggie thinks about what her father thinks, and how Charlotte functions in the thoughts of both about the other. But what is the source of Bob's secure knowledge? Charlotte is Fanny's special friend, and the Prince also (or he used to be), but not Maggie. So how does Bob really know what Maggie is prepared or not prepared to do? After all, neither he nor Fanny is present during this conversation—indeed, Fanny has left quite precipitously to avoid hearing it. Bob's confidence about what he knows comes perilously close to the novel's narrator's confidence. And then toward the end of this speech, Bob stops knowing: "[Maggie] must have believed then her father knew nothing." I don't mean that he doesn't know what Adam knows; I mean that he doesn't know what Maggie believes, even though he has just guaranteed her motives in a scene he did not witness, nor could have heard about from another witness.

This movement into and then out of the omniscient narrator role continues throughout the serial. At the beginning, Bob presents himself as a human participant and describes his sources as Fanny, and some scenes in which he directly participated, but as he says, "only on the fringe" (A 1:40), and he is puzzled about what his narrative strategy ought to be: "Let me sort this thing out in my head and decide where to begin" (A 3:45). The challenge is not simple: "I can't begin at the beginning because that's too far back" (A 4:25). He concludes, talking to the camera, "You'll just have to pick it up as you go along, feel it out, fit it in, as I did" (A 4:52). He's just a storyteller, and not very good with words. Yet at other times, Bob has very privileged knowledge. Perhaps most strikingly, he knows the contents of the telegram that the Prince sends Charlotte about the proposed marriage to Adam. Most of the language in the serial (A 1:23:47*ff.*) comes directly from the meditations of the novel's narrator about what the "wire" meant: for example, that perhaps it meant that for the Prince his daily life "was uphill work for him," and that if he and Charlotte become nearer, he would then "live still more under arms" (17/212). In the novel, no one reads the telegram but Charlotte, and no provenance appears in the BBC version for Bob's knowledge.

Another example with powerful thematic force is one I mentioned above: the image for Charlotte's life with "a long silken halter looped round her beautiful neck. He didn't twitch it, yet it was there" (38/508). (In the BBC version, Bob says "a long silken cord.") The eyes watching Charlotte and Adam are Maggie's in the novel, but the text waffles on the source of the famous image itself: "the likeness of their connection would

FIGURE 3.4. *The Golden Bowl* (1972) (B 1:05:54): "Yes, you see—I lead her now by the neck ... lead her to her doom, and she doesn't as much as know what it is."

not have been wrongly figured if he [Adam] had been thought of as holding in one of his pocketed hands the end of" the cord. In the BBC version, Bob says, "Maggie saw it was as if he held the end" (B 1:05:08). So the image is Maggie's here, and Bob knows that, and knows that Maggie saw, "as Charlotte must have seen" (B 1:04:50). He doesn't in this case quite *know* what Charlotte saw. But he does see—literally, as it turns out—that Maggie imagines her father delivering the terrifying words, "Yes, you see—I lead her now by the neck." Bob's imagination brings to the screen Maggie's imagination of the face of a unforgiving Barry Morse (who plays Adam) delivering these words. The choice to show Adam's face has enormous consequences, since the film's viewer tends to forget that the image is only in Maggie's mind. Instead, the words that continue come, in the frame, from her father: "[I] lead her to her doom ... and she doesn't as much as know what it is" (figure 3.4). In the novel, these exact words are only Maggie's translation of her father's "soft shake of the twisted silken rope." Pulman's choice to show Bob's vision of Maggie's vision of her father's vision is a stunning example of deep intersubjectivity in film. Pulman's screenplay for the BBC wants it both ways: Bob really knows but is putting the pieces together, like the viewer. Bob has extraordinary powers and can see what Maggie imagines, but he is also an ordinary person (well, retired Army).

The issues of traceability and authority are connected, and both link closely to the representation of deep (or less deep) intersubjectivity and the operations of the oblique angle. Bob's role may in strict narratological terms be inconsistent, but it raises the epistemological questions in a powerful way: who knows, and how does that mind know what others know, and what others know or misknow or know in part about yet others? Lee Mitchell Clark agrees, in one of the few scholarly treatments of the BBC serial, that "by foregrounding Bob's role as narrator, an important dual thematic strain is sustained throughout: of people watching others, who watch others in turn" (298). Bob takes our hand through the labyrinth as the viewer's guide and partner, as if such penetration were possible for us ordinary viewers (Bob says it is). This is a remarkable innovation, a remarkable addition to *The Golden Bowl,* to turn the screw, perhaps, another time, on the moral and ontological problem of others.

Behind Bob the BBC version of the story does present, quite clearly when one notices, the hand of the architect behind the scenes, the enunciator of the story. But that agent in James's novel is actually quite anthropomorphic, referring to itself frequently as "I" or "we" ("that gravity the oppression of which I began by recording"; "and I must add, moreover, that she at last found herself"; "we each have our own way," to write down a few examples [1/14; 26/323; 30/373]). The architect in the serial, however, does not have a persona or a pronoun. That agent manages the cuts between shots, the frame, and the camera's movement or position. One example is the tracking shot early in the story that moves behind a wall of leaded-glass windows while Maggie and Adam walk on the other side, discussing a letter from Charlotte, a topic Maggie broaches because Adam has asked, "What's on your mind?" (A 58:55–59:08). The tracking shot follows Maggie and Adam through the distortions of the leaded windows, so that the images match well the story's sense of what it requires to discern what is in fact on others' minds. Tracking shots are very rare in the serial, and indeed in "heritage" television, so that this choice stands out with special emphasis. There is similar moment in Jack Clayton's *The Innocents,* when the mobile camera, accompanying Miss Giddens on her walk to Bly, moves behind a large tree and watches her in a parallel movement, and it stops and watches her walk away (9:05). For a moment the viewer has the sense that someone is spying on the governess within the diegesis (though it's not clear who that could be), and in fact the camera often imitates a point-of-view shot in the film. These choices emphasize the theme of looking and watching as voyeur, but not in this case (in *The Innocents*) looking at looking. Decoding the web of perceptions of perceptions in the embodiments of deep intersubjectivity is not a project of this film, in which exchanges between characters usually reach a dead end with Deborah Kerr's anxious, overwrought body movements and those widening, shocked eyes that do not look *at* someone, but really look inward.

Frame composition also provides a comment, as in the example we discussed at length above of the bust of the young African serving woman who occupies that frame with Fanny and the Prince. Figure placement matters throughout the story, as in the frames in the middle of the serial in which Charlotte and the Prince sit at a table in a dinner party on the same side, even holding hands, while Maggie and Adam do the same on the other side of the table (see A 1:30:07, for example). The frame whose design comments most powerfully on the relationships among our four principals in *The Golden Bowl* occurs at the end of the last episode, at the farewell scene. First the camera sees the Prince and Charlotte through a window at Portland Place (Maggie and the Prince's home), and then moves left, in another rare tracking shot, to the next window, which is open, and at which Maggie and her father review their choices. Maggie and Adam are at the edges of the frame, and the Prince and Charlotte are enclosed in the center, in the shot's deep space (somewhat out of focus—this is not *Citizen Kane*—and also out of earshot). The words of father and daughter express satisfaction at their position, their control over the narratives of both couples. Adam concludes, "Now we see," and Maggie echoes, "We see" (figure 3.5). But there is no seeing of what the other sees, no looking at looking. Instead they both look out the window, not at each other, along parallel planes, and their faces (aside from a few brave smiles) write the sorrow of their parting. We see their seeing, but it is melancholy, isolated, absent any exchange. There certainly is no braiding of perceptions between the foreground and the background. Separation is the rule here, visually and thematically.

These few examples suggest how film narrative can—perhaps the emphasis should be *can*—explore some of the same conflicts in these late James novels. Obliqueness and the over-the-shoulder gaze occur in both novels and films, and suture edits these moments into narratives of absence and loss and perhaps very limited espousal. (The work of suture is in some texts more thoughtful than in others, and one outcome of this study for me is a new understanding of the remarkable

FIGURE 3.5. *The Golden Bowl* (1972) (B 1:20:32): "Now we see."

achievement—inadequately recognized—in both form and content of the BBC's 1972 *The Golden Bowl*.)

What is the nature of intimacy and community when connection to the other (and the other's connection to others) is so problematic? This thread links this chapter to the next, which in an extended case study looks at another series of gaps between characters' consciousnesses, with complex uses of narrative indirections. In these examples, suture is a narrative strategy that reveals deep wounds and losses across the large body of Peter Pan tales, from the multiple versions that James Barrie wrote to film iterations many years later.

CHAPTER 4

The Wounds of Peter Pan

Suture and Loss

> To be born is to be wrecked upon an island.
> —J. M. Barrie, Preface to *The Coral Island*

> Wendy: Peter, why did you come to our nursery window?
> Peter: To try to hear stories. None of us knows any stories.
> —J. M. Barrie, *Peter Pan*, I.i 477–78

> Wendy: I have to grow up tomorrow.
> —*Peter Pan* (Disney, 1953)

In J. M. Barrie's play *Peter Pan,* only fairies can touch Peter. When Peter tells Wendy he doesn't have a mother, in their first scene in the Darling nursery, and she immediately tries to hug him, Peter pulls back and says, "You mustn't touch me." When Wendy asks why, he replies, "I don't know," and Wendy observes, "No wonder you were crying" (*Peter Pan* 98).[1] Here at the beginning of the Peter Pan legend, touch touches on consolation, prohibition, the loss of mothers, proud isolation that might be narcissism, and mourning. At the end of the play (at least in the 1928 version), Wendy still must repress the embrace: "Oh, Peter, how I wish I

---

1. Citations will occur in this text to frequently quoted works with this code: PP: Barrie, *Peter Pan* (1928 play text, in *Peter Pan and Other Plays*); PPKG: *Peter Pan in Kensington Gardens* and PW: *Peter and Wendy*, both in Barrie, *Peter Pan in Kensington Gardens / Peter and Wendy*; DPP: Disney's film *Peter Pan* (1953); HPP: P. J. Hogan's film *Peter Pan* (2003).

could take you up and squdge you!" But as Peter again draws back, she answers, "Yes, I know" (PP 153). Yet Barrie suggests that the reverse is also possible, because characters *can* touch Peter in Barrie's 1911 novella *Peter and Wendy,* perhaps most poignantly after the battle with the pirates when Peter kills Hook. Peter proudly "strutted up and down the deck" of the pirate ship, but despite this triumph, "he had one of his dreams that night, and cried in his sleep for a long time, and Wendy held him tight" (PW 205). For Barrie's Peter, touch is both possible and impossible, disturbing and comforting, invasive and protective. So touch opens the door onto the need for the oblique, and in the Peter Pan stories, its special version will be what I have called the Oblique II, the extraordinary use of eavesdropping, especially in the form of what I call the ricochet effect.

Touching is deeply problematic in *Peter Pan* and echoes J. Hillis Miller's complex meditations on touching in Jacques Derrida, in Jean-Luc Nancy, in Edmund Husserl, and in Merleau-Ponty and Levinas in *For Derrida*. Miller's chain of meditations emphasizes the gap between bodies and consciousnesses that bedevils any version of community. Crossing or even narrowing this gap raises always for Derrida (and Miller) the topic of the character and role of what Derrida calls the wholly other. Miller sees in Derrida a deep oscillation in the midst of this labyrinth of readings: "Derrida's wavering between a resolute quasi-solipsism and a conviction that some 'wholly other' or other may nevertheless break through those monadic walls" (xix). The result of that breakthrough would be "a command from the wholly other that is both impossible and yet may perhaps arrive" (8). Barrie's title for chapter 1 of *Peter and Wendy* echoes Derrida's wish (if the past can echo the future): "Peter Breaks Through" (PW 71). But how does this breakthrough happen, and what are its consequences? This is the dilemma posed in my first citation above, from Barrie's 1913 preface to yet another edition of R. M. Ballantyne's *The Coral Island,* first published in 1858: "To be born is to be wrecked upon an island."[2] The human condition is to be wholly other, starting the world anew with each birth. When and how does a movement away from the center, to and for the other, occur? What conditions would make such a move possible? What forms of the oblique might provide necessary protection? Or cover for certain kinds of aggression?

The problem of the ontology of touch, of touching touching, of contact with and experiences of the other (whether "wholly" or not), lies at the

---

2. For those lacking easy access to this 1913 edition, Barrie's Preface now appears in Anne Hiebert Alton's recent edition of the play. This quotation occurs on p. 380.

heart of *Peter Pan*'s island story. How can Peter and Wendy and the Lost Boys touch if they are still wholly other? How can a skeptical, longing narrator tell this tale? Touching crosses boundaries and invades bodies, and so opens possibilities for abuse and violation, possibilities that suggest the most vexed and important questions about *Peter Pan*. Jacqueline Rose has argued that the narrative form of Barrie's Pan stories, especially in *The Little White Bird* and *Peter and Wendy,* is a kind of molestation of child narratees (this last word—*narratee*—is mine, but *molestation* is hers). I will talk a lot about narratees in Barrie and their placement amidst the ricochet of story and language. Touching (even if by tale and word) as violation of children is a theme inside and outside the diegesis of Barrie's tales, as might not be surprising in a writer who was a friend of the author of *The Turn of the Screw*. (In 1909 Barrie invited James to write a play for him, and the year before they attended a performance together of Barrie's play *What Every Woman Knows*.[3]) We know Miles and Flora in *The Turn of the Screw* know too much because they say taboo words, and here, as in Barrie, the stories of family and abandonment risk excess and lack, saying too much and saying too little, knowing too much and knowing too little. One great interest of narrative lies in these degrees of knowing and misknowing, of violation and encounter and what Merleau-Ponty called espousal, these partialities layered on partialities, these degrees of error and mistaking others' mistakes and on occasion not entirely mistaking their mistakes.[4]

The chapter that follows is a series of reflections on the narration of fragments of consciousnesses as they encounter the other in the Pan stories; on the role of multiple narratees in Barrie and the Pan films and their complex, sometimes threatening relationships; on the nature and function

---

3. For the story of Barrie's invitation to James to write a play for the repertory company Charles Frohman and he were organizing in 1909, see Leon Edel's foreword to *The Outcry* in *The Complete Plays of Henry James,* pp. 761–65. In a letter of December 4, 1908, James refers to an evening of dinner and theater with Barrie, "attending his own production," and on this date Barrie's hit play *What Every Woman Knows* was running in London (*Letters* V, 505; Mackail 405).

4. As I argued in discussing narrators in Henry James in chapter 3, this range of knowledges is guaranteed in narrative, if not in our lives, by a text's narrative confidence, which is perhaps another word for that narrative agency that somehow always stages even a story's aporias. This range of knowing and misknowing with all its partialities and rhetorical ploys is also my primary interest in embedded narratives, in which might be called the first level of deep intersubjectivity, in contrast to critics in the cognitive school who are interested in further layers of embedding. See Lisa Zunshine's essay, for example, on how many recursive steps (I know that you know that Fred knows that Susan knows . . .) human cognitive wiring can reasonably negotiate ("Can We Teach" 30–33, especially 31 for the possibility of "cognitive vertigo").

of what I call the ricochet effect among these narratees; on the risks of violation the ricochet effect threatens; and on the effort to suture story fragments and also subjectivities in both print and film narrative, especially in forms that have traditionally been limited to print (free indirect discourse) or to film (shot / reverse shot conventions) but which I argued in chapter 2 are homologous. The Peter Pan stories, then, offer the most complex and varied examples of suture in this book, in the form that I named the Oblique II, and provide excellent illustrations of the effects, formal and thematic, of these strategies.

They also offer remarkable evidence that narratological choices have thorny and significant ethical implications. As I say later, Barrie's Peter Pan texts are edgy and dangerous for all audiences because they suture multiple consciousnesses in narratologically innovative ways that put all of us at risk. Obliqueness, indirection, difficulty: these are persistent motifs throughout this chapter and this book. The forms of oblique deep intersubjectivity here will, I hope, remind readers of examples of the risks of shame and loss they have found in this book, as well as the occasional, hard-won hope for community.

i. BARRIE'S PETER PANS: "WOULD NOT" OR "COULD NOT"?

The quarrel over voice, authorial audience, and narrative form in the Peter Pan stories has only deepened in the thirty years since the Great Ormond Street Hospital for Sick Children in London lost control of the J. M. Barrie play in 1987. The Barrie texts, themselves a tangled web of versions, revisions, and evasions, have been joined by further revisions and evasions, from Steven Spielberg's *Hook* (1992) and an all-woman production of the play in London in 1991 (Rose ix), to two more recent films, P. J. Hogan's live-action *Peter Pan* (2003) and Marc Forster's *Finding Neverland* (2004), both also complex reinterpretations. The Barrie texts begin in a series of false starts, incomplete middles, and multiple, contradictory ends that suggest an intense effort to make coherent a story that defies conventional narration. These texts range from the unpublished *The Boy Castaways of Black Lake Island* (1901) and the novel *The Little White Bird* (1902) to the novella *Peter and Wendy* (1911) and then the play text *Peter Pan* (1928), first published years after the triumphant debut of the play in 1904, after many successful productions around the world, and also after Barrie contracted for other writers to produce redactions of the play in print for school-age children.

These tellings and retellings point to a circling around some material that might seem to be almost unnarratable. The recent re-visioning and evading in film add to the sense of a compulsion and even desperation enacted in these forms. The narrative drive in the Peter Pan stories is deep and broad and raises fraught questions of boundaries between a general adult and a more specifically child audience (real or implied), as more and more extensively theorized by children's literature scholars in recent years. The Peter Pan stories contain a mix of consciousnesses, adult and younger, sexualized and not, sentimental and cynical, intra- and extra-diegetic. These Peter Pan stories will provide another and quite different example of what I named deeply intersubjective suture in *The Silence of the Lambs* and in Henry James. My own view will hold that no narrative strategies can heal the wounds of time in Barrie's Peter Pan stories, but characters and narrators try, and their efforts and evasions partly explain our wider confusions about Barrie's Peter Pan texts, as well as the related but different confusions of the film versions.

Clarifying the nature and function of narrative fragmentation in the Peter Pan stories is a vexed project because Barrie's texts, especially *The Little White Bird* and *Peter and Wendy*, have been accused of fundamental violations of narrative expectations: in particular, a failure to understand or respect boundaries between narrator and narratee. Breaching this boundary inside a story may not seem serious, but the issue becomes clearer when we remember that implied readers—authorial or narrative audience—eavesdrop closely over the shoulder of a narratee, and that the competent flesh-and-blood audience will then try to align itself with these listeners in the text. (I will review below the specific meanings for these terms for audiences.) Given this queue of aligned recipients, when does talk of time, eros, and abandonment cross an age-inappropriate boundary? Who might be so positioned as to hear something damaging or abusive? Could narrative form in *Peter Pan* become itself a form of "molestation," Jacqueline Rose's arresting word (70)?[5]

Behind my claims lies an echo of Rose's further diagnosis, that the evasions of Barrie's Pan texts (which I will argue are not evasions) mirror

---

5. Alison Kavey argues that Rose's attack on *Peter Pan* grows out of a confusion of Barrie with his character, so that pedophilia in Barrie (a claim that, she correctly maintains, the historical record does not support in any simple way) gets transferred unproblematically to Barrie's work. Kavey is right to criticize simplistic biographical readings of Barrie's story, but Rose grounds her doubts about *Peter Pan* not in claims about Barrie's life, but in close reading of specific language in Barrie's texts (see Rose 34–39, for example).

the anxieties of real-world adult readers who fear the fluidity, never to be transcended, of their own selves, especially their erotic selves. For Rose the Barrie stories point to "what is always at some level an impossible task—the task of cohering the fragmented, component and perverse sexuality of the child," a process that is "fictional..., at best precarious, and never complete" (14). Rose identifies what she sees as the bad-faith negotiations between children and adults in the real world for whom the label "literature for children" functions as a "decoy." This label ("for children"), Rose argues, helps adults avoid admitting to the important function for *them* of reading texts to flesh-and-blood children, which is to promote "a fantasy of origins" (and sexual wholeness), which then solidifies "the very constitution of the adult as subject" (137–41). I see these tangled relations between audiences also *within* Barrie's texts, relations that are foregrounded so problematically that any decoy function would only be possible with serious underreading.

The tangle of consciousnesses appears in two arenas in Barrie's Peter Pan stories: within the story-level itself, the diegesis; and in the relations between the fluid enunciating or narrative voice or agent, more or less explicit in each story's form, and the authorial or implied audiences for these narratives. Each of these levels offers its own labyrinth of possibilities, especially since Barrie's texts take so many different forms. First there are the fragments and insertions: the unpublished collage of text and photo, *The Boy Castaways of Black Lake Island* (1901), followed by the tale within a tale, the Peter chapters of *The Little White Bird* (1902), followed then by the extraction of those chapters into a separate volume, *Peter Pan in Kensington Gardens* (1906), still bearing the marks of this rupture. In addition, two "whole" Pans exist in print, the novella *Peter and Wendy* (1911) and the play text *Peter Pan*. The novella, albeit often misnamed *Peter Pan* in its many republications since 1911, retains more stability and wholeness as a text, compared to the others, though the narrative voice that tells the tale is in narratological terms more puzzling than any other version's narrative or enunciating agency. Barrie's play text has a long, complex history of its own, from early drafts through the Christmas 1904 premiere to extensive rewritings and variations up to the 1928 publication (see R. D. S. Jack's *The Road to the Never Land* for the best account of the text's evolution). But even the 1928 text was not "whole" in one simple sense: the "Afterthought," a sort of Act VI, performed once in 1908, was only published, as *When Wendy Grew Up*, in 1957, long after Barrie's death in 1937, though in a prose form it appears as the last chapter in *Peter and Wendy* (PP vii).

Despite these complications, or perhaps because of them, key strategies for narrating how characters experience the trauma of time emerge in these stories in their extensive repetitions and renarrations. *Peter and Wendy* will serve as my primary print text partly because it is the first "complete" Peter Pan text that Barrie published, and it remained unrevised. At the same time, my argument will refer to the play text(s) because Barrie's 1911 novella self-consciously problematizes the "original" Pan story so intricately with its dramatized, self-referential, and apparently inconsistent storyteller and with its multiple narratees.

The Peter Pan story begins with the loss of mother and home. This loss is the beginning because it is the first event in the fabula, in the story line; it is also the injury that motivates many of the story's narrative arabesques and indirections. And it opens a gap whose ambiguities the stories tell and retell and never forget. Whether these stories can suture the gap is the great question. The mother-wound in *Peter Pan* is both her presence and absence, the generating and abandoning of the child, her care and carelessness (a paradox mirrored in Peter's character, although he is a little thin on the care side). These doublenesses surface also in different versions of the beginning of Peter's story: how do the Lost Boys get lost? This origin gets defined in two different narratives. In the first, Peter chooses to "[escape] from being a human when he was seven days old" (PPKG 12) and continues to make that choice, as when, for example, Mrs. Darling offers to adopt Peter too at the end of the play, in addition to adopting the other Lost Boys. Peter replies, "No one is going to catch me, lady, and make me a man. I want always to be a little boy and to have fun" (PP 151). In the other narrative, Peter only wanted to have fun for a few years, always expecting the window to remain open for his return. This second version appears at least three times in the Pan texts, first in *Kensington Gardens* (PPKG 40), and again when Peter tells the same story in chapter 11 of the novella, and in the play, in Act IV, when Wendy has urged the Lost Boys to return home.

> Wendy, you're wrong about mother. I thought like you about the window, so I stayed away for moons and moons, and then I flew back, but the window was barred, for my mother had forgotten all about me, and there was another little boy sleeping in my bed. (PP 132)

So, which is it? The boy who *would* not grow up, or the boy who *could* not grow up? Here, at the beginning of the Peter Pan fabula, fundamentally different stories obscure our way. The play's subtitle, printed for the first production's program in December 1904, was "The Boy Who Wouldn't Grow Up," but Andrew Birkin records an entry in Barrie's notebook for 1921 with another subtitle: "The Man Who Didn't [crossed through] *Couldn't* Grow Up" (Birkin 116, 290; emphasis in original). Adding to the ambiguities here, in 1928 the play text cites Peter's defiant line delivered to Mrs. Darling, quoted above ("No one is going to catch me, lady!") and then adds the stage direction, "So perhaps he thinks, but it is only his greatest pretend" (PP 151). (Of course, the line is not a stage direction—it is unplayable—but rather a kind of narrator's commentary. One of P. J. Hogan's most interesting choices in the 2003 film is to give this line to Wendy near the film's conclusion.) This comment is oddly missing in the novella, replete as it is with many other narrator judgments, but the Darling children's return home concludes with the famous description of Peter watching at the window: "He had ecstasies innumerable that other children can never know; but he was looking through the window at the one joy from which he must be for ever barred" (PW 214). A Peter who "must be for ever barred" from this joy is not a Peter who could choose it.

Earlier in the Pan tales, in *Kensington Gardens,* Peter is in fact deeply uncertain about what he wants at a moment when he *has* flown home through the open window and watches his sleeping mother. Barrie's narrator comments, "I quite shrink from the truth, which is that he sat there in two minds. Sometimes he looked longingly at his mother, and sometimes he looked longingly at the window" (PPKG 38). The first line of Barrie's novella defines only the outcome, not the cause: "All children, except one, grow up" (PW 69). In all of the Peter Pan texts, then, the breaking apart of mother and child gives birth to different stories, even with different subtitles, told and retold as if to confirm their unresolvable differences.

"Could" or "would" point to other uncertainties in the Barrie universe: Is home a nest to be cherished or an enclosure to escape? Which way does the window look? In to the circle of the family, finally loving but anxious (how to afford all these new boys, and what *will* the neighbors think?), or out to the realm of open air and flight? And why is narrative so necessary that Peter must return to Wendy's window "to try to hear stories," because "none of us knows any"? The Cinderella tale that Peter seeks to complete has the dark side (Bruno Bettelheim refers, for example, to a version in which Cinderella flees the father who wants to marry her [245]), but it also paints growing up in much brighter colors than Peter does. Peter needs Wendy's stories but hates Wendy's good-night story on the island (because it's a story of faithful mothers and home restored). Storytelling is an important motif for the Peter Pan narratives, because stories order time and family and identity inside the diegesis, but also because the texts present complex and, for many readers (authorial or flesh and blood), puzzling, even troubling, narrative choices, especially in *Peter and Wendy*. My purpose is to explore these formal choices, that is, how they deploy strategies of indirection and link them to the fractured lives they narrate.

ii. *PETER AND WENDY* AND BARRIE'S MULTIPLE NARRATEES: WHO IS LISTENING TO THIS STORY?

Storytelling is fractured in Barrie's Peter Pan stories, and is most fractured in Barrie's 1911 novella, *Peter and Wendy*, partly because of its deviousness over which readers it addresses—perhaps in the real world too, but especially inside the text: readers overt or covert, implied or dramatized. These fractures start small but grow and grow until they are enormous. They become the occasion, I will argue, for a particularly subtle use of deeply intersubjective suture that is exploited in a wide array of formal and thematic choices in Barrie, and later in the Peter Pan films. The effects of these fractures for presumed audiences have troubled many real-world readers of Barrie. Here is a brief sample of those voices: Barrie's narrator in *Peter and Wendy* is "repulsive and offensive" (Wall 27); Barrie's "dual-address narrative ... dart[s] strategically, even sadistically, between mature and naïve modes" (Holmes 140); Barrie's "collapse of narrative voices" occurs in "moments of narrative indeterminacy" and "narrative confusion" (Wasinger 219); "the harshness of [Barrie's] message often shocks new readers" and amounts to "almost an assault in a children's book" (Holmes 143). These writers repeat in some form Rose's initial description of *Peter and Wendy* as "an attack on, or at least an affront to, the very concept of children's literature" (86).[6] All of these protests share the belief that *Peter and Wendy* is a text for children to read or to hear.

---

6. The concept of children's literature is, of course, a vexed topic. In a recent provocative essay in *PMLA*, "On Not Defining Children's Literature," Marah Gubar reviews the problematic history of proposed definitions and proposes her own elegant, Wittgensteinian approach, which focuses on identifying "family resemblances" for children's literature, many of which texts would share, but none of which would characterize all members of the genre (212). However, I doubt Gubar would want to allow "assault" and "molestation" in her family.

But this presumed answer, that *Peter and Wendy* is a text for children to read or hear, oversimplifies a complex narratological problem: who *are* the novella's audiences? Behind this question lurks another that will require careful attention as well: what are the narratological rules for a children's tale (that is, a story not only *about* children and childhood, but *for* flesh-and-blood children to read or hear), even if adults are also an audience? Are the accusations against Barrie's Peter Pan texts irrelevant because they blame those stories for violating the rules of a game they never sought to play (because they're not "children's literature")? A key issue in this debate will be the relation between intra-textual and extra-textual audiences: inside the work there can be specific listeners (say, the Lost Boys around the campfire) or a less dramatized narratee ("I don't know if you have ever seen a map of a person's mind" [PW 73]), and then there is the implied reader, who can be divided, according to Peter Rabinowitz's thinking, into narrative audience (who believe the story is real) and authorial audience (who know the story is a work of art). As will be clear soon, the relations among these audiences become very complicated in the Peter Pan tales, so that the possibilities for alignment by different real readers become very complicated as well. It is these alignments that become oblique and risky.

So, to begin: who is the narrator in *Peter and Wendy* addressing? Everyone agrees that identifying the text's addressee is difficult, for a variety of reasons. One reason is the way the text seems to address different listeners at different times, or even at the same time; another reason is that the role the narrator adopts seems to shift also. Yet another problem is the way the text itself may seem to claim that its intra-textual listener has a particular relation to a real audience outside the text. This claim has a special twist when the text appears to include in the landscape of its readers the figure of an adult (implied as well as real-world) reading to a child, also implied as well as real-world. The power relations among these figures (at least four of them) can become extraordinarily intricate, as Peter Hollindale describes vividly:

> The adult reader is a helpless intermediary between Barrie and the child, caught in storytelling crossfire and receiving bullet wounds intended for him or her alone. Under the surface of the children's book is a sharp and sometimes ferocious dialectic, exploring the collision and relation of the child and adult worlds. (PW xxi)

We will be tracking the threads that suture these subjectivities together in complicated, oblique, and risky networks.

To get a clearer take on the argument here, and on the astonishing complexity of Barrie's work, let us begin with a closer examination of the famous first paragraph of *Peter and Wendy*:

> All children, except one, grow up. They soon know that they will grow up, and the way Wendy knew was this. One day when she was two years old she was playing in a garden, and she plucked another flower and ran with it to her mother. I suppose she must have looked rather delightful, for Mrs. Darling put her hand over her heart and cried, "Oh, why can't you remain like this forever!" This was all that passed between them on the subject, but henceforth Wendy knew that she must grow up. You always know after you are two. Two is the beginning of the end. (PW 69)

It is immediately clear that this narrator is not speaking only to children, or not even to children at all, in this paragraph. The famous opening line stakes a general claim, in the manner of a George Eliot narrator, that makes sense only to a listener who has some foundation for an idea about "all" children. What kind of reader thinks in abstractions about "children," and could that reader be a child? Because the word *children* has a wide range of meanings, its use as a topic for reflection and as an identification of an audience is fluid. Although real-world fifteen-year-olds, say, and real-world two-year-olds vary enormously in cognitive sophistication, it is unlikely that a "child" listener of two, or even of six, would be able to grasp this claim and make some sense of its strange exception. Perhaps an older child, or a "young adult," in twenty-first-century usage, could navigate these abstractions and ironies. But the discourse of this opening paragraph, like much of *Peter and Wendy,* excludes the audience of younger persons—how young I will discuss soon—that *children* usually refers to. Hence the story's specific inclusion of this particular audience at scattered moments is so significant.

In fact, Barrie's language in *Peter and Wendy*'s first paragraph identifies its use of *children* quite narrowly. The two-year-old Wendy is its example of children who are "they" to the narrator, who therefore is speaking over "their" heads to someone else; that is, Barrie's narrator explicitly addresses the first sentence to not-Wendies. So much for *Peter and Wendy* as a classic of literature *for* children to read or hear. The narrator claims that Wendy learned she must grow up from her mother, when she was two, but Wendy does not understand the implications of her knowledge. Only one segment of this paragraph represents Wendy's thought ("henceforth Wendy knew she must grow up"), but this representation is directed at the readers who understand the narrative arc that extends from this moment: "Two is the beginning of the end." Time—process, mortality, decay—looms here, as it does in Wendy's mother's lament: "Oh, why can't you remain like this forever!" But the two-year-old does not know what it knows, that there are ends to beginnings. Here, as in much of *Peter and Wendy*, the narrative voice specifically excludes the young child (including children a good deal older than two), speaking over its head so to speak to an audience aware of the implications of life narratives.

Since later in chapter 1 the narrator changes direction to include somewhat younger children as narratees, it would be useful at this point to expand Seymour Chatman's famous framework of the narrative process, from *Story and Discourse,* and discuss the value of such an expansion. I want to add categories and concepts developed by Peter Rabinowitz, mentioned before, in "Truth in Fiction" and *Before Reading,* and by James Phelan in *Narrative as Rhetoric*. First, I want to divide the text's "implied reader" into two different groups, the narrative audience and the authorial audience. The first group—the narrative audience—believes the story is real, and, as I wrote before, might, after seeing *Rear Window,* look up Lars Thorwald's phone number in the Manhattan directory of 1954 if it could find one. This narrative audience in *Peter and Wendy* is more typically the younger reader (or listener—who is too young to read the tale), the child who really believes Peter flies to Neverland. Certainly real adults will choose to play the role of the younger child—indeed, the seductiveness of this opportunity is a big reason Jacqueline Rose finds children's literature as a genre fundamentally dishonest. The narrative audience will align itself easily with the character listeners in the story—say, the Lost Boys listening to Wendy—and will also align itself easily with the younger narratee addressed by the narrator ("If you could keep awake (but of course you can't) you would see your own mother doing this") (PW 73). The (younger) narrative audience, having aligned itself with the young narratee, will typically draw the younger real reader to this position, as James Phelan argues (see below). The charge leveled against *Peter and Wendy* especially, but against other versions of the story too, is that drawing the younger audience (younger narratee, narrative audience, and real listeners) into these positions sets them up for an ambush.

The second group, the "author's hypothetical audience," in Rabinowitz's terms, or the authorial audience, knows it is listening to a constructed tale, and so will not expect to find a report in the *New York Times* from 1954 about Mrs. Thorwald's disappearance. It tries to align itself with the expectations of the story, understanding the cultural allusions or pretending to; as Rabinowitz says, "we are often lazy" and so pretend to understand Spanish politics of the 1930s while reading *For Whom the Bell Tolls* rather than looking up the historical background ("Truth" 131). The authorial audience for *Peter and Wendy* will understand the conventions of this tale, and because it also plays the role of the narrative audience, it will both believe Peter flies and also know better. Particularly because of the ability required to frame narrative choices and understand conventions, not many younger flesh-and-blood children will be able to occupy the authorial audience position. When, in the theatre, Peter asks the audience to clap to show they believe in fairies, it's a nice question which role the adults are playing when they clap (often, in consort with the children sitting with them). Perhaps they play both roles (narrative and authorial audience) at the same time, in a poignant and unusual example of deep intersubjectivity.

The authorial audience will also recognize the ploys of the tale's narrator, its multiple voices and ironies, even the way it uses the role of the child narratee to allow a space for flesh-and-blood children to enter the story, a concept particularly developed by Phelan, who writes in *Narrative as Rhetoric,* "second-person narrative almost always retains the potential to pull the actual reader back into the addressee [implied reader] role" (138).[7] The authorial audience may admire this devious and clever narrator, or not. Later we will discuss the playfulness of this narrator—perhaps a vindictive playfulness, according to some. The value of this extension of the Chatman grid is the subtlety it allows for pathways of alignment from inside the story to real readers. The dichotomy of younger child and melancholy, time-aware adult moves right through the novella, organizing each narrative level, from narratees inside the text, to the text's implied readers—the narrative (younger children will cluster here, with grown-ups) and authorial (mostly just grown-ups) audiences—to the different groups of real readers. These different pathways help explain why the Peter Pan story has so many different versions, so many different kinds of audiences, and so many different interpretations.

---

7. In chapter 7 of *Narrative as Rhetoric,* Phelan discusses a range of issues and terminologies for second-person narration, including Gerald Prince's different framework for naming various audiences in the chain of narrative communication. Phelan divides implied readers as Rabinowitz does, and argues that the relationship between narrative audience and narratee can be fluid and complex, including important overlapping (139*ff.*).

How specifically does *Peter and Wendy* construct its labyrinth of subjectivities? Barrie's text presents at least two implied audiences, the philosophically minded adult who has reflected on life narratives that lead to "the end," and younger listeners too. Just how young is this second group, and what do we know about them? Here the narrator is describing Mrs. Darling's nightly task of tidying her children's minds, "repacking into their proper places the many articles that have wandered during the day" (73). The narrator then moves from Mrs. Darling to "every mother" and to a specifically younger narratee: "If you could keep awake (but of course you can't) you would see your own mother doing this." Her project, the narrator says, is much like "tidying up drawers":

> When you wake up in the morning, the naughtinesses and evil passions with which you went to bed have been folded up small and placed at the bottom of your mind; and on the top, beautifully aired, are spread out your prettier thoughts, ready for you to put on. (73)

What are the descriptors for this "you"? It is a child still at home, unable to keep itself awake even if it wants to, one whose caretaker takes on the responsibility of cleaning and folding clothes for the next day. When, according to some customary timeline of maturation, do real-world children or children in Barrie begin to fold their own clothes? Wendy herself has passed this marking boundary, unlike John and certainly Michael, and indeed does darn socks and oversee meals in Neverland; she could probably even keep herself awake if she wanted to.

The narrator's language for this younger child audience's moral life is not entirely consistent: "naughtinesses" is the diction of earlier childhood, but "evil passions" suggests the darker tone of an older mind. The narrator later speaks of drawing "a map of a child's mind," with certain zones of consciousness: "There is also first day at school, religion, fathers, the Round Pond, needlework, murders, hangings, verbs that take the dative, chocolate-pudding day, getting into braces, say ninety-nine, threepence for pulling out your tooth yourself" (73–74). These specifics suggest for this child narratee a particular range of middle-childhood, middle-class experiences (in early twentieth-century Britain, of course): going to school, studying Latin, losing baby teeth, casting aside childish clothes ("getting into braces"). This Barrie child has entered school, but not puberty.

But *Peter and Wendy*'s approach to children, as narratees and as implied (again, typically the narrative) audience, continues to shift. In fact,

Barrie's narrator continues to include *and* exclude this middle-childhood child (say, ages five to twelve) from his direct address. A few pages after mapping the child's mind, the narrator observes, "Children have the strangest adventures without being troubled by them. For instance, they may remember . . ." (75). So the pronoun of reference for children has shifted again from "your tooth" to "they may remember." At this moment, Barrie's narrator speaks to an adult implied audience who refers to children as "they." Even more explicitly in this same scene, the narrator speaks of "these magic shores [where] children at play are for ever beaching their coracles. We too have been there; we can still hear the sound of the surf, though we shall land no more" (74). This "we" not only excludes the child at play, it occupies a position that most real-world children at play will *not* want to occupy imaginatively while playing at adultness. (An example of this play at being grown-up occurs when Wendy wants to do the "correct thing" like "people in our set.") Growing up at this moment, on these magic shores, means remembering loss, a state of consciousness the narrator's "we" never voices to its child narratees, not even the older children like Wendy.

Chapter 1 of *Peter and Wendy* characterizes its older, more knowledgeable audience not only in these moments of direct address but also with the gaps it expects that audience to complete or at least leap across. For example, in chapter 1 the narrator, looking back at the Darling family story, concludes, "There was never a simpler, happier family until the coming of Peter Pan" (72). Yet the previous three pages have described several disturbing problems. First, because the Darling family income is not generous, "for a week or two after Wendy came it was doubtful whether they would able to keep her, as she was another mouth to feed," and Mr. Darling makes an extensive list of the costs for "keeping Wendy," for example worrying over mumps as first one pound, then thirty shillings, then putting down "measles [at] one five" (one pound five shillings) (71). Wendy's just been born, and she almost joins the other lost children in Kensington Gardens (not the Lost Boys in Neverland, who are of course all boys). But "at last Wendy just got through, with mumps reduced to twelve six, and the two kinds of measles treated as one" (71). And already the core issue of Mr. Darling's fragile masculinity surfaces, both in the public sphere ("He had his position in the City to consider") and in the domestic sphere ("He had sometimes a feeling that [Nana] did not admire him") (72). If these anxieties add up to the simplest, happiest possible family in this world, then family life cannot be not very simple or happy.

The gap between that claim, "There was never a simpler, happier family," and the preceding narrative presumes a memory that notes the discrepancy. Equally important, the specifics I have cited above (How much *do* mumps cost? What is a child worth? the cute but unconventional economy of casting the Newfoundland dog as nurse) also presume a listener who is familiar with social codes, complex ethical dilemmas, and the conflict between public and private forms of identity. Reading and remembering across several pages and across different kinds of category gaps require complex interpretative skills that in the real world few ten-year-olds possess, and Barrie's text does not presume that they do. That is, I see no evidence that Barrie's narrator expects the five- to twelve-year-old child who is losing its baby teeth to grasp the sadness and losses that the older listener should hear in the narrator's subtle language and structural ironies.

What kinds of narrative skills and conceptual vocabulary, then, with their associated cultural assumptions, do such gaps and complicated linkages require? These manipulations of the story often imply various kinds of contrasts and evasions, for example. In doing so, they point toward gaps, inconsistencies, conflicts—that is, ironies—that require an understanding of formations, or at least theories of the formation, of the self and its social environment. These understandings seem to me demanded by the text. Different real-world readers of my book will apply different experiences to decide what skills it is "plausible," to use Jim Phelan's word from a different argument, to think a younger or older child or young adult or older adult (in whichever roles, from narratee to implied audiences to flesh-and-blood reader) could bring to these gaps and ironies and scrambled events.[8] We also can apply various kinds of knowledge (or claims to knowledge) to describe the skills and cultural assumptions real-world readers of different ages and educations might have brought to the texts in an earlier historical period, say in 1911. But what signals might we unearth from the texts themselves about the skills invited from the various positions that its participants adopt along the chains of alignment we have charted?

In chapter 1, *Peter and Wendy* continues to address different kinds of listeners, again from narratees to implied audiences to flesh and blood. But the qualifications posted for the different narratees (younger and older) present the differences most clearly. Not only do these narratees

---

8. See Phelan's *Reading People, Reading Plots* for a discussion of how stories create characters who are at least "the illusion of a plausible person" (11). I am extending this notion to apply to the illusion of a plausible narratee or authorial audience.

possess by implication different attitudes and knowledge, but Barrie's narrator sees them as seeing the world in ways that are deeply contradictory. As I noted before, sometimes the text's pronouns shift their reference quite overtly, so that "our" or "you" refers at one point to middle-span children (perhaps age five to puberty) thinking about what it will be like to be older, and at another point to an older audience remembering what it was like, or what they think it was like, to be seven. And sometimes the text addresses both narratees at the same time. A good example of this doubleness occurs when Nibs describes what he remembers of his mother:

> "All I remember about my mother," Nibs told them, "is that she often said to my father, 'Oh, how I wish I had a cheque-book of my own.' I don't know what a cheque-book is, but I should love to give my mother one." (117)

Middle-span children listeners (in the narrative audience and flesh-and-blood children) will grasp Nibs's experience of not knowing what those adults are up to. But Barrie's language also addresses the audiences that understand what a checkbook is, and that even will remember (and understand) not understanding.

Furthermore, within that adult audience is a smaller cohort of listeners who, like Barrie, know Ibsen—Barrie's first success with London critics was a one-act parody of *Hedda Gabler, Ibsen's Ghost*, in 1891 (Birkin 21). For that smaller group of adults, the mother's desire for a checkbook of her own echoes, perhaps proleptically by way of Virginia Woolf, Nora's unhappiness in *A Doll's House*. The language becomes an aside about gender convention and the privileges, perhaps to be questioned, of masculinity. The edginess and danger in Barrie surfaces when these readings collide, when the adult bitterness about gender or mothers or narrative conventions sabotages the assumptions of the eavesdropping younger narratee. There is also a similar but reverse danger to the adult eavesdropper, who may overhear uncomfortable words from these children that violate adult beliefs or illusions about children's consciousnesses. Certainly some adult audiences will delight in the polyvocal narration, noting the text's construction of multiple narratees and multiple voices and enjoying the narrator's ironies and wit. Eavesdropping is a narrative ploy with multiple outcomes.

Barrie's unusual use of multiple narratees enables a text to speak to several audiences in several registers at the same time, and *Peter and Wendy* offers many variations of such multiplicities. Michael Egan describes one particular form of double address: a narrator speaks ostensibly to a child, "but glances sidelong at the adults listening in and winks" (these positions can be conceived as belonging to narratees, implied readers, and real-world reader positions: see the diagram in section 5 of this chapter) (Egan 46). But in *Peter and Wendy*, in fact, the reverse pattern is more common: the narrator addresses older narratees directly, with a deeply ambiguous sidelong glance at the younger narratee. A good example occurs in chapter 3 of *Peter and Wendy*:

> When people in our set are introduced, it is customary for them to ask each other's age, and so Wendy, who always liked to do the correct thing, asked Peter how old he was. It was not really a happy question to ask him; it was like an examination paper that asks grammar, when what you want to be asked is Kings of England. (92)

The initial "our" here identifies a class consciousness that is most formed in the adult or older audiences (again, from narratees to narrative/authorial audiences to flesh-and-blood readers), and the word (*our*) remembers how children, like Wendy, sometimes imitate its expectations. The subsequent example of Peter's discomfort then refers to the experience of school examinations of the middle-span middle- or upper-middle-class child narratee, and the final "you" in the citation addresses the younger narratee in a way that invites the schoolchild flesh-and-blood listener to join the narrative audience. But the move from "him" (Peter) to "you" is also deeply complicating because "you" is a space for two consciousnesses: the adult narratee who remembers the wounds of school life and the child narratee who is living them now. This point echoes Phelan's summation of his narratological study of second-person narration's fluidity: "it moves readers between the positions of observer and addressee": "In short, it's not easy to say who you are" (*Narrative* 137). Suturing multiple subjectivities once again becomes risky.

Some audiences—the more sophisticated—will delight in this disorientation and role-playing, and others will find the interplay troubling. The younger narratee (and by extension, younger narrative and flesh-and-blood audiences) is invoked, and then as it were invited to sit in a chair and overhear the adult voice. This move, characteristic of *Peter and Wendy*, is the core of the ricochet effect, one of the more serious examples of oblique intersubjectivity. The younger audiences may simply overhear, or may be able to include themselves in the other narratee's audience, either through a misunderstanding of the adult language or through a conscious choice by the younger narratee to role-play at adulthood. To see the significance of the fundamental experience of shame in this episode requires, however, the wider understanding of the older audiences: Peter knows he doesn't want to talk about his age, but understanding why he doesn't, and how embarrassing it is to have prepared for one set of test questions but not the ones you are asked, requires the perspective of the adult audiences. The meaning of "customary" also presumes a broader knowledge of social performance. And only the adult audiences grasp the structural irony of comparing Peter's discomfort to that of the schoolchild he *can* never become (and, according to one thread of the Pan texts, *will,* that is, chooses, never to become). The younger real audience, invited into the story by the position of the child narratee to join the narrative audience, lacks the cultural knowledge, narrative skills, and understanding of loss to join the authorial audience. But it may overhear enough—for some, perhaps to be exhilarated by the promises of adult understandings, but for others, like Tootles, to be scared.

So there is space in Barrie's language here as earlier for several narratees to orient themselves against a recognizable horizon in Barrie's story. Or to disorient themselves, against multiple horizons. Eavesdropping poses dangers for all the listeners in *Peter and Wendy* who have been so carefully invoked and gathered together, though the dangers are different for children than for adults. Eavesdropping can provide pleasures, too, even the pleasure of observing or experiencing the dangers, and the pleasure (the deeply intersubjective piece) of observing others observe (or not observe) the dangers.

Barrie's text articulates with sometimes painful clarity its distinct narratological choices, in its complex and risky efforts to explore the cost of knowing, or not knowing, the stories of mothers and fathers, of family life, and of sexual affiliation. The costs of knowing or not knowing are significant, both within the diegesis (Peter's choice, if it is that, not to know and not to remember) and outside it. Barrie's apologists want to exonerate him from the charge of exposing children to despair and erotic terror. But perhaps this effort is a mistake. In a different context, R. D. S. Jack offers the view that Barrie "had mastered an art which is both populist and misanthropic" (12). Perhaps Barrie's narrative choices are offensive on purpose. After all, what does this design design its audiences to overhear? How does it suture consciousnesses together in deeply intersubjective intimacy, and at what cost?

It is time to study specific examples of this narratological practice of the ricochet effect, a remarkable example of deeply intersubjective suture, and to begin to ask what is at stake thematically in Barrie's use of it. Its exploration of families and adult sexuality as threatening, of the double role of mothers as loyal yet betraying, and of anxiety about masculinity are the most important.

iii. EAVESDROPPING: TARGETING CHILDREN IN "WENDY'S STORY"—PRACTICE I

> Off we skip like the most heartless things in the world, which is what children are, but so attractive; and we have an entirely selfish time.
> —*Peter and Wendy* (167)

> "It's an awfully good story," said Nibs. "I don't see how it can have a happy ending," said the second twin.
> —*Peter and Wendy* (165)

Our specific examples of narratees, audiences, and narrative structure in *Peter and Wendy* will knit together our various narratological and thematic concerns in remarkable illustrations of Barrie's subtlety. Our first example occurs in chapter 11, "Wendy's Story," when the simmering anger and anguish over the roles and losses of mothers surfaces most extensively in the novella. The problem expresses itself in a battle of stories: between Wendy's story, in which the older John and Michael find their mother's window still open for them years later, and Peter's story, of the window shut, barred, and the lost boy forgotten (or so Peter thinks) and replaced. Both narrators are pleased with their stories, and both compensate in one direction or another. These contrasting archetypes remind us that throughout *Peter and Wendy* there are two kinds of stories about mothers, as nurturing and as forgetful. And there are two kinds of readings of both stories: nurturing mothers are comforting or smothering; forgetful mothers free their children or abandon them.[9] Barrie's multiple

---

9. James Kincaid explores with wit and depth the mother as smothering in his chapter on *Peter Pan*: "The mother I construct from the play is both oafish and deadly, a cross between Edith Bunker and Medusa. Wendy comes into the play as an intruder, a disturber of the peace and play, sets up a school, and is last seen on a broomstick, where she should have been all along" (285). But Kincaid disallows the other archetype, and does so by ignoring important threads in the tales. Yes, Wendy's motherliness can be prim and schoolmarmish, as the Disney film tends to emphasize. But Peter's anger at what he perceives as his mother's abandonment points to wounds that Kincaid's

narrative strategies expose these readings. Along the way, these stories may well explore productive hybridity and gender play, as some critics argue (Wasinger especially), but they also explore the deep, ambiguous wounds of erotic and family life. One kind of oblique intersubjectivity, of profoundly crisscrossing consciousnesses, becomes very specific now.

The battle of stories about mothers in chapter 11 of *Peter and Wendy* cuts deeper than almost any other moment in the Peter Pan tales. Its intricate narrative strategies are a testimony to what is at stake here. To take up the thread of different audiences in Barrie, this scene offers examples of intradiegetic narratees, that is, specific characters who listen and overhear. In this case, the eight children clustered around Wendy at the opening of chapter 11, as well as the eavesdropping Peter, hear "Wendy's Story." In some ways, the most obvious quality of this scene is the way Barrie's text foregrounds the act of storytelling, as first Wendy and then Peter perform their mother narratives. But more important are the labyrinthine layers of narratee responses, sometimes overt, sometimes covert, in the scene's interpretations of its two stories, and then interpretations of these interpretations, expressed first by the character narratees (including Peter), then by Wendy the storyteller, and at one more remove by Barrie's narrator, and finally at a maximally covert level on the horizon of the diegesis by the implied readers.

The characters who listen to Wendy's tale (about the grown-up Michael, John, and Wendy who find their mother's window still open years later) express deeply contradictory feelings about this story. Pleased vanity is an early response to the "discovery" that the tale (which of course the Lost Boys have heard many times) is about them: when Wendy confirms for Tootles that he was one of the "lost children," he exults, "I am in a story. Hurrah, I am in a story, Nibs" (165). Wendy then appeals to Tootles and the other Lost Boys to return the favor of this attention: "Now, I want you to consider the feelings of the unhappy parents with all their children flown away" (165). But the boys do not return this reciprocity of care: is this self-ness, what appears as narcissism, a moral flaw, or a "natural" outcome in young animals? This question lies in the background throughout Barrie's Peter Pan stories (if not in the later adaptations, which on this score are much more sentimental, or perhaps only optimistic). The boys do know they should pretend a little, that there is some value to performing for their audience, but the performance

---

celebration of play ignores. And Peter's loss of home is by no means only a release into freedom, as his tears, bad dreams, and even compulsive forgetting suggest.

is quite perfunctory: "'Oo,' they all moaned, though they were not really considering the feelings of the unhappy parents one jot" (165). "One jot" is an emphatic note from Barrie's narrator, whose problematic tone we'll address later. Suffice it to say here that there is a violent jerk to "one jot" that voices a kind of deep annoyance at these free, yet sometimes bratty, spoiled boys. The climax of the boys' contradictions is the response to Wendy's lament, "Think of the empty beds!": "'It's awfully sad,' the first twin said cheerfully" (165). Given the contradictory values in this story (freedom in Neverland is good, home is good), the second twin's narratological analysis of the tale's plot structure is in fact quite astute: "I don't see how it can have a happy ending" (165).

Wendy's response to the boys' reading is to urge them to believe more deeply in mothers, and her version of the now-adult children's return exaggerates its narrative frame to make that point. Wendy is "an elegant lady of uncertain age alighting at London station," and John and Michael are "two noble portly figures accompanying her, now grown to man's estate" (166). The telltale exaggerations in Wendy's story include the absence of any adult family entanglements (the three grown-up children return with no retinue of spouse or progeny), and the adult children's joyful response to the open window: "So up they flew to their mummy and daddy; and pen cannot describe the happy scene, over which we draw a veil" (166). The concluding cliché (drawing the veil) is almost a note of parody, a nudge in the ribs of at least some listeners, I suspect, from the narrator. The other character narratee, of course, is Peter, who groans during Wendy's narration and finally bursts out with his alternative story to set the record straight: mothers do *not* keep the window open.

There is another set of twists and turns in tone to examine. The narrator's voice becomes more explicit in its interpretation of Wendy's story, in a dazzling commentary that changes gears repeatedly.

> That was the story, and they were as pleased with it as the fair narrator herself. Everything just as it should be, you see. Off we skip like the most heartless things in the world, which is what children are, but so attractive; and we have an entirely selfish time; and then when we have need of special attention we nobly return for it, confident that we shall be embraced instead of smacked. (166)

Once again "we" and "you" and "they" become deeply unstable, but not in a way that erases narrative roles or is finally confusing; the various meanings are quite clear, like cleanly separated strata in some kinds of rock formations. Furthermore, these instabilities have rich thematic value in Barrie's text. All three pronouns dance through this paragraph, first, second, and third person, and their relationships are deeply revealing. The narrator's "they" in the first sentence is quite clear and apparently stable: it is the overt narratees (minus Peter) listening to Wendy who add up to a good representation of younger children listeners generally. The narrator's plural first-person "we" seems to take up the perspective of "they" enthusiastically: "Off we skip . . ." But what is the role of the intermediary "you" ("Everything just as it should be, you see")? This narratee must be the older listener, who can evaluate norms: how *should* things be? I think the narrator takes along the older audience, diving into the "we" that was "they" (younger children listeners), but always with the residue of complex, older consciousnesses.

The following sentences move back and forth between "we" and "they," participating with and then evaluating the children's own contradictory responses to Wendy's story, that is, to mothering. The first sentence is the most labyrinthine: "Off we skip like the most heartless things in the world, which is what children are, but so attractive." "Heartless" is not a word that the Lost Boys could apply to themselves: it requires a cognitive and social perspective that they certainly have not acquired in Neverland. It's as if the sentence presents the kind of hybridity that Bakhtin analyzed, when "two styles, two 'languages,' two semantic and axiological belief systems" occur "within the limits of a single syntactic whole, often within the limits of a simple sentence" (*Dialogic Imagination* 304–5). The narrator's line also articulates a complex, even contradictory consciousness, one that Tootles could not explain or grasp with much clarity: the Lost Boys are not in fact without feelings, not even without feelings for others. But those feelings include immediate, insistent impulses toward pleasure, and equally insistent feelings of fear and anger, none of which the younger child has usually learned (or is yet able) to bracket and understand. So "heartless" is partly the older world's judgment on youthful narcissism expressed so directly. If "heartless" pulls the narrator's audience back from the younger audience's "we," the next clause solidifies that separation ("which is what children are"—even more clearly a thought that the Lost Boys would not have).

The most puzzling words in this sentence are the final evaluation, "but so attractive." Again, in this judgment the narrator steps out of the younger child consciousness and looks at it from a complex—and somewhat bitter—older perspective. (Though children in Barrie *can* perceive others' perceptions of them as attractive, and behave seductively as a result, that seductiveness doesn't mean to the child what it means to the adult observer.) Barrie's stunning move here—once again reminding us that this narrator is a rhetorical choice by an implied author—is to suggest how the older consciousness is deeply riven by like *and* dislike of the attractive, heartless child, and the use of "attractive" here is both a sign of admiration and an accusation. This conflict colors the narrator's return in the next clauses to the children's "we," in words that carry a sour, angry tone, as if their narrative perspective retains traces of the adult's anger at the child *as* it voices the child's narcissism: "and we have an entirely selfish time." Note the anger in the word of categorical degree, "entirely." The final clause of the paragraph confirms the narrator's anger at the child, I think: "and then when we have need of special attention we nobly return for it, confident we shall be embraced instead of smacked." "Smacked," like the phrase "one jot" above, ends the paragraph with a snap, a slightly violent whip of syntax that also suggests some pleasure at the child's experience of consequences for its performance of "nobly."

These children are capable of only some degree of calculation, but their calculation minimizes the risk they take, and the narrator watches with considerable coolness as the children suffer when their calculation misfires: "So great indeed was their faith in a mother's love that they felt they could afford to be callous for a bit longer." In this new paragraph that follows immediately after "we shall be . . . smacked," the narrator's abrupt move away from "we" establishes that cool distance even more dramatically: "they felt they could afford to be callous" suggests that "smacking" may be deserved. Indeed, the narrator's swift changes from "we" to "they" and back may induce a kind of whiplash in the careful reader, like the syntactic snap I mentioned above that echoes the deserving smack to be delivered. Barrie's older audience may participate in the joyful, heartless skipping of the younger, "so attractive" children, but it also recognizes their manipulations and seductive performances. To the extent that the older audience *has* skipped heartlessly, the barbs overheard by the "so attractive" child audience also pierce them. The ricochet ricochets.

Skilled implied readers will notice the twists and turns of tone and judgment and address of Barrie's supple narrator. This audience will also notice larger structures and rhythms in this scene, even will notice, if especially skilled, the linkage of specific language to the issue of lost mothers and fathers. For example, here is Peter when he seeks to calm the noisy boys so they will settle down to listen to Wendy's story: "'Little less noise there,' Peter called out, determined that [Wendy] should have fair play" (164). This phrase, of course, was Mr. Darling's in the nursery of Act I of the play (PP 91), a line of paternal authority that John used in his performance of fatherliness earlier in Act I (PP 89). The novella omits both lines, so perhaps this audience verges closer to the implied readers, particularly the authorial audience subset, constructed not only by *Peter and Wendy* as a whole, but by the Peter Pan tales as a group. At the minimum, this sophisticated implied reader of *Peter and Wendy* must be familiar with the (as yet unpublished in 1911) stage version in order to recognize Mr. Darling's line. Peter does *not* use the line in the parallel scene in the play (see 4.1, PP 130); by adding the line here, the novella stresses the complex father roles shadowing Peter, and also the shadowy power of Barrie's narrator. Most importantly, for Peter to play Mr. Darling is ironic on several levels, not the least of which is the way the parallel gets rejected later when Peter refuses Mrs. Darling's offer to adopt him and help him grow up to be, perhaps, like Mr. Darling (in a way, Peter finally accepts her offer in Steven Spielberg's *Hook*).

The older authorial audience will also pick up the sexual overtones of Wendy's story. When Wendy begins her tale, she says, "They were married, you know, and what do you think they had?" Nibs, "inspired," cries, "White rats" (164). Nibs's failure to identify correctly a human couple's progeny is a kind of cute Disney nod to the adult who accompanies the child in the real audience, and congratulates the older listener who understands not only where babies come from but also how children of a certain age misunderstand where they come from. In the scene immediately preceding chapter 11, Peter extensively misunderstands what Tiger Lily and Wendy and Tinker Bell want from him. The boy who will insist mothers are unfaithful imagines again and again that each of these characters wants to mother him, and is puzzled by their disdain at his error. When Peter asks what the correct answer is, Wendy replies, "It isn't for a lady to tell." Still, Tinker Bell might reveal it, Wendy adds, because "she is an abandoned little creature," to which Tinker Bell retorts, as translated by Peter, "She glories in being abandoned" (162). All of this wordplay (not present in the play text) over abandoned creatures deepens the Peter Pan story's struggle with women's sexuality, mothering, and males' conflicted responses to them. "Being abandoned" functions in two ways syntactically: "abandoned" is an adjective describing Tinker Bell's moral status, and a passive verb, which reminds the thoughtful reader of children who have been abandoned. This double play will raise the question for that audience, is there a link between strong sexual energy in women (usually ominous in nineteenth-century culture) and the abandonment of children (that fundamental ache throughout the Pan stories)?

Children, like older people, may construct such a connection, or a version of it that they can understand, because they need a framework in which to make sense of their abandonment. The phrase ("being abandoned") raises an even larger issue, the possibility that birth is such a discarding, as the line at the head of this chapter (from Barrie's essay on *The Coral Island*) suggests: "To be born is to be wrecked upon an island." The adult audience's understanding of children's sexual ignorance will connect these patterns and fears. Furthermore, that older audience's wider knowledge of the Pan story pulls together similar threads from other corners of the tale. So, as Peter not only asserts mothers' faithlessness but boasts how very well he can do "without one," this reader remembers that at the end of Peter's victorious duel with Hook, when he finally falls asleep, "he had one of his dreams that night, and cried in his sleep for a long time, and Wendy held him tight" (170, 205). So much for Peter's boast. Peter is a target as well as the other heartless children who are so attractive but really deserve to be smacked. All simultaneously defy and need the touch, as mothers offer and withdraw that touch. But there is enough anger and sadness to go around in Neverland.[10]

The truth of this claim becomes even clearer when Barrie adds the multiplicities and ambiguities of free indirect discourse (FID) to his narratological arsenal. To pursue this claim, we now turn intensively to the role of the young eavesdropper. What is the response, in the story-world or the real world, of those middle-range young children who have heard that they are heartless but so attractive, that they may deserve to be smacked because they were entirely selfish, because they thought they could afford to be callous to their mother? FID stages an eavesdropping that targets them, indeed as well as their adult companions, in dazzling constructions of a kind of narrative chiasmus that illustrates more vividly than almost

---

10. Here are a few of the many other moments in the Pan tales that ricochet in similar anger or sadness: "Peter called, 'Mother! Mother!' but she heard him not; in vain he beat his little limbs against the iron bars.... When we reach the window it is Lock-Out Time. The iron bars are up for life" (PPKG 40); "There is a saying in Neverland that every time you breathe a grown-up dies; and Peter was killing them off vindictively as fast as possible" (PW 168) (an example whose anger targets the adult audience); "Then Wendy and John and Michael found the window open for them after all, which of course was more than they deserved" (PW 212); "When Margaret grows up she will have a daughter, who is to be Peter's mother in turn; and thus it will go on, so long as children are gay and innocent and heartless" (PW 226).

any other moment in this book how intimate, and how dangerous, suturing subjectivities can be, however oblique the threads.

iv. EAVESDROPPING: FREE INDIRECT DISCOURSE AND MOTHERS, THE TOADS—PRACTICE II

Barrie's narrator deploys free indirect discourse to extend the implications of eavesdropping and the ricochet effect in chapter 11 of *Peter and Wendy* and throughout the novella. FID is a very good tool for playing with multiple audiences and multiple registers of perception, and the status of mothers and the theme of children's abandonment are worthy subjects for this play in chapter 11. J. Hillis Miller comments, in *Versions of Pygmalion,* that FID offers an "uncanny power" because it allows an audience to peer safely into another's consciousness: "to possess from within the mind of another without that other's knowledge" (40). Here is another example of the principle of overhearing, of eavesdropping, with a slightly illicit overtone (since the person exposed does not know someone is listening in. The claim that the Pan stories expose the secrets of home, especially of the abandoning mother, is fundamental to the accusations that Barrie, especially in this novella, abuses the eavesdropping younger child audience. The topic of FID may at first seem out of place in discussing a story whose primary forms are a play and films. But Barrie's novella makes complex and extensive use of free indirect discourse, in a way that expresses much about the core contradictions of the Peter Pan puzzle.

The role of FID in *Peter and Wendy* is significant because most of the novella's characters express themselves in lots of direct speech, much of it transported unchanged from the stage play. There is very little direct thought of characters, and also very little indirect speech or indirect thought, if we accept Gerald Prince's definition of those indirect forms as reportage of a character's thought or speech "with more or less literal fidelity" (*Dictionary* 43). Virtually all of the novella's indirect reporting of character thought or speech gets colored by the special tone, whether whimsical or ironical, of Barrie's narrator, and most of this reporting is summary anyway, not a version of the character's specific images or words. This description is true of most of the examples we have discussed so far: "henceforth Wendy knew that she must grow up" (69); "that was the story, and they were as pleased with it as the fair narrator herself" (166); "so great was their faith in a mother's love that they felt they could afford to be callous for a bit longer" (166). In this last line, for example, Barrie's thoughtful reader is not confused about the source of the phrase "they could afford to be callous" nor of the irony expressed in the word "afford." This word is the narrator's, not the Lost Boys'. The language in the narrator's indirect summary or analysis is nearly always clearly his, even if layered as happens in free indirect discourse alongside the character's. There is no doubt about the provenance of the sentence's tone or comment *on* the character. For example, when Peter calls the boys together to tell *his* version of the mother-love story, the narrator says, "They all gathered round him in affright, so alarming was his agitation; and with a fine candour he told them what he had hitherto concealed" (167). Because the novella almost never proposes to recount exact thoughts or speech indirectly, the narrator rarely uses what Seymour Chatman calls "tags," as in "He thought that it was time to go" or "She said that she feared the rain" (199–201) The last citation is about as close to a traditional tag for indirect thought as Barrie comes: "with a fine candour he told them what he had hitherto concealed."

FID occurs in *Peter and Wendy* not as a result of reported thoughts or speech in which the tags drop away and the character's special diction becomes mixed with the narrator's, so that the relative authority of each can come into doubt. Instead, the characteristically double-track quality of FID typically arises in Barrie when the narrator's summary follows the direct speech of a character and picks up the character's diction. A good example occurs in the narrator's summary in chapter 1 of the conclusion to Mr. Darling's accounting exercise to see if the young parents can keep Wendy: "But at last Wendy just got through, with mumps reduced to twelve six, and the two kinds of measles treated as one" (71). This indirect thought mimics Mr. Darling's diction and syntax ("with mumps reduced to twelve six") compared to his direct speech ("I dare say it will be more like thirty shillings—don't speak—measles one five" [71]). The question of the overt narrator's possible commentary arises with the edgy phrase "at last Wendy just got through," with its comparison of child-keeping to some kind of race or competition, a comparison that Mr. Darling would not make, at least not consciously. At some point, the tone of the summary and the repeated diction becomes uncertain or multiple, as the patterns of irony and commentary from the narrator's earlier practice seem to infiltrate the summary.

A complex example of these narrator patterns and signals is exclamation points (which will figure significantly in chapter 11). Exclamation points, as Chatman has said, are usually a marker of the character, not a narrator who is covert, since if the exclamation point is the narrator's, the strong feelings expressed by it would draw unusual and distracting attention to that narrator. "The logic of covert narration permits only the character to exclaim," writes Chatman, using his example from Joyce's "The Dead" as support: "Gabriel's warm trembling fingers tapped the cold pane of the window. How cool it must be outside!" (*Story and Discourse* 202). Barrie's narrator in *Peter and Wendy* is, of course, not covert, and expresses strong emotions and opinions throughout the story. So at key moments in the summary of character psychology or feeling in this text, an exclamation point that emphasizes an emotion may constitute an expression of the narrator's practice—in contrast to the Joyce example above—rather than a representation of the character's feeling. Or it may not. We'll look at a telling example of how *Peter and Wendy* manipulates this uncertainty in a moment. In Barrie's own way, then, free indirect discourse destabilizes commentary and tone also. And when the issue is the faithfulness or faithlessness of mothers, voiced in a venue where smaller children (flesh-and-blood listeners who enter the audience by way of the text's narratees and also its younger—narrative—implied audience) may be eavesdropping, much is at stake in this destabilization. It matters greatly, in the example below, *who* is claiming mothers are toads, and how different audiences are supposed to make sense of the claim.

Let's look at this sequence from chapter 11 of *Peter and Wendy*, beginning with Peter's reaction to Wendy's story about the faithful parents and concluding with the Lost Boys' reaction to his competing narrative. My paragraphs imitate the Barrie text's paragraphing to retain its emphases.

> So great indeed was their faith in a mother's love that they felt they could afford to be callous for a bit longer.
>
> But there was one who knew better; and when Wendy finished he uttered a hollow groan.
>
> "What is it, Peter," she cried, running to him. . . . [Then Peter, saying to Wendy, "You are wrong about mothers," tells the story he had "hitherto concealed."]
>
> ". . . so I stayed away for moons and moons and moons, and then flew back; but the window was barred, for mother had forgotten all about me, and there was another little boy sleeping in my bed."
>
> I am not sure this was true, but Peter thought it was true, and it scared them.
>
> "Are you sure mothers are like that?"

"Yes."

So this was the truth about mothers. The toads!

Still, it is best to be careful; and no one knows so quickly as a child when he should give in. "Wendy, let us go home," cried John and Michael together. . . .

"Not tonight?" asked the lost boys, bewildered. They knew in what they called their hearts that one can get on quite well without a mother, and that it is only the mothers who think you can't. (166–67)

The status of the narration's key claims is the core problem here, how to read words like "knew" and "true," and whose voice claims the iconic exclamation point after "toads": Peter "knew better"; "I am not sure this was true, but Peter thought it was true"; "so this was the truth about mothers. The toads!"; and "they knew in what they called their hearts that one can get on quite well without a mother." Most critics have read the narrator's cynicism as pretty universal even if contradictory: that is, the narrator expresses some bitterness about the "callousness" and heartlessness of children who may indeed deserve some smacking, but at the same time shares Peter's anger at the heartlessness of mothers and other grown-ups and their world of schools and offices. For Peter Hollindale, the link between these two kinds of cynicism is thematic: "Domestic life has its absurdities and fantasies, just as the Neverland does, and the game of adult life is as full of them as childhood" (*PW* xxiv). So each heartless audience can observe the absorbing games and heartlessness of the other, and each deserves its humiliation.

Once this confrontation between cynics has defined battle positions, how do the different audiences that I have identified respond? Perhaps, like Peter Pan, they are paralyzed between "could not" and "would not" grow up. Perhaps, like Barrie's friend Thomas Hardy's almost-contemporary character Tess, they simply can yearn to "have my life unbe" ("Tess's Lament," *Complete Poems* 177). But maybe a narratologically more careful reading of Barrie can sort through these options. Karen Coats is a rare reader who identifies the threads of children's hatred (or perhaps *anger* is a better word) in *Peter Pan*. Let me be clear: she means both hatred felt *by* children, and hatred, or anger, *at* children, but located (and perhaps quarantined) in "beings that hate both the state of childhood and children themselves" (3). Her primary example of such a being is Hook as misanthrope.

But when this deep dislike (*of* children) surfaces in the much more reliable voice of the story's "omniscient" narrator, our celebration of the text's honesty may waver. The big question then returns: what kinds of boundary crossing do these eavesdroppings require? Hollindale claimed that despite Jacqueline Rose's protest, "the barriers between child and adult have largely fallen since 1900" (PP xxiv). But I think he's wrong about some topics with some audiences, especially that cohort of middle-younger children in Barrie's audiences, about ages five to nine. The issue is still very much alive about age-appropriate exposure (I use this word advisedly) of these younger children to certain kinds of eroticism, cynicism, and suffering. The issue is not the adult overhearing the child's anger, but the child (finally, the flesh-and-blood child) overhearing the adult's despair about family and abandoning mothers (and the adult's anger also, at "the toads!").

The problem of eavesdropping is significant because the interpretive skills of the younger child audience (narratee, implied, or flesh and blood) may not be up to sifting the subtleties of free indirect discourse. And Barrie's text is more subtle than most readers have acknowledged. The difficult task in parsing complex examples of free indirect discourse is to separate, as much as possible, the two languages combined in it: the character's thoughts or words that the narrator is repeating or summarizing, as distinct from the narrator's characteristic diction or syntax, especially if they provide a commentary on the character's language. Sometimes the line between these two consciousnesses is pretty clear, as later in the scene at hand, when Wendy, "forgetful of what must be Peter's feelings," hastens to prepare for their departure home. Barrie gives us two paragraphs that tidily separate our two languages:

> Not so much as a sorry-to-lose-you between them! If she did not mind the parting, he was going to show her, was Peter, that neither did he.
>   But of course he cared very much. (167)

The first paragraph is quite clean in its representation of Peter's feelings and language, in repeating, for example, his syntax of determination ("he was going to show her, was Peter": a free indirect discourse version of "I'm going to show her, I will"). In this paragraph, I take the exclamation point, following the Chatman principle (despite the overt narrator), to express Peter's anger. The next paragraph changes tone in undermining the claim of the previous sentence, as the narrator delves beneath Peter's bravado to identify his true feelings, guaranteed by the narratorial "of course," an appeal to an older audience's understanding of intersubjective layers of pretense in proud, willful children. The move to a new paragraph also typically marks a shift in tone or narratee—although not always in this text.

In the vexed example at the heart of our discussion, the new paragraph does not necessarily mark clearly whose consciousness it expresses. "So this was the truth about mothers. The toads!" Which of the narrator's narratees does this line primarily address, and with what tone? The previous two lines are the boys' question in direct speech, and Peter's answer ("Yes."). The rhythm of the next indentation suggests this line is the boys' response to Peter's answer, and the introductory "So" confirms this connection to the Lost Boys who are trying to make sense of Peter's story. That is, this line summarizes their understanding of Peter's "truth." The fact that the text moves from direct speech to indirect allows the narrator to take a position about the boys' own summary. The move to free indirect discourse signals the possibility of a new layer of narrator commentary—why else move into indirect mode? If so, where might that commentary seep into Barrie's language?

The prime candidate is the final phrase, "The toads!" The exclamation point seems to me to express primarily the Lost Boys' intense feelings. But what is the source of the image of the toad? Is it the boys' image, or the narrator's, a choice to express, perhaps parodically, their anger? "Toad" is so different in register from typical images for bad mothers that the jolt of unevenness in its tone can provoke laughter. But at whom? Mothers? Or at the children who might use such a phrase? The best answer may indeed be "both," but the syntactical isolation of the exclamatory phrase emphasizes its immoderate tone and its translation of childhood angst, even if its over-the-top-quality also is designed to seem funny. On balance the context and structure of this language seem to me to emphasize the child's perception, filtered through a mildly distanced, partly parodying older consciousness. Throughout this scene, Barrie's narrator subtly distinguishes between the younger child's perceptions (whether in the Lost Boys who are listening, in the narrative audience, or in the real audience following the lead of the narrative audience) and the older reader's understanding, and also between the older audience's understanding of the younger child's perception and vice versa. Hence free indirect discourse and the story's use of multiple audiences becomes an example of consciousness of consciousnesses, in the form I have called deep intersubjectivity, here in the form of multiple vectors of eavesdropping.

The same layers of distinctions clarify the text's use of "knew": as in "there was one who knew better" (than Wendy about a mother's love), or "they knew in what they called their hearts that one can get on quite well without a mother." In both sentences, "knew" is a paraphrase of the child's self-understanding. It is not the narrator's guarantee that what they know is an accurate account of the world. That is, *they* say about their stance that they "know." The second sentence makes the distinction clear, because the narrator's commentary intrudes explicitly in the subordinate clause "in what they called their hearts." The "knowledge" that "only the mothers" think you need them is clearly marked here as a defensive exaggeration. Barrie's narrator earlier makes such a distinction explicitly about the word "true," in Peter's story of the barred window: "I am not sure this was true, but Peter thought it was true."

Putting aside the illogical pretense of the narrator not to know what happened in Peter's past, we then wonder what "this" refers to; what exactly may or may not be true that Peter perceives to be true? Is it the claim that there was a boy sleeping in the bed? That the window was barred? Neither of these options seems reasonable, unless Peter is a *very* unreliable narrator. But another option does make sense given what we know about Peter's character: his claim that "mother had forgotten all about me." Peter's compensatory story about mothers who forget their children functions in his psychic life as the story that for him makes sense of his life. But for the astute adult reader, a quite different story makes even better sense of the nursery as Peter finds it: the mother (and father), upon losing one child, decide to protect the next child more thoroughly, partly because they *do* remember the lost child, not because they have forgotten him. Barrie's narrator acknowledges the older reader's more complex understanding (and so Peter's version of his mother's consciousness may indeed not be accurate) while also understanding Peter's need to believe his version is the right one. The same kind of need drives the exclamation, "The toads!" Barrie's use of free indirect discourse here allows space for the narrator's commentary that marks this need. I have disagreed throughout this book with the argument that FID expresses no narratorial consciousness; instead, I have agreed with the view that it allows ample space for the simultaneous presence, along with the represented character thought, of markers of the agent of "narratorial *mimicry*," that is, markers of the "presence of an imitating voice" (Gunn 35, 40), and as a corollary the presence of an evaluating agency.

What is stunning, and disturbing, about Barrie's use of the two-voiced streaming of FID is that his multiple audiences, from intradiegetic narratees to implied audiences to flesh-and-blood listeners, can hear both tones and be troubled by both, especially if sorting out their provenances requires literary and cognitive skills that some audiences may not possess. The line ("So this was the truth about mothers") is not simply someone's direct attack on mothers, the toads, but is one symptom of a struggle between stories about and hopes for mothers. This scene suggests how readings of readings might produce such an outburst, which itself demands further reading. Threading its way through this hermeneutical minefield would be difficult even for the educated authorial audience that remembers Napoleon and has read Ibsen, and nearly impossible, it seems to me, for that other audience, both implied and real-world seven-year-olds. The inevitable next step to take is to admit that Barrie's child audiences will get wounded in the ricochet of bitternesses and angers in *Peter and Wendy*, as in chapter 11. Telling stories about telling stories about growing up (or not) is serious business.

Eavesdropping and its consequent ricochet effect functions to some degree in *Peter and Wendy* to shock its audiences, including its children. Real-world audiences, especially parents and caregivers, will have to decide if this shock amounts to molestation, as Jacqueline Rose claims. But Barrie's narrative ploys definitely touch his narratees, whether in mourning or anger or both. In Barrie's world, heartless, callous, so attractive children deserve to be smacked, and Peter's mother-story scares *his* (intradiegetic) audience. Barrie's own real-world audience before *Peter Pan* was always grown-ups, both for his fiction and his plays, and the first-night audience for *Peter Pan* in 1904 was, as usual, also adults. Barrie sprinkled into that group a surprise collection of children, seduced with free tickets, so that each audience would be able to overhear in person the other's voice, or hands (Barrie worried that no one would respond to Peter's plea, "If you believe [in fairies], clap your hands!" [Birkin 114; PP 137]). By 1911, however, Barrie was certainly aware of the child audience for *Peter Pan* in the real world, since he had licensed retellings of the story published explicitly for a younger market (PW xxx, xxxi).

The ricochet effect, therefore, even on December 28, 1904, and certainly in *Peter and Wendy*, consistently and precisely targets all of its audiences, including the skilled adult authorial (implied) and real readers, with its anger and sadness about mothers and families and the need for and fear of touching. *Peter and Wendy* isn't confused or badly narrated or resentful. Its narrator (and the implied author who designed the narrator) is quite clear about its double voiced free indirect discourse and its multiple listeners. These strategies point to yet another version of deeply intersubjective suture, one different from the ranges of opacity we found in Henry James or the exploration of racism we found in *Nothing But a*

Man, though here as there we cannot escape the pain of suture by invoking a story of the Absent One.

These three threads trace a similar pattern in the oblique, risky narration of intersubjectivities: suture, shot / reverse shot conventions, and free indirect discourse, especially when they function to construct multiple subjectivities. The value of connecting these three concepts is to identify strategies in narrative for telling the stories of multiple selves. What shot / reverse shot editing conventions as a practice of film narrative and free indirect discourse in print narrative share, as I began to explore in chapter 2, is the "over-the-shoulder" posture among consciousnesses perceiving and perceiving perceptions perceived, in the intricate interplay of anger and shame and espousal and wounds received, given and sometimes healed. Suture navigates the chiasmus of shot / reverse shots and free indirect discourse in order both to elide and also connect (however partially) multiple centers of perception in these various paradigms of shame, espousal, and perhaps molestation. My project here is not to "answer" Jacqueline Rose or Martha Stoddard Holmes, but to provide a more narratologically precise and phenomenologically subtle approach to the vexed issue of tone and audience in Barrie's Peter Pan tales (and then to provide a foundation for evaluating the same issues in the Peter Pan films).

V. EAVESDROPPING AND THE RICOCHET EFFECT: THEORY

Understanding just who is eavesdropping on whom and when now requires more careful theoretical work, because much is at stake here. I defer an exact navigation through the work of narratological precursors like Seymour Chatman, Barbara Wall, Jacqueline Rose, and Perry Nodelman to the Appendix. But I will offer now my own revision of the famous Chatman diagram to clarify the labyrinth of consciousnesses of consciousnesses that complicates Barrie's story in such a stunning way. My goal is to move beyond Perry Nodelman's sense of a covert risk to the child narratee (63) and Barbara Wall's (and Rose's) sense of an overt risk to the child narratee (Wall 25; Rose 71), and do fuller justice to Peter Hollindale's claim that the Barrie text is edgy and dangerous for all its audiences (PW xxi–xxiv). *Peter Pan* is to and for and about all of us, suturing multiple consciousnesses in narratologically innovative strategies that put all of us at risk.

In order to outline the ricochet effect and Barrie's use of it, I will clarify the grid I have developed for narrative communication (see figure 4.1).

SUTURE AND LOSS | 155

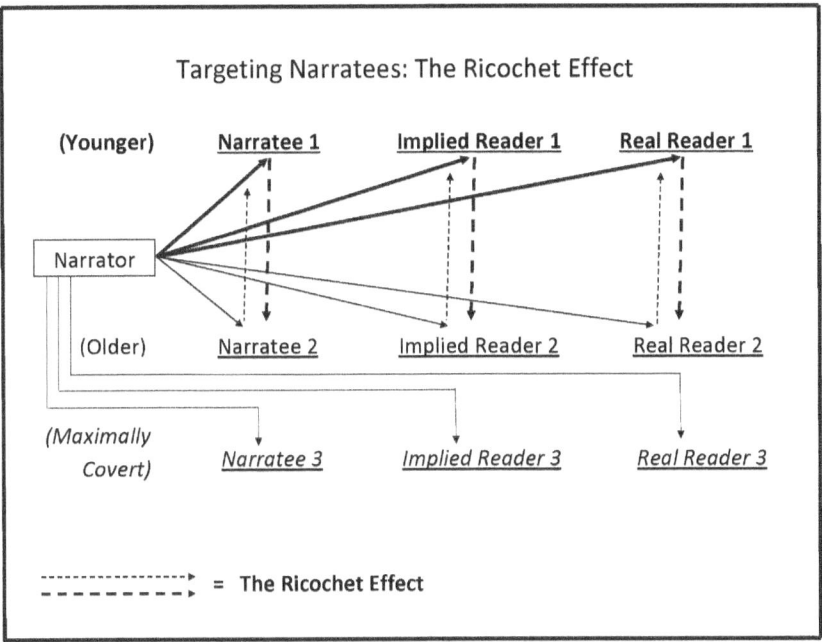

FIGURE 4.1. The Ricochet Effect

The chain of participants, via Seymour Chatman, Peter Rabinowitz, Gerald Prince, and James Phelan, now looks like this, moving from author to reader: real author—implied author—narrator—narratee(s)—implied readers (narrative audience and authorial audience)—actual readers. With narratees that possess clearly different characteristics (some cannot stay awake to see their mother fold away their clothes; others remember childhood as a magic land they will never see again), the pathways for alignment through the next levels are multiple—some real adults, for example, will enjoy the pretenses of the narrative audience and while playing that role will ignore the contradictory worldviews of the text's narratees. Other adults as the authorial audience will understand only some of the manipulation of conventions, cultural allusions, and ironies addressed to them and may be annoyed by some of them. Yet others will understand better, and more importantly, be deeply delighted by manipulation of conventions and narrative form. After all, it's 1911, and some of the real audience will have read *Lord Jim* and "The Turn of the Screw." Some younger real children who don't know enough or possess the necessary cognitive skills to join the authorial audience will be delighted to accept the invitation of the narrative audience role, made more accessible by the younger child narratees in the tale itself. Some may have an intimation of what's going on over their heads (though they still may not know what a checkbook is or why a mother would want one), some will want to know more, some will also be exhilarated by the wit of Barrie's play with form, and some will be troubled. In this array of possible roles and responses (from delight to puzzlement to fear), the ricochet effect refers to one pathway of alignments within the broader phenomenon of eavesdropping, a process that, as we will see shortly, Barrie himself names and reflects on.

Eavesdropping occurs directly or indirectly at each level of our narrative grid and is the precondition for the unease that I cited earlier from a wide range of Barrie critics. Sometimes eavesdropping occurs literally inside the story, as characters overhear other characters' conversations. But in *Peter and Wendy*, the important issue is not the characters' but the narrator's voice. As the narrator speaks first to one and then another listener, who hears or reads these addresses, and who might therefore overhear the words addressed to the other? There are no representations in *Peter and Wendy* of a response by one narratee to the narrator's address to another narratee, so overhearing at this level may only be implicit. But the group of potential eavesdroppers becomes more defined once we move to the narrator's implied readers that we've discussed before, the narrative audience and the authorial audience, and the circle of eavesdroppers widens when we include the listeners in the real-world audiences. "Eavesdropping" is a significant image, with its implications of illicit and perhaps voyeuristic participation in the story. Eavesdropping as an aural concept links to the figure of Peeping Tom, whose punishments are manifold in folk and popular culture (think of Stella's graphic description in Hitchcock's *Rear Window* of the "red-hot poker" visited upon voyeurs). Jeremy Hawthorn's study of readers as Peeping Toms is useful here, in his discussion of various kinds of ethical implications for the behavior of these intruders, though the "disquiet" he sees in real audiences gets evoked by observing spying inside a film or story's diegesis, not intrusion at the level of implied audiences (7).

Eavesdropping occurs in a range of situations, more or less illicit, and is more or less pleasurable to different listeners, inside or outside a story. Using the phrase "ricochet effect" for a subset of these behaviors ups the ante because they become more dangerous. Some ricochets will be more threatening than others, and the effects in some cases may be more exhilarating or enlightening, or less so, but the implication of danger remains.

Also, "ricochet" implies less agency: the eavesdropper often chooses to overhear (though certainly not always), but ricochets threaten people who would not have known they were at risk and didn't choose to place themselves in harm's way. A major part of the discomfort with *Peter and Wendy* arises at this point, with the observation that certain real people have been invited to the feast unaware that their chairs have been positioned so that they cannot avoid overhearing some seriously disturbing voices. Because of these different and complex possibilities, eavesdropping will be a fundamental image to address the multiple processes of deeply intersubjective suture in the Peter Pan stories.

Barrie himself uses *eavesdropping* in a wonderful moment of narratological vertigo from *Tommy and Grizel,* his 1900 novel about confused sexuality that so moved D. H. Lawrence (for Lawrence, see Sedgwick 182). Barrie's narrator uses the word to describe the relation between his protagonist, Tommy, and his creator. Character reading in this example is inherently incomplete, indirect, and slightly illicit: "[Tommy] knew what he was at that moment as you and I shall never be able to know him, eavesdrop how we may" (225). Eavesdropping is a role for both "you" and "I," narratee and narrator, as if for a moment both are intradiegetic personae engaged in the same sneaky behavior in the character's vicinity. The narrator further confuses the role of storyteller and listener by pretending, here as elsewhere ("I suppose" in the citation above; 69), not to know everything about these characters, confirming that he is only another eavesdropper himself. To cast himself in this role is an elaborate if intermittent pretense that emphasizes fragmentation, incompletion, and intense moments of vaguely unethical voyeurism. Barrie's narrator, in both *Tommy and Grizel* and *Peter and Wendy,* is a persona, almost a character narrator, a voice that refers to itself as "I" repeatedly and that addresses, in the manner of *Tom Jones* and *Vanity Fair,* various listening presences that sometimes are part of the diegesis (hence are intradiegetic narratees) and sometimes are outside the tale he is telling (and hence are extradiegetic narratees). Barrie's narrator, in any case, is another choice by the implied author, like any other narrator, whose voice has certain qualities and effects. I see its whimsy, erratic shifts in tone, and knowingness to be aspects of its character that the knowledgeable audiences will observe, but that may puzzle others who expect a more conventional narrator.[11]

---

11. I do not mean to raise the vexed issue of the reliability of an omniscient narrator, even though I have used the phrase "character narrator." In this case, Barrie has given

To clarify the roles and levels among all these listeners, I want to discuss further the work of the authorial audience. It attends to the patterns of the *syuzhet* and interprets their nonlinear sequence, it notices the different "you's" the narrator addresses, and it connects Wendy's reference to Napoleon to Barrie's play text. This authorial audience, the self-aware and semiotically subtle subgroup of the implied readers, is the addressee of the implied author, another figure "inferable from the entire text" (to use Gerald Prince's words) who is something of a ghostly presence behind a voluble, overt, self-identifying narrator like *Peter and Wendy*'s. But because *Peter and Wendy* gives us this dramatized, self-aware narrator who is deeply conscious of various audiences, it is clear to me this narrator is consciously addressing this skilled authorial audience who, for example, notices (at its most subtle and informed) when *Peter and Wendy* deletes language (about touching Peter, say) from the play text of *Peter Pan*. Barrie's narrator is aware of this deep-cover listener, hovering behind Tootles and the child who can't keep awake, who is the most attentive eavesdropper of all.

Seymour Chatman observes, in his extended discussion of narratees, that "the narrator-narratee relation can parallel or confirm in some way the themes of the object story" (*Story and Discourse* 259), and that confirmation occurs in *Peter and Wendy*. Barrie's narrator changes tones for different audiences, especially for the narrative and authorial audience, while both are invoked almost simultaneously (we will look at examples where the narrator swivels from one to other between two sentences), so that one cannot avoid eavesdropping on another, and indeed the narrative form seems to intend to cross—violate, some would say—this boundary. He then manipulates language for each audience to suggest and then avoid complex dilemmas of eros (sexuality), family (mothers especially), and gender (the masculine especially). The layerings of manipulation, avoidance, and aggression, often responding to responses between voices, provide some of our richest examples of deeply intersubjective suture. The slipperiness of the form is exactly the deeper theme, and suggests how the Peter Pan story, even in its most popular, evasive versions in paraphrased children's books and films, explores a series of losses and compensations. The key symptom of the tangle of tones in *Peter and Wendy* is its multiple audiences, and how the text manipulates, segregates, and targets each of them. We need another variation on the Chatman diagram, with more

---

us, I think, a quirky, complicated, self-aware, and clearly omniscient voice, similar in many of these qualities to the narrators of, indeed, *Tom Jones* and *Vanity Fair*.

levels than Barbara Wall's revision, to explore the narrative complexity of a text with so many different kinds of readers and listeners. Here is my proposal (see figure 4.1: The Ricochet Effect).

This diagram outlines each of the various angles along which the narrator's voice may get deflected. In the first column on the left, narratees (mostly intradiegetic, but perhaps a "you" addressed directly by Barrie's narrator) may overhear an observation directed at another narratee because both narratees reside in the same aural space that the narrator presumes. This commonality is clear inside the story-world (the Lost Boys listening to Peter and Wendy in chapter 11) but is only implied at the level of the narrator's other addressees. In the second column, moving to the right, one implied reader overhears opinions delivered to the other implied audience (and the ricochet can threaten either the more naïve or the more sophisticated audience, though the younger listener has more to lose); in this case, the argument that both audiences exist (in some sense) within earshot of each other is somewhat hypothetical. At the third level, younger and older real audiences are often necessarily within earshot when the older person is reading the text to the younger. In this instance, the notion that the narrative and authorial audiences can overhear language directed either to the younger or older real audience is much less hypothetical. These examples of eavesdropping can be conceived as an overhearing (by the younger listeners) of the disturbing language spoken to the authorial and/or more adult audience, on the one hand (and again, this is the more fraught outcome), or an overhearing (by the more mature listeners) of troubling language delivered to the narrative audience and/or the younger real reader, on the other hand (as in my example in footnote 10 about Peter's pleasure in killing as many "grown-ups" as he can).

The value of this model is its map of the way some narratives acknowledge, more or less overtly, the presence in their audience of listeners who may not be able to read the text, and the presence of older receivers of the text who may be needed to perform the text, or may be asked to do so as part of the conventions of a particular reading community. Once we acknowledge these layers, we open the door for multiple relations among these audience members that can take on a dizzying set of permutations, each with its own dynamic processes. One audience may misread or underread a sign that another audience may hear very differently, either in delight (perhaps at the expense of the first or some other audience), or in disillusion or sadness. To take examples from real-world audiences, any one of us—parents, caregivers, teenage babysitters—will understand what I mean if we have edited out words or even episodes from a text while reading it to a child, or have heard that child laugh at some implication that the text managed to slip past us, signaling the child as it were over *our* shoulder. Because of the ricochet effect, many older readers have specifically chosen to edit *Peter and Wendy* when reading it to younger children the second time (usually there was an uncomfortable, even disastrous first time). The edits target not only moments that might disillusion or sadden a child. The real-world adult reader may be uncomfortable being seen to see the child's smile at a particularly subversive thought of Peter's, and in any case, the parent knows, what seven-year-old benefits from Peter's encouragement to resist the burdens of school life?

Barrie's multiple narratees inhabit a story-world in which both ends of the generational span are at risk of overhearing sad, tormenting, or angry claims about parents and children. But the risks for implied or real-world child listeners, with their economic, social, and emotional vulnerabilities (however different their variables of class, education, and cognitive development), seem to me significantly greater than the risks to older audiences. I think Barrie's texts take those risks purposefully, expecting at some level the consequences in the protests that I have recounted. *Molestation* is the wrong word for us now, in the second decade of the twenty-first century, because it suggests surreptitious and damaging, specifically sexual (and sexualizing) attention.[12] But younger children (and adults, of course) *are* targets in *Peter and Wendy,* and the weapon of choice is free indirect discourse. Each of Jacqueline Rose's examples at the beginning of her chapter 3 illustrates what she calls "a momentary loss of narrative *control*" that leads to "a possible confusion of tongues" (70). But each example is a classic moment of free indirect discourse, and the complexities, however dangerous, illustrate exactly the opposite outcome: the *presence* of narrative control employed for profound if troubling thematic ends.[13]

---

12. The difficulty lies in the new uses of *molest* in the last forty or fifty years. According to the OED, the origin of *molestation* to refer to a primarily sexual abuse is American, and its first examples date from 1945. Writing about children in 1983, Rose, I think, uses the word in this newly dominant American sense, but the abuse is epistemological, not physiological. Her examples of confusing narrative voices in free indirect discourse are very similar to mine: examples of irony and anger and "voices [that] contradict each other" (71). The damage to children in Rose's view comes from the boundary crossing of narrative voices, which Rose identifies in itself as an impurity in this case: the "formal play of the modern adult novel" is fine in its place, but "the writer for children must keep his or her hands clean" (70).

13. See the Appendix for further context in narrative theory and more development of this discussion about the ethics of boundaries.

Tracing these elements of suture, especially eavesdropping and the ricochet effect, in some important Peter Pan films is a logical next step, to see how the complexities of the oblique work themselves out at least in some representative examples in the narrative form that provoked this theory of suture.

vi. THE PETER PAN FILMS: NARRATING LOSS AND ANXIETY

> Miss Nina Boucicault as Peter Pan . . . had the touch of heart-breaking tragedy that is there in the story or fable from beginning to end.
> —Denis Mackail

> Peter: I want always to be a boy and to have fun. You can't catch me and make me a man.
> Wendy: You say so, but I think it's your greatest pretend.
> —P. J. Hogan's *Peter Pan* (2003)

Denis Mackail's description of the first Peter Pan, played by Nina Boucicault in December 1904, emphasizes the sense of loss that most of the film versions of the story have avoided. Barrie himself thought of Peter as "a tragic boy" (Birkin 117), and in his notebooks he wrote, in 1922, "It's as if long after writing 'Peter P' its true meaning came to me—Desperate attempts to grow up, but can't" (Birkin 297). Many writers have noted the pain and loss that surrounds *Peter Pan,* though none has done so more effectively than Andrew Birkin. Most visible are all the deaths, from Barrie's own promising older brother at thirteen and the play's producer Charles Frohman's death on the *Lusitania* in May 1915; to the Llewellyn-Davies family litany, the father Arthur from cancer in 1907, the mother Sylvia in 1910, son George's death in France in March 1915, the apparent suicide of son Michael in 1921; to son Peter's suicide in 1960, long after Barrie's death. But there are even more immediate brackets of death and loss around the Peter Pan texts: Barrie was writing and revising *Peter and Wendy* precisely during the final decline and lingering death of Sylvia, mother to his five "Lost Boys." In the summer and fall of 1904, during the final composition of the first performance text (to be much revised, of course, in subsequent years) and during the extensive preparations for the expensive first production of *Peter Pan* (of whose success neither Barrie nor Frohman was at all confident), Barrie continued to reflect on his unhappy marriage. In one example of these reflections, Barrie made expansive notes in July 1904 for a short tale on the tenth anniversary of his wedding. Some telling details of Barrie's scenario: the husband has forgotten the anniversary; the wife asks, as an anniversary present, that he stop kissing her; the wife talks about "the agonies of years of forgiveness, self-deceptions, clinging to straws, &, & how all these have gone" (Birkin 108).

This note of loss points to a thread in the Peter Pan stories that I have not emphasized yet and want to trace in the Pan films: their anxiety over adult sexuality. And is this anxiety a stimulus for forms of narrative indirection, of the oblique? All of the Barrie Pan tales, from *The Little White Bird* to *Peter and Wendy* and the final play text, include powerfully erotic elements that contribute to the experience of loss and to the complexity of the mother theme that we have discussed. The implications of these motifs about adult sexuality are unavoidable, however strenuously characters and films may seek to avoid, or placate, or displace them. The erotic elements do get picked up by the Pan films, including significant explorations in the Disney version of 1953. But these erotic motifs vary from the Barrie versions because they sometimes present loss and the textures of erotic life differently. My theory of adaptation, as I explained in chapter 3, does not fault a film for changing its source; whatever alterations occur are part of the thematic and aesthetic fabric of the new work. What matters is not arriving at a verdict of unfaithfulness to some Platonic ideal of Barrie's originals, but identifying the changes as acts of interpretation and reconstruction, in some ways similar to the rethinking implied in Barrie's own multiple versions of his tale.

The erotic in Barrie's Pan stories is always connected to the threat of time and to a looming, limiting other. It is contradictory and disturbing. That is why the erotic is troubling to the freedom and narcissism of the child, especially the lost boy. A common error in Peter Pan criticism erases Peter's sexuality, as if he were as careless of the erotic as he performs himself to be (however unintentional or unself-aware that performance is). But Peter's character is deeply erotic, even when he denies it. For example, Peter seeks out Wendy because he lacks "female companionship," a phrase that occurs in both novella and play, and he works hard to persuade her to come with him, but then he forgets her name on the flight to Neverland. Peter's connection to narrative and time underlines his contradictory relation to eros: he seeks (he wants to know what happened to Cinderella) and yet avoids time. He says at the end of the play, "I always want to be a little boy and to have fun," but Peter is not a *little* boy. (David Munns emphasizes the aging of Peter in modern Pan versions from, say, six earlier in Barrie to twelve now [220].) But Peter has not been a small boy between two and six since *The Little White Bird*. Peter's exaggeration of his childishness is a mark of his need to evade time even as he seeks immersion in it. In the play, in an example I mentioned earlier, Barrie's commentator draws attention to this contradiction; when Peter says this line ("I always want to be a little boy"), the "stage direction" reads immediately, "So perhaps he thinks, but it is only his greatest pretend" (PP 151). The pretense here is, of course, Peter's *version* of his desire, his claim that he really does want to remain a little boy forever. Furthermore, "pretend" underscores Peter's self-awareness as he constructs for Mrs. Darling a pre-erotic self that much of the preceding story discredits.

Other threads of erotic energy in both play and novella also link characters together in ominous or disturbingly intense ways. Tiger Lily wants to be "something" to Peter, but "she says it is not my mother" (PW 162), and so do Tinker Bell and Wendy. *Peter and Wendy* especially emphasizes a deep sexual energy in both Tiger Lily and Tinker Bell that is more intense than the play's version of these characters. Tiger Lily "was the most beautiful of dusky Dianas . . . coquettish, cold and amorous by turns; there is not a brave who would not have the wayward thing to wife, but she staves off the altar with a hatchet" (PW 116). Conventional gender patterns are wonderfully tangled in this line: the virginal Diana (also a huntress) employs a warrior's weapon (the hatchet) against the men who want to make her a wife—is there a slight suggestion that she might emasculate them? Later the pirates capture her "boarding the pirate ship with a knife in her mouth" (PW 143). A line that Barrie excised from an early version of the play suggests Tiger Lily's purpose in evading these suitors: in answer to Peter's question, "Now then, what is it you want?", she replies (twice), "Want to be your squaw" (PP xii).

Perhaps Tinker Bell's erotic intensity (and sexual maturity) are also daunting to Peter. Tinker Bell, who later says she "glories in her abandonment" (because she will tell Peter what Tiger Lily wants), appears first "gowned in a skeleton leaf, cut low and square, through which her figure could be seen to the best advantage," a figure "slightly inclined to *embonpoint*" (162, 88). Tiger Lily and Tinker Bell are *women*, older and sexually mature in a way usually downplayed or avoided in films of the story. Both characters, that is, embody a focused, conscious, active female sexuality that links them to an erotic other. Peter too seeks "female companionship," but then evades it; again, as we saw above, he approaches and retreats. He seeks and abandons. This pattern is only slightly more complex because he approaches and retreats from two versions of the erotic object: the mother and the daughter, for whom his roles are,

FIGURE 4.2. Disney's *Peter Pan* (14:18): "But . . . that means no more stories!"

respectively, son and lover. He seeks both and avoids both, sometimes at the same time.

The Peter Pan films contain extensive traces of these complexities, and the most complex traces occur in the versions by Walt Disney (1953) and P. J. Hogan (2003). Disney's Peter Pan, for example, is a significantly erotic figure, in ways perhaps surprising given stereotypes of Disney and the 1950s. The initial suggestion of his erotic force is his figure, the way he's drawn: his costume especially is strikingly revealing, with a plunging neckline and short shirt sleeves whose peek-a-boo edges expose an almost-buff body (see figure 4.2). Peter's outfit emphasizes his physical embodiment that has a sort of centerfold masculinity, an earlier and somewhat younger version of Burt Reynolds in *Smokey and the Bandit*; with a gold medallion around his neck, he could serve tables at a 1970s steak and salad restaurant. I do not mean to suggest a homoerotic dimension as such, though the Peter Pan figure comes to carry those tones, as Marjorie Garber has explained in *Vested Interests*. The other signal of Peter's erotic force in Disney's film is the register of his voice. It is a man's voice, or at least an older boy's voice, low enough to mark him off from John and Michael and the younger boys, safely consistent in texture to distance it from the scratchy wobbliness of the boy's voice right at the transition into

FIGURE 4.3. Disney's *Peter Pan* (37:17): "Hello, Peter!"

puberty. It is not the voice of the young women who had always played Peter on stage.[14]

The combination of these features makes Peter's role in the sexiest scene in the film almost flamboyant. That scene, at the Mermaid's Lagoon, places Peter at the center of a circle of flirtation ("Oh, Peter, where have you been?" "Oh Peter, did you miss me?"), and he laps up the attention exultantly (DPP 37:30). The mermaids, often clad only in their hair, pirouette with Peter in a fully reciprocal dance of pleasure and desire (figure 4.3). But, interestingly, Peter does not join such a dance of desire with Wendy. His relation to her throughout the film is written and embodied without the erotic. There is no yearning for the prim Wendy, and more importantly, no unhealed wound of maternal abandonment, no wistful backwards look at the Darling nursery. Disney rewrites Barrie's

---

14. Susan Ohmer describes at length the anxiety about Peter's "sexual ambiguity" that Disney story analysts and animators felt as the studio was preparing its version of the story (173). Walt Disney told Hedda Hopper, "It's been traditional for a girl to play the part of Peter on stage, but we're making him a real boy" (174). Indeed, as Ohmer says, the studio was so anxious about Peter's maleness that it altered his story and character (including the deeper voice) in a number of ways so that "Peter is not a boy but a young man" (174).

FIGURE 4.4. Hogan's *Peter Pan* (17:41)

evasions by aging Peter and deepening his erotic energy. Disney's Peter is more like a married man, and the complexities (and the evasions) occur in *that* relationship, with Tinker Bell. *Does* he wander? What about those mermaids, and this new girl Wendy? The anger and fear that younger audiences may overhear occur in the marital strife between Peter and Tinker Bell.

P. J. Hogan's 2003 live-action version of *Peter Pan* makes Peter even more explicitly erotic, though perhaps younger than the Disney Peter. His voice, also deeper than the prepubescent boys', cracks from time to time, and he often returns to the games and pantomimes of a younger boy, much more than Disney's Peter does. His body is on even fuller display than the body of Disney's character, in tune with the directions of Barrie's play text ("In so far as he is dressed at all it is in autumn leaves and cobwebs" [PP 97]). And the object of this Peter's erotic energy is unmistakably Wendy, from the beginning of the film to the last frame. In the nursery, Hogan's mise-en-scène develops this young love: more than flirtation, not yet courtship, not quite conscious of its sexual implications. Specific close-ups frame first Wendy's and then Peter's face in the bed frame's heart (figure 4.4), and earlier Peter hovers intimately over the prone Wendy in her bed, his body stretched over hers in another suggestive pose. (This shot is a good example of a narrational wink at the older implied viewer, over the shoulder, as it were, of Peter, who is certainly not himself aware of the sexual implications of the closely framed bodies.) This over-the-shoulder watching occurs especially when the audience looks through the surrogacy of a Hook who with the casting of Jason Isaacs becomes significantly younger and more erotic than is usual for Hook.

Jeremy Sumpter's Peter captures Barrie's ambivalent character in other ways, embodying the young male on the cusp of puberty as at times younger, and at other times older. This Peter, for example, does value social rituals, even as he scorns them. So in the lovely midair dance sequence that Hogan adds to the story, Peter bows to Wendy in a clumsy imitation of ballroom etiquette, like a boy at his first cotillion class. Yet, still like Barrie's Peter, he refuses to go to school and play suitor to Wendy; Hook, in Hogan's thoughtful development of Barrie's character, competes effectively with Peter for Wendy's affections, in a dazzling version of the play's Oedipal web (since he also plays Mr. Darling), because he understands the adult moves she desires from a suitor. This Peter also celebrates his narcissism, as Disney's does not, by relishing Barrie's lines that emphasize Peter's "cockiness," like "Oh the cleverness of me!" (PP 99).

These two films adopt, extend, and then also deflect the sexual energy in Barrie's stories in their interpretation of women's erotic force. This deflection appears in versions of the indirections we have pursued: in eavesdropping that ricochets, for example. Disney's Wendy, like Peter, approaches and retreats from adolescent sexuality. The early conflict in the film, of course added to the play's scenario, concerns her father's wish that she move out of the nursery into a room of her own (she tells Peter, "I have to grow up tomorrow" [DPP 13:15]). Her own flirtations with Peter seem modest and prim, as if she is resisting a romantic attraction by leapfrogging sexual awakening to take on a motherly, or at least safely domestic role, expressed in for example her rapid-fire small talk (additions to the play text). In the mermaid's lagoon sequence, Wendy's plain blue nightgown and awkward body movements are an almost embarrassing contrast to the mermaids' colors and dance-like gestures: *they* are comfortable in their bodies, she is not, and Wendy is quite aware of these contrasts, especially as she watches from the wings, as it were, the spectacle in the lagoon. This moment of watching Wendy watch (and overhear) promises the pleasures (and dangers) of the voyeur: what will Peter reveal, and maybe the mermaids' tresses will slip a little?

Of the other women in Peter's life, Tiger Lily is more childlike than Barrie's figure (no huntress warding off suitors with a hatchet), though she does dance with Peter at the Indian camp. Tinker Bell is, however, an older partner with a woman's figure and a consciousness of her erotic role in the eyes of the other. She primps in the mirror in the Darling nursery, and is embarrassed that she's too hippy to squeeze through the keyhole of the drawer when she gets shut inside Wendy's dresser. Tinker

Bell and Peter are in fact the film's primary romantic heterosexual couple (rather than the Darlings). In Barrie Peter is flummoxed by the demands of three women (or near-women)—Wendy, Tiger Lily, and Tinker Bell. In Disney he's the older male already securely partnered. Neither Wendy nor Tiger Lily is a threat to Tinker Bell, as Peter assures her after Hook's bomb explodes and she expects him to leave her (Peter is translating her question): "Wendy? The boys? I've got to save you first. You mean more to me than anything in this whole world" (DPP 1:06:36).

The Disney film raises the stakes for erotic maturity in some disturbing ways: Wendy faces a deadline (the classic Hollywood formula) for growing up, and Peter is the older male already linked to a voluptuous and volatile Tinker Bell. One twist of the story screw and we'll be in *Mildred Pierce*. Indeed, Hook invents a conventional story of marital infidelity for Tinker Bell when he persuades her to betray Peter Pan in their confrontation in Hook's cabin. Hook first worms his way into Tinker Bell's graces with his lachrymose soundtrack music (he can still play the piano). More important is his summary of her melodramatic story, right out of the daytime radio handbook, which demonstrates "the way of a man with a maid, taking the best years of her life and then casting her aside, like an old glove" (DPP 54:31). This striking and powerful moment is the clearest example in Disney of the ricochet effect, a bitter comment about marriage addressed to a previously confident marital partner, who is distraught over Peter's apparent infidelity. Disney's two audiences overhear Hook, and his cynicism about married men could disturb the younger narrative audience, even if they do not quite understand it, because it disturbs Tinker Bell, who bursts into tears (figure 4.5). Tinker Bell's sense of betrayal alerts her audience to a fragility in the family she has formed with Peter and the Lost Boys.

The film deflects these fears in ways that sometimes reemphasize them. Wendy herself is never genuinely sensual, so that the film downplays any erotic pressure from her to grow up "tomorrow." Her father's irresponsibility and childishness in Barrie gets erased (his protest about taking his medicine, "Nobody coddles me!"; his literal banishment to Nana's doghouse), so that Wendy has less need to find a safer home. Wendy is in fact never competition for Tinker Bell, to whom Peter proves loyal. So Tinker Bell's deep fears in a sense are more powerful in their irrationality; for this full-figured woman to feel so insecure before the waifish, prim Wendy is troubling. The film also deflects the need for Wendy to mature by rewriting the deadline of the opening. However, it acknowledges its announced and then avoided theme in the ambiguity of this rewriting: Mr. Darling

FIGURE 4.5. Disney's *Peter Pan* (57:34): "But we mustn't judge Peter too harshly. It's that Wendy who's to blame."

changes his mind about insisting that Wendy move out of the nursery, agreeing with his wife, "She's still a child." Yet Wendy announces, "I am ready ... to grow up." Mr. Darling smiles his change of heart, deferring maturity with his line, "All in good time ..." (DPP 1:15:16). Wendy interrupts him to watch Peter's ship sail away, and Mr. Darling never finishes his sentence. The film never suggests what "good time" might mean.

To Mr. Darling, it clearly means "not now," and the weight of the film endorses immaturity. The Lost Boys decide not to come home (in contrast, of course, to Barrie's play), the father subverts his daughter's choice to leave Neverland (and enter time) by returning her to childhood, and the more serious erotic (even marital) energy of Peter Pan and Tinker Bell goes back to Neverland, safely removed from the world of real time, or at least removed from the temptations of another Wendy. To be fair to Disney's film: accompanying each of these evasions is a nod to that older audience that knows the conventions of *Now, Voyager* and *Helen Trent*. The result is indeed a suturing of consciousnesses. Children eavesdropping on Mr. Darling, for example, may note the evasion of Wendy's deadline, and of Tinker Bell's fear of betrayal in a world where married men abandon their partners for new and younger women. Our map of the ricochet effect helps identify different kinds of threats and different degrees of evasion.

The mother theme, which in the Barrie texts, especially the novella, is so troubling, is also less of a threat in Disney. Eavesdropping by narratees and implied audiences does occur, but Peter has no bitter memories with which to challenge Wendy's song, "Your Mother and Mine" in the "Wendy's Story" scene in the Lost Boys' underground home. Disney films have always addressed at least two audiences, the younger child and the child's attending chauffeurs or ticket purchasers, and *Peter Pan* addresses these two audiences also, though less extensively and obviously than many other Disney films. There is the echo of Hollywood melodrama in the line cited above about "casting aside" a longtime female partner "like an old glove," for example. The film even provides an overt, voice-over, very adult narrator who announces at the opening that "all this has happened before, and it will all happen again, but this time it happened in London" (DPP 1:49). This narrator's world-historical perspective clearly addresses an older audience listening beside the child viewer; some children, even younger children, safely ensconced in the narrative audience, will overhear this line and have a glimpse of its perspective. But their ability to understand it is limited, and it doesn't threaten them. This voice-over narrator never offers a disturbing opinion of "the truth about mothers" or, for that matter, about children, "the most heartless things in the world . . . , but so attractive." When Tinker Bell frowns at her figure, disapproving of her hips, this narrator winks at the adults conspiratorially, without drawing the small-child audience's attention to the wink, and without threatening to trouble somewhat older children even if they noticed.

P. J. Hogan's *Peter Pan* seems initially to take a different direction. Because sexual energy is more complex and threatening, maybe some ironies will ricochet. Not only is Peter an erotic force, but Wendy is too. A particularly important addition to her character is her innovative storytelling. Wendy's version of "Cinderella" that Peter seeks to hear has a marvelous new scenario in which a band of pirates led by the one-handed Captain Hook meet Cinderella in a great battle in which Cinderella wields her sword heroically to save the day. Later in the film, Hook is such a magnetic, seductive presence for Wendy that she momentarily considers joining the pirate crew under the moniker of Red-Handed Jill, a fierce warrior who will tell her companions stories. Hogan develops a brief hint in the novella ("Perhaps it is tell-tale to divulge that for a moment Hook entranced her") into a rich scene of seduction in which Hook's attraction for Wendy hovers between the loverly and the fatherly (PW 178). Wendy as Red-Handed Jill has come a long way from Disney's prim girl in the blue nightie. When she grows up, this Wendy wants to be a novelist, though her aunt Millicent warns her parents, "Novelists are difficult to marry."

Hogan's Wendy therefore carries more authority (pun intended) than other versions, not only in rewriting "Cinderella," but in joining Peter in battle at Marooner's Rock, and in confronting Peter with the words quite literally of Barrie's narrator in the play, as I mentioned before. When Peter says to Wendy, "I want always to be a boy" (Hogan cuts the "little") "and to have fun" (from Act IV of the play), Peter adds his lines to Mrs. Darling from Act V, "You can't catch me and make me a man," and Wendy replies with the stage direction from Act V, "You say so, but I think it's your greatest pretend" (PP 151; HPP 1:08:18). Hogan also concentrates the story's erotic energy on Wendy and Peter by sidetracking Tiger Lily and even Tinker Bell, and then adds in Hook.

The seductive dinner scene between Wendy and Hook sets up the most complex moment of voyeurism in the film, as audiences watch the intimate give-and-take between guest and host. This Hook, who is much closer to Wendy's age than other versions of the character, is wittier and more knowing about her life. He comments, for example, on growing up: "a barbarous business: all the inconvenience ... and the pimples" (HPP 1:02:20). A buff, virile Hook in his late thirties is a quite credible rival to Peter for Wendy's affections. Hogan's Hook is a strangely precise reversed-image of Mr. Darling the mousy tongue-tied bank clerk, so that when Isaacs-as-Hook invites Wendy to join the pirates, her response has a Oedipal edge: "I wonder what mother would think?" (HPP 1:03:10). There is a small ricochet here, an Oedipal echo (lover-as-father-as-lover) that probably simply flies over the head of younger audiences. Still, Hook presents himself as a true *lover* to Wendy when he announces, "Peter cannot love" (HPP 1:02:02). That is, he is not the better qualified *father* that he is in, for example, Spielberg's variant. Hook's powerful erotic presence in this scene (see figure 4.6) and throughout the film crosses several uncomfortable boundaries.

But then Hogan's film retreats from the high-stakes romance it has constructed in ways that reemphasize its contradictions. It approaches and avoids the deeper wounds and losses of the Barrie tale. The major revision here of the Barrie story is Peter's emotional growth, partly in response to Hook's challenge ("You'll die unloved, like me"), so that in the climactic battle with Hook, Peter's recovery of his ability to fly is paradoxically linked not to his separation from the world of flesh and commitment, but his immersion in it, to the degree that he carefully and

FIGURE 4.6. Hogan's *Peter Pan*: "There, there. It doesn't have to be this way. Didst thou ever want to be . . . a pirate?"

consciously chooses to kiss Wendy. Like John, Peter turns pink after kissing, but Wendy's dedication of the kiss to Peter already presumes their separation: "This is yours, and always will be." Peter's growth into feeling is *not* a movement into time; he matures without growing up. In a choice that is either brilliant or evasive or both, Hogan's screenplay simply ignores this contradiction, but this irony echoes through the ending. Like Barrie, Hogan never resolves the difference between the boy who *would* not and the boy who *could* not grow up.

But the bifurcation is less angry than Barrie's versions, though retained in the film's editing. The resentment of mothers and mothering is almost entirely missing, and Hogan repeats Steven Spielberg's decision in *Hook,* like Disney's, to cut the famous line, "To die would be a great adventure," from the end of Act III in the play. Instead, at the end of this film, as at the end of *Hook,* Peter says, "To live would be an awful big adventure." Barrie himself had written this line in the extended stage direction at the end of Act V, to explain why Peter does not understand Wendy.

> It has something to do with the riddle of his being. If he could get the hang of the thing his cry might become "To live would be an awfully big adventure!" but he can never quite get the hang of it, and so no one is as gay as he. (PP 153–54)

That is, Barrie's Peter does *not* say the words. Hogan's mise-en-scène for this line presents a pensive Peter, head resting against the Darling window frame (see figure 4.7) as we watch over his shoulder the reconstituted

FIGURE 4.7. Hogan's *Peter Pan* (1:40:25): "To live would be an awful big adventure."

Darling family. This Peter becomes a voyeur of the "one joy from which he must be forever barred," though in compensation he has "innumerable ecstasies" (PW 214). However, Hogan's shot / reverse shot editing in this sequence suggests some suspension of resolution: he cuts back and forth, from face to face, along an oblique eyeline match, Wendy to Peter to Wendy, in a kind of shadow ricochet, as the viewer overhears the unresolvable conflict between time and Neverland. Inside the window and outside, home and Neverland: the realms cannot meld. Peter still cannot "quite get the hang of it," the riddle remains.

Hogan's editing in this final sequence acknowledges separation: there are only shot / reverse shots across space, only separate images of Wendy and Peter looking at each other, unlike the moments in the forest waltz where they share the frame in the same shot, as in the lyrical (if somewhat blurred) moment before the full moon, a moment of embrace completely missing in Barrie (see figure 4.8). The only figure to move into Peter's frame with him now, at the end, is his buddy Tinker Bell. The film's older implied viewer, like the older Wendy who narrates, sees the larger frames and cycles; the implied architect behind Wendy even gives the knowledgeable and alert viewer nudges, as when Millicent enters an earlier frame carrying a copy of H. G. Wells's *The War of the Worlds*. The camera does not hold the older audience hostage while forcing it to eavesdrop on the angry or protesting voice of the younger characters in the story. Nor does the younger child audience overhear the older narrator's bitter skepticism about heartless children and abandoning, unnecessary mothers.

Hogan's nod to Barrie's uncertainties lies in the absence of an explanation for Peter's flight away from Wendy and her family (which the other

FIGURE 4.8. Hogan's *Peter Pan* (55:34)

Lost Boys have happily joined). Peter seems to choose not to return with the other Lost Boys, yet the film's concluding scene repeats Barrie's line about the "one joy from which he *must* be forever barred" (emphasis added). This contradiction resonates to some degree, but without Barrie's backstory of forgetful/possessive mothers, not so deeply. Wendy does ask Peter if he will forget her (a line from chapter 17), and he promises not to, but in Barrie's novella, of course, Peter forgets people (even Hook) all the time. In the final disconnected frames, Wendy asks if Peter will return, and he answers, with his cocky smile, "To hear stories—about *me*!" The disconnection (in the film's editing, and in human relations) never gets sutured, and so the authorial audience may wonder quite why Hogan's Wendy wants to pass the story along to her children and their children.

In my argument, the important narratological threads in these Peter Pan story-worlds are, as I have traced them, the complex role of eavesdropping and the ricochet effect, sometimes complicated by free indirect discourse, among multiple audiences. These narrative devices are all examples of suturing together consciousnesses among audiences that take an over-the-shoulder stance toward each other or their narrator in ways that echo film narrative's shot / reverse shot conventions. We have come a long way from Jean-Pierre Oudart's Absent One in sutured narrative, so that a more flexible, subtly graded approach to multiple consciousnesses in narrative allows us to measure degrees of loss, to outline absence against a fuller screen, and also to acknowledge anger, bitterness, aggression, even against children, in our models of the oblique as narrative practice.

But suture is also an image that promises linkage, often in a crisscrossing form, in the manner of Merleau-Ponty's chiasmus. Some of these linkages are simpler, without a recursive layer of responding consciousness(es), as in the voyeur's primal stance of observation, and so I talked in chapter 1 of elementary suture as one end of a spectrum. However, almost all of our examples constitute response to response(s), in layers of consciousnesses that become more intricate, though of course not necessarily more profound. These responses to responses include the loneliness of the voyeur, say the solitary Jeff watching Miss Lonelyhearts in *Rear Window* (one wonders who is the more genuinely lost), or Mark watching through his murderous film camera in Michael Powell's *Peeping Tom,* and are powerful studies of human desire.

The layers of threadings or of complex stitches in the examples of suture in this book have mostly emphasized intrusion, or loss, violation, or absence, but if absence, an embodied absence, felt in the body, not the absence of Lacan or "Lacan" as constructed in film theory of the 1980s. We have seen anger and shame sutured inside the frame in *Nothing But a Man,* and then the intricately graded layers of misperception of misperception in *The Golden Bowl,* of looks "misconstrued together," to echo the Stephen Sondheim lyric. And in the Peter Pan stories, we have seen the effects of eavesdropping by way of over-the-shoulder perspectives or free indirect discourse. The ricochet effect has laid the wounds of family and eros before unsuspecting audiences.

But I promised in chapter 1 that this book would also counter the generally dark tones of modernist and postmodern narratives of the last one hundred years. Deep intersubjectivity, however oblique and risky, can tell stories of espousal and connection, even if imperfect and limited. So let's conclude by turning to comedy and rebirth, to the *komos* of sacrifice and hope. How do the promise and threat of suture function in the narrative practices of comedy? Since comedy is finally about the possibilities for healing and community (however partial and problematic), this chapter will clarify a thread that runs through this book from Oudart's Absent One to Derrida's wholly other: the hopes for connections with others. And let's return to film for our primary example, where suture began as an image for storytelling strategies in film theory, as I discussed in chapter 2. My final case study examines how suture works in the special instance of film comedy. We will trace the promise and limits of sewing up, of linking across the frame, in a masterful exercise of suturing across the gaps of death and denial, in Joel and Ethan Coen's *Raising Arizona* (1987).

CHAPTER 5

Suture and Film Comedy

Raising Arizona and the Derridean *Komos*

> The character of the *pharmakos* has been compared to a scapegoat... beneficial insofar as he cures—and for that, venerated and cared for—harmful insofar as he incarnates the powers of evil—and for that, feared and treated with caution. Alarming and calming. Sacred and accursed.
> —Jacques Derrida, "Plato's Pharmacy"

> These were the happy days, the salad days as they say.
> —*Raising Arizona*

Suture and comedy gain their power from similar gaps and contradictions. Suture promises a threading across the lips of a wound, and so does the *komos*, even when the agent of rebirth is the ambiguous scapegoat of Derrida's *pharmakos*. For Derrida, in "Plato's Pharmacy," the *pharmakos* walks along various boundary lines, "between inside and outside" (133), "the invisible and the visible" (127), between poison and counterpoison (125), even between "Socrates's words and the viper's venom" (118). Of course in Derrida's argument, this liminality points toward the *pharmakos* as generator of the supplement, "the movement, the locus and the play: (the production of) difference" (127). For Derrida, the "ambivalence of the *pharmakon*" has "authorized" a "crossed connection-making," indeed, "this chiasmus" (127). The contradiction of the scapegoat is the contradiction of the ancient ritual of the *komos*, as Francis Cornford explains: "the *Pharmakos*, by some primitive conjunction difficult for us to grasp, is a representative both of the power of fertility and of the opposite powers of famine, disease, impurity, death" (69).

But the contradiction unwinds into time as a narrative of the Mobius strip, of the chiasmus: "death is flowerlike, flowers are deadly." Suture is the narrative strategy of chiasmus, hooking together the sides of the wound without erasing their scar. The gaps occur between elements of the fabula, or of multiple fabulas (say, *Bleak House* rather than *Great Expectations*; Inarritu's film *Babel* rather than Nolan's *Memento*), or between enunciations of the narrative camera, but especially in my study of intersubjectivities, between characters, between subjects, minds, consciousnesses, in the form that I named in chapter 1 as the Oblique III. The loops connecting sides of the chiasmus, or frames in the shot / reverse shot sequence, may close the gap a bit or a lot, as they crisscross the intervening absence in lines at oblique angles. But traces of the rupture always remain to some degree, because as Merleau-Ponty understood, transcendental connection never happens in a world of embodiments. And the *komos* costs.

A full phenomenology of comedy and its chiasmus is beyond the scope of this book, but some thoughts about their elements will frame this chapter. The focus on comedy's later link to laughter has often obscured its primal connection to an earlier story of rupture, violation, and loss. Phenomenology's interest in the experience of the body and the other has grounded much of this study, and this chapter will work with Derrida's notion of these topics by way of his concept of Plato's pharmacy, and in the book's epilogue, a conversation between him and Jean-Luc Nancy, J. Hillis Miller, Paul Ricouer, and Emmanuel Levinas. In this chapter, I want to draw special attention to the deep connection between Derrida's pharmacy and the Cambridge Ritualists like J. G. Frazer and Jane Harrison (my special interest will be in Francis Cornford's work)—a connection that has gone unexplored, although Derrida discusses it extensively (see notes 56, 57, and 59 in "Plato's Pharmacy"). Indeed, this much-studied essay ("Plato's Pharmacy") has received almost no recognition for its fundamental contribution to theory of comedy. This connection (between Derrida and the Cambridge Ritualists) allows us to explore how forms of the oblique can tell the story of body and the other and others, at least in this exemplary and deeply self-problematizing narrative, *Raising Arizona*, and to measure what kinds of intersubjectivity and community are possible in these stories.

But the notion that comedy can be a kind of narrative of suture, a form of the oblique that explores chiasmus (an image from Merleau-Ponty and also Derrida, as we saw above), can benefit from two challenges. The first comes from Rene Girard, especially from *The Scapegoat,* which specifically identifies the failure of "Frazer and his disciples," who "[conceal] the most interesting meaning of [*scapegoat*]," and which for them has meaning "in the ritual sense only" (120). In Girard's view, they ignore the real meaning of the *komos,* which is collective murder. Frazer sees in Christianity, according to Girard, "the ultimate triumph of that superstition," rather than the dismantling of it that Girard argues for in his book (120). Leaving aside Girard's argument for the way Christianity (or Christ) dismantled the trope of the scapegoat, I will focus on the depth of loss and suffering in Cornford, and link the body in the *komos* to bodies in *Raising Arizona.* That is, comedy here is not only ritual; it is embodied experience. And these bodies have gender, class, ethnicity, as we will discuss below. But Girard's challenge is significant: What is the cost of this violence, this sacrifice? What happens when the other becomes the outsider? Perhaps the very difficulty of these questions provides an explanation for the value of the oblique narrative, as evasion, some might argue, or as the straightest approach possible, as Henry James argued (see chapter 3). Girard wants to move beyond comedy and the scapegoat, rejecting "the foolish genesis of bloodstained idols," to a world where only "the murderers remain convinced of the worthiness of their sacrifices" (212). Such a utopia has not yet arrived, and is it true that all sacrifice becomes murder? The stories of the *komos* are not so simple, I think, from *The Odyssey* to *Waiting for Godot* (which, remember, Beckett subtitled "a tragicomedy"). But the question of a costly violence hangs in the air as we talk about rupture and the possibility—or contradictions—of postmodern community.

A second challenge arises from Erving Goffman's rich notion of stigma, another framework for thinking about the body and the other. For Goffman stigma is a kind of violence that causes ripples throughout the body of a community. The stigmatized respond in multiple ways, others respond to that response, and the stigmatized responds further to that response to his wound. The Other—"the 'visibly stigmatized' one"—becomes a seed in an intricate network of consciousnesses:

> Each potential source of discomfort for him when we are with him can become something we sense he is aware of, aware that we are aware of, and even aware of our state of awareness about his awareness; the stage is set then for the infinite regress of mutual consideration that Meadean social psychology tells how to begin but not how to terminate. (18)

In Goffman's analysis, groups of stigmatized persons often form a "deviant community" inside the larger "normal" community, and the relations between the two are always fraught (145). Goffman's study is appropriate here because he thinks so carefully about the body of the stigmatized, as, for example, in his wonderful discussion of "passing," which can apply to various situations in which a particular body may "pass"—that is, not only a light-skinned person of color, but, for example, a blind person whose blindness is not immediately visible, or "black-skinned Negroes who have never passed publicly [who] may nonetheless find themselves, in writing letters or making telephone calls, projecting an image of self that is later subject to discrediting" (74). Body as social identity opens upon a larger phenomenology of differences, from genders to ethnicities to class markers. Goffman's book's subtitle—"Notes on the Management of Spoiled Identity"—raises complex questions of power and ideology in the marking of bodies in always deeply intersubjective lifeworlds: who spoils, on what grounds, as a part of what larger rhetoric? At its best, looking at narratives of multiple embodied consciousnsesses need not erase their specific genders, ethnicities, sexualities, or classes, but would include attention to these influences on their stories. Furthermore, the stigmatized are often convenient scapegoats, and so the issues raised by Girard recur. All of these questions help define the answer to the question, what is the cost of the *komos*, where medicine is also poison? How far apart are the threads of the chiasmus? Can the wound be sutured, and what would healing mean in the various communities of the story? A phenomenology of cost and difference is part of the matrix of the *komos* in a Derridean narratology.

This chapter will trace the kinds of hope that a comedy of suture can offer, at what price, in a particularly complex film narrative. The hope is never unfiltered or naïve here. Derrida describes well this elusive future of the scapegoat, of the poison/counterpoison: "We will watch [the *pharmakon*] infinitely promise itself and endlessly vanish through concealed doorways that shine like mirrors and open onto a labyrinth" ("Plato's Pharmacy" 128).

Raising Arizona articulates a version of this elusive promise. It makes use of a deeply fractured narrative form to approach the problems of comedy, itself a vexed and fractured genre. The vexations date to the beginning of the *komos* and its conception of the *pharmakon*, as Derrida's essay points out, features that comedy's narrative form then and now mirrors. The cracks, however, have opened wider in what for lack of a better word I will call a postmodern time. *Raising Arizona* exhibits a range of symptoms that might be more usefully conceived as consequences of what Derrida conceived as the rupture of the sign: a wide play with narrative conventions in the context of the disappearance of Lyotard's master

180 | CHAPTER 5

narratives, in this instance the governing forms of the *komos*; greater and more problematic self-referentiality; and an explicit play with forms of ungrounding that produce a kind of vertigo that might qualify as ontological as well as epistemological, to use Brian McHale's idea about how the postmodernist advances from the modernist ("Structure" 246).[1] If we remember that notion of rupture in Derrida's "Structure, Sign and Play in the Discourse of the Human Sciences," one of the threads of the idea is "the absence of the transcendental signified which extends the domain and the interplay of signification *ad infinitum*"; this absence produces another kind of vertigo, in the midst of which we tell tales as bricoleurs (249).[2]

So comedy now becomes bricolage, improvised with "the means at hand," adapting the tools we have inherited, without center and master narrative (Derrida, "Structure" 255). Suture as narrative form in film will be a good way to measure and understand the vertigo of the *komos* as improvisation, and this film offers examples of such improvisation: how to make comedy in the absence of the sacred origin, even though that origin was always problematic. This text meditates on different threads in the complex tradition of the *komos*: for the Coen Brothers' film, the question is the role of sterility and death in rebirth (hence the pun of their film's title: raising Arizona, or razing Arizona?). The film ends with a dream whose status problematizes community and time even more deeply: does H. I. simply repress the Lone Biker's apocalypse, or is there really a land of peace and healthy families somewhere, sometime? Despite the Derridan notion of narrative as bricolage, *Raising Arizona* nonetheless sutures its fragments together into a recognizable kind of comedy. Improvising may be all that's left of the *komos,* and yet perhaps that's enough.

i. ETHAN AND JOEL'S PHARMACY

> This is *komos* pure and simple, a revel without a cause.
> —Erich Segal, *The Death of Comedy*

> [W]e have laughed to see the sails conceive
> And grow big-bellied with the wanton wind;

---

1. See *Postmodernist Fiction* 9–11 and McHale's "Postmodern Narrative" 456–59.
2. My discussion combines vocabulary associated with both postmodernism and poststructuralism, as did Dick Hebdige years ago, for example, in *Subculture: The Meaning of Style* and in *Hiding in the Light,* and, much later, Christopher Butler also, who specifically addresses "Deconstruction" in *Postmodernism* 16–19.

> Which she, with pretty and with swimming gait
> Following—her womb then rich with my young squire—
> Would imitate, and sail upon the land,
> To fetch my trifles, and return again,
> As from a voyage, rich with merchandise.
> But she, being mortal, of that boy did die.
> —Shakespeare, *A Midsummer Night's Dream*, I.ii 128–35

Raising Arizona, Ethan and Joel Coen's 1987 film, is a remarkable experiment in narrative, especially film narrative, because it functions as both ancient and poststructuralist comedy. In both roles, the film hopes for wholeness, or for a fiction of wholeness, albeit stitched together from the available fragments, in the midst of stories of the liminal, the daemonic, the indecent, the magical, and the masked. The *komos* and the Derridean seem to speak different languages because the ritual function of the *komos* was rebirth, as F. M. Cornford's study of Attic comedy emphasizes, as a way to recreate life in the midst of death in archetypal narratives such as the struggle between winter and summer, the Young and Old King, or the "carrying out of death" (Cornford 9–15).[3] In contrast, ungrounded postmodern narrative emphasizes bricolage, irony, and the Derridean loss of the Logos. As if to dramatize this loss of center, *Raising Arizona* plays with codes and discourses in many semantic fields, from soundtrack music to film genres (a quality *Raising Arizona* shares with other Coen movies, especially *Blood Simple* [1985], *Miller's Crossing* [1990], and *A Serious Man* [2009]), to class speech codes to narrative rhetorics.[4] As sutured narrative, *Raising Arizona* will loop into and around bodies and subjectivities as it maps types of threads and types

---

3. Cornford on Attic comedy, Kenneth Reckford on Aristophanes, C. L. Barber on Shakespeare's festive comedy, and Bakhtin on the carnivalesque (*Rabelais and His World*) provide the theoretical framework for my discussion of the traditions of comedy. The Cambridge Ritualists have returned to academic favor, to some degree, and provide useful approaches to ancient comic ritual. See Jeffrey Henderson's introduction to the recent edition of Cornford. See also Robert Ackerman.

4. J. Hillis Miller has recently written about another important narrative, Toni Morrison's *Beloved*, which also appeared in 1987, a year that Miller calls "the heyday of what is called 'postmodernism'" (*Conflagration* 232). Miller observes that many of the formal elements often seen as markers of the postmodern (pastiche, depthlessness, various kinds of discontinuity, a "calling attention to the problems of fictionality") appear in earlier narratives, like Cervantes's "The Dogs' Colloquy" or Sterne's *Tristram Shandy* (233). But both *Beloved* and *Raising Arizona* create a deeper ontological vertigo than these predecessors; the primary preconditions for this vertigo are Derrida's rupture of the sign and Lyotard's loss of credible master narratives.

of gaps between those threads, where chiasmus becomes a dialectic of absence and presence.

Comedy is the name, with a long history, for a collection of genre practices whose doublenesses have provoked many reflections: on the ancient Greek *komos* as sacrifice and renewal (Cornford); on the *komos* as revel, village, and sleep (Segal); on revel's carnival as outside time yet lost to the unbelieving modern world (Bakhtin's *Rabelais*); on revel's fools as natural and artificial, unconscious and manipulative (Erasmus and Kaiser); on revel's humor as enclosing and anxious (Freud); on lifemaking as death-making (Shakespeare, *A Midsummer's Night's Dream*). But Derrida in "Plato's Pharmacy" ponders in the most eerie way on the loop from the archaic to the poststructuralist, on the slippage in *pharmakon* between remedy and poison, in *pharmakeus* between magician and sophist, in *pharmacia* between fountain and labyrinth. As Derrida tries to define Socrates's place in the drama ("a *pharmakeus*? A magician? A sorcerer? Even a poisoner?"), he finds in the chain *pharmakeia-pharmakon-pharmakeus* an echo of the sign absent from Plato, and in the *pharmakos* ("scapegoat") another deferral of sacrifice and healing ("Plato's Pharmacy" 117, 129). Under the sign of the supplement, then, what is the power of Socrates's alchemy to transubstantiate his hemlock ("Plato's Pharmacy" 126)? From *pharmakon* (medicine, remedy, poison, perfume) to comedy: the yellow-brick road of the supplement points to the remapping of genre practices in the age of the Post: postmodern, or even postpostmodern. Irony, then as now, subverts faith, and a desire to believe in belief subverts subversion but can also do the reverse. In the Coen Brothers' pitch-perfect version of this double-bind, H. I., at the end of *Raising Arizona*, ponders on his dream homecoming: "It *seemed* real. It *seemed* like us. And it seemed like . . . well . . . our home" (139).[5]

So the relation between Derridean play and the rituals of the *komos* in this film is not simply parody or irony; archaic comic rhythms are not a privileged ground, but neither are they only another discourse. The echoes of the ancient Greek *komos* raise the stakes in the post game. This hybrid narrative explores the boundaries of "revel-songs" (*komoidia*: *komos* ["revels"] + *aidea* ["sing"]), in H. I. and Ed's and Gale and Evelle's excellent adventure, in order to have its cake and eat it too, to believe and question, to recuperate the ancient carnivalesque into a new narrative of play with its oblique stitches and indirect connections (Reckford 444).

---

5. Page number citations refer to the Coen Brothers' screenplay; time citations refer to the film.

An interest in border territory, in boundaries and the outsider, is one common thread in the ritual comedy of ancient Greece and the comedy of the ruptured sign: here *Raising Arizona* speaks both languages, tells both stories, so to speak. So how do these narrative conventions coexist, how do these languages translate into each other, given that dilemma of the ruptured sign? Let's begin by studying one archaic narrative code, in the collection of border crossers in this film, whom to speak of as scapegoats, masked daemons, and irreverent fools is to underscore their links to Attic comedy.[6] Border crossing also points to another loop in Derrida's chiasmus, in the pathway of the *pharmakos,* between "the invisible and the visible" and "between inside and outside" ("Plato's Pharmacy" 127, 133).

Although H. I. is the film's most important liminal figure, surrounding him are other figures who crisscross boundaries as well, often in demonic and carnivalesque excess, like the figures in archaic festive play who, according to Kenneth Reckford, "dressed up as animals or as daemonic creatures" (446) and to whom disguises gave "free rein to invective and obscenity" as they brought to life the dark side of carnival (455). A good example of the daemonic tale-bearer is Bud, the machine shop earbender (played by Emmet Walsh), clothed in soot, mask raised, framed against the sparks and fire behind him, whose grotesque story about finding a human head in the middle of a highway defines one kind of excess in comedy. The story might even function as an example of "*aischrologia,* the magical combination of obscenity and insult that promotes fertility and wards off bad influences (Reckford 455). But the most important supplemental figures of insult and excess are the brothers Gale and Evelle, and the Biker from Hell. Their inversions and invasions, in detail and spirit and particularly in their bodies, articulate *Raising Arizona*'s embodiment of a chiastic approach to gender.

The figures of Gale and Evelle exhibit, in all their contradictions, a strange, exhilarating, dangerous comic energy that mixes embodiments of multiple genders. For example, Gale, in John Goodman's beefy,

---

6. For a different approach, see Gilmore. He conceives comedy as a work that is "very funny" and that "ends in a good place" (10); his theoretical models come from Plato, Aristotle, and Dante. For Gilmore, jokes in this film provide "perspective on the kinds of things that cause us anxiety" and open the way to "tenderness for Hi and Ed" and others (16). Thomas S. Hibbs sees the film as even happier than Gilmore does; it is "the Coens' early pure comedy" in which "the few noir elements ... are subordinate to a larger narrative, a story of fidelity and the hope for fertility" (38). In my approach, rooted in Derrida, Freud, and Cornford's account of the Attic *komos,* death, sacrifice, and hostility between people are unavoidable components in the ritual of rebirth.

pomaded, tattooed incarnation, is stereotypically "masculine," and yet he is sometimes coded as feminine and also maternal. "Gale" is more commonly a woman's name than a man's, and Gale dispenses self-help column advice with a mock sincerity that subverts the tough-guy image ("But sometimes your career gotta come before family," Gale tells the prison therapist [7]). Gale and Evelle together function as a domestic couple, especially after they steal Nathan Jr. from H. I., when, for example, Evelle asks detailed questions about the use of disposable diapers. Indeed, Evelle is more maternal than Gale, sheltering Nathan Jr. in the trailer's bathroom while Gale and H. I. fight over the baby, and hugging him delightedly later in the car when Nathan smiles at him. Gale and Evelle's frantic last words in the film, as H. I. and Ed race off to recover Nathan Jr. (forgotten for the second time, after the bank robbery) are "He's our baby too" (119).

Their competition with H. I. and Ed for Nathan highlights their coupledom, but Gale and Evelle are more than a parody of the "family unit" with its rigid gender conventions, though they are that too. Both couples kidnap a child by invading a home, both steal diapers, and all four play the role of innocents about raising children who need the comforting wisdom of Dr. Spock even as they endanger Nathan. But Gale and Evelle's wild, forgetful, and somehow generous energy adopts Nathan Jr. in some ways more easily than H. I. and Ed do: they show no hesitation over renaming him, for example. When they recover Nathan Jr. the first time, after the diaper robbery, Evelle begs, "Promise we ain't never gonna give him up, Gale! We ain't never gonna let him go," and Gale replies, "We'll never give him up, Evelle. He's our little Gale Jr. now" (113). In contrast, H. I. and Ed didn't have a name for Nathan, and bungle the challenge when Gale and Evelle, fresh out of prison, ask. This energy—anarchic, life-making perhaps—leads to their explosive birth from the prison (by way of a sewage drain: a gender-bending version of a birth canal?), and to a sequence of invasions, thefts, and exhilarating high-speed car chases that echo H. I. and Ed's. Sexualities and genders mix and circulate here in dazzling combinations and "crossed-connections," to use Derrida's language again. The crisscrossing scripts of gender may begin to address some of the issues about gender assumptions that feminist phenomenologists Judith Butler and Laura Doyle raised in chapter 3. Reading the gender of bodies subverts convention in all kinds of ways in this film.

Leonard Smalls, the Biker from Hell, is the other figure who crosses boundaries, not only in his daemonic, insolent freedom (feet up on Nathan Arizona's immaculate desk) but also in his role as the scapegoat.

Cornford has given an extensive description of the function and archetypal imagery of the scapegoat, whose expulsion from the community makes possible the celebration of the *komos*. What Cornford grasps from his sources in Frazer (*The Golden Bough* and *The Scapegoat*) is the fundamental doubleness of this figure (also Derrida's theme), and the implications of that doubleness for comedy. In the narrative of renewal, which Cornford calls the "carrying out of death," the scapegoat functions with in fact two versions of this doubleness: in the first, it is paired with the *eiresione,* the olive branch of promised fertility, and in the second, its own images suggest both death and rebirth: strings of figs, says Cornford, hung with barley cakes and cheese on the sacrificial men, who were then beaten about the genitals, and finally burned; their ashes were scattered to the winds and sea, for purification (11). The mysterious connection of the scapegoat to health appears even in its name in Greek, *pharmakos*; the Greek root *pharmakon* is both a poison and a drug, a conjunction on which Derrida meditates at length. Cornford phrases the puzzle concisely, in language I cited before: "the *Pharmakos*, by some primitive conjunction difficult for us to grasp, is representative both of the power of fertility and of the opposite powers of famine, disease, impurity and death" (11). Fertile death, the death of rebirth; razing Arizona, Arizona raised; the flower in the desert, the rocky places where no seed can germinate: throughout this chapter, we will repeatedly encounter the magic, or hope, or delusion of chiasmus that Derrida argued was "authorized" by the ambivalence of the *pharmakon* ("Plato's Pharmacy" 127).

That threading of the chiasmus, often oblique as it also "undoes itself" in connecting to the "wholly other" (to use another Derridean phrase), is a fundamental project of the *komos* and this film. This is Derrida's description of that project:

> The ceremony of the *pharmakos* is thus played out on the boundary line between inside and outside, which it has as its function ceaselessly to trace and retrace. *Intra muros / extra muros*. The origin of difference and division, *the pharmakos* represents evil both introjected and projected. Beneficial insofar as he cures—and for that, venerated and cared for—harmful insofar as he incarnates the powers of evil.... The conjunction, the *coincidentia oppositorum*, ceaselessly undoes itself in the passage to decision or crisis. ("Plato's Pharmacy" 133)

The Coen Brothers' Biker bodies forth this *"coincidentia oppositorum,"* Cornford's "primitive conjunction," in detail and form, beginning with his first appearance in H. I.'s dream after the kidnaping, when H. I. went to sleep "thinkin' about happiness, birth and new life," but conjures up instead a nightmare of pain and loss. H. I. thinks the nightmare is Florence Arizona's, but it is his as well, given the tattoo he shares with the Biker, and the Biker's story (told to Nathan Arizona, that he "fetched" $30,000 as a baby—"and that was 1954 dollars" [96]). The Biker's association with maternal loss extends the paradox of Derrida and Cornford. His other tattoo proclaims, "Mama Didn't Love Me," and yet, despite this shadow of abandonment, Nathan Jr. smiles securely in the Biker's custody, fixed to the front of his bike. Ed links the motifs of new life and loss as well when she comforts Nathan Jr. (awaking after that nightmare of H. I.'s) by singing a lullaby about a man sitting at the base of a scaffold, awaiting his own hanging (the lyrics are not included in the published screenplay): "My race is run, for I did murder that dear little girl" (27:41) That is, the "powers of fertility" and those of "disease, impurity and death," combine in sometimes stunning and disturbing patterns. Their indirect connection is the puzzle and terror of comedy's chiasmus.

The Biker's association with babies becomes more and more complex, however, in the film, beginning with the bronzed baby shoes that hang from his vest. This connection suggests the theme of fertility in an especially ambiguous way. The Coens' camera (or Barry Sonnenfeld's) begins by emphasizing the shoes twice: first, when we first see the Biker, and the camera cuts from the tattoo "Mama Didn't Love Me" to the shoes, and second, when the Biker enters the Unpainted Arizona store, and the camera, tracking from the center rear, moves to the left and reframes Smalls to outline the shoes (see figure 5.1). In all his scenes, the film's mise-en-scène outlines Smalls's body, especially his upper body, as dark, apocalyptic, fearful: bullet belts crisscross a deeply nonmaternal breast, for example. And yet from those belts hang grenades whose bulbous and textured surface is almost a parody of fruitfulness. In fact, all of Smalls's appendages, his depending ornaments, echo the scapegoat's ambiguous location between expulsion and rebirth: the grenades, two shotguns, the looped chains, and the baby shoes. H. I. observes of the Biker during his first dream that he was hard on the "helpless and gentle creatures," especially rabbits, in a particular echo of Steinbeck's *Of Mice and Men,* as Rodney Hill has shown, and he repeats that observation while watching the sun rise as Ed sings her lullaby. And then the Coens' soundtrack records a baby crying in the distance (29:56). Do the cries belong to Smalls the purchased child, to Nathan's brothers, to Nathan Jr., or to some archetypal world-child?

FIGURE 5.1. Baby shoes (RA 57:51)

That same sound recurs behind the third and final shot of the baby shoes in the film, after Smalls is destroyed by the explosion of the fruitful grenade, or fig or pineapple, its core removed accidentally when H. I. begs for mercy. The shoes fall to the asphalt, in slow motion and artificial lighting, and a baby cries in the distance (1:22:27) as the film fades with a precise graphic match from the shoes to the exactly superimposed tips of a ladder settling in a window, as Ed and H. I. return Nathan Jr. So the lone Biker of the apocalypse, as H. I. calls him, is also associated with a baby's voice, with pain, loss, and rebirth. He is an agent of violence, an outsider (he calls himself an "outlaw" to Nathan Sr.), whose armor and paraphernalia of bullets and grenades and baby shoes echo that other figure who promises sacrifice and cleansing in strings of figs and barley cakes. A particularly remarkable quality of this sacrifice is its absence of ambiguity. Leonard's death itself produces no melancholy, no sadness over the loss of the Outsider. *Raising Arizona* is not the step beyond the scapegoat myth that Rene Girard seeks. Nor is the stigmatized Biker with his marked body a source of the deeper consciousness that Erving Goffman described. The *komos* costs, but Leonard is not the price. The unclosed gaps in the chiasmus lie elsewhere in this film.

The Biker also promises vengeance and apocalypse as the daemon masked behind beard and grime who breathes fire from cigar and motorcycle and armaments. When that apocalypse occurs, the Biker's ashes scatter to the winds, captured in carefully oblique, rapid camera setups, in a purification that allows H. I. and Ed to return the "extra" baby and find a less compromised rebirth. After all, stealing a baby has from the beginning of the film suggested questions of anger and compensation (where *are* those grandparents?). Evelle reminds Ed about the cycle of anger when he comments about breast-feeding, "Ya don't breast feed him, he'll hate you for it later. That's why we wound up in prison" (57). The sting of cliché doesn't eliminate the broad anxiety about abandonment in the film. *Raising Arizona*'s liminal, desperate festivities, here as elsewhere, point to an archetypal past and, in H. I.'s final dream-vision, to an archetypal future. The Biker's double relation to that future is exactly figured in Cornford's *pharmakos*: a dark self to be burnt away even as it reenacts, perhaps reinflicts our losses. In the Derridean chiasmus, poison and cure loop through each other.

As I said before, H. I. is the key liminal figure in the film, repeatedly crossing the line between prison and freedom, for example. It is significant that H. I. meets, woos, and wins Edwina precisely in the space between prison and outside. But the *komos* seems to occur early in this story, in the eleven-minute prologue, to be exact, not at the story's end, and its issue is problematic. Certainly *Raising Arizona* is full of classical archetypes and images suggestive of the *komos*: H. I. and Ed meet in November, and the kidnaping occurs in April, during spring rainstorms. H. I.'s bright Hawaiian shirts offer a kind of erotic energy, especially the water-bearing one, complete with ships inside bottles, that he wears while wooing Ed. Their gender-bending traces another kind of life-making boundary crossing: Ed is not commonly a woman's name and her femininity is not immediately apparent in her police officer's uniform, while H. I. is associated, however parodically, with the circle of confession and therapy in prison, where the "facilitator" asks the men to talk about their feminine side, and one convict confesses, in a strange deadpan voice, to experiencing menstrual cramps.

This comedy of the desert has a subversive, oblique Derridean form that threatens to uncharm the magic of the ritual of sacrifice and rebirth. Can the threads of inside and outside, of "sacred and accursed," be drawn together across the gaps of the chiasmus? Maybe the cure doesn't work; maybe the medicine poisons. The darkness of anger and death has a place in the master narrative of the *komos,* but postmodernism's "depthlessness," the anti-"natural" tenor, the absence of *telos*, and the poststructuralist logic of the supplement, with its disconnected signifier, do not. So to speak of *Raising Arizona* as a postmodern comedy is in one sense an oxymoron, as I implied earlier. Postmodern *humor*, yes, we can conceive: the laughter of uncertainty, of anxiety, of discourse decentered; laughter that does *not* heal or illuminate: the student of this anti-comic humor is Freud, for whom melancholy and uneasiness always color the jokework, whose purpose is to express and deflect hostility and anger despite powerful repressive forces (see 100, 115).[7] *Raising Arizona* offers plenty of (in this sense) postmodern laughter, the laughter of the supplement. But what would it mean to talk about a postmodern *komos*? And what fissures would require the care, so to speak, of suture, the threads crisscrossing the lips of the wound?

ii. POSTMODERN SUTURES

> Postmodernists are good critical deconstructors, and terrible constructors.
> —Christopher Butler, *Postmodernism: A Very Short Introduction*

> There is no coinciding of the seer with the visible. But each borrows from the other, takes from or encroaches upon the other, intersects with the other, is in chiasm with the other.
> —Merleau-Ponty, *The Visible and the Invisible*

> I dunno, maybe it was Utah.
> —*Raising Arizona*

Out of the myriad uses of *postmodern* circulating now (see Hillis Miller's two-page list: *Conflagration* 233–34), let me pick four notions. One, postmodern art offers no governing meta-language(s) or discourse(s) (Maltby 8–9; Jameson 65)—a notion similar to Dick Hebdige's poststructuralist claim for a style that is "ruptural," because "'signification' is in a constant state of assemblage, of flux" (*Subculture* 126). Two, postmodern narratives function in a world without workable master or meta-stories, whether of scientific or political or philosophical origin (Lyotard says "the grand narrative has lost its credibility" [37]). Three, nature becomes "nature," as irony and parody add their characteristic scare quotes: nature is images, simulacra, ideology, culture. Linda Hutcheon has written, "Even nature, postmodernism might point out, doesn't grow on

---

7. Jokes "make possible the satisfaction of an instinct (whether lustful or hostile) in the face of an obstacle that stands in its way" (Freud 100). Woody Allen has also reflected on laughter that does not confront or heal the sources of anxiety, but rather evades them: "Comedy tends to defuse a subject; and it avoids the pain of a subject in a very clever and entertaining way" (interview, *Sixty Minutes*, December 1987).

trees" (*Politics* 2). Four, postmodern narratives have made a shift from a focus on the epistemological ("How can I interpret this world of which I am a part?") to the ontological ("Which world is this?") (McHale, *Postmodernist Fiction* 9–10). McHale traces this shift in both postmodern thematics and its enabling poetics, and I will look at both topics (*Postmodernist Fiction* 26–27). These qualities of the postmodern combine in one particular device, the parodic pastiche, which seems especially characteristic of postmodernism, as Hebdige has said, and Jameson too, though *his* pastiche is nonadversarial, political neutral, unlike Hebdige's (*Subculture* 125; Jameson 64–65). Investigating *Raising Arizona*'s postmodernism along these lines, in its persistent use of multiple languages and of multiple signifying practices, allows us to come at Derrida's chiasmus from a different angle.[8]

These multiplicities imply the loss of a coordinating discourse, as well as the loss of a legitimizing narrative as the context for that master discourse. What is left is bricolage improvised out of the ruins of old sign systems. But without a governing discourse for these improvisations, without Cornford's master narratives, and without a grounding nature, what is left of the *komos*? What is at stake is the possibility of a comedy of the desert: Arizona raised, not Arizona razed. To evaluate this possibility, let's look at how the film's multiplicities work to destabilize inherited signifying practices, so as finally to ask if any strategy of suture can connect these fragments, however oblique the threads may be.

Raising Arizona decenters discourses in at least three different semantics: specific English vocabularies, music codes, and film genres. The collision within and among these discourses provides much of the exhilaration of the film. In the first semantic field, some of the English vocabularies are Shakespearean and Biblical (King James translation) languages and, in strong contrast, the idiom of various human service professions, often at the level of psychobabble and sociological cliché. These idioms raise questions of rank and class, because they occupy such different registers, often in the same person's speech (usually H. I.'s). These language practices usually presume a certain kind of education or training, in contrast to, for example, the Earbender's style. H. I.'s uneven but generally sophisticated diction, like the Biker's, seems at odds with other class

---

8. R. Barton Palmer does a similar review of postmodernisms, from Jameson and Eagleton to Hutcheon, Hebdige, and McHale, and also claims that the Coens are postmodern, but in a way that does *not* "aggressively flatten [...] the past," and "eschews the slick, shallow invocation" of canonical screwball film directors like Sturges, Capra, and, I would add, Hawks (59–60).

markers these characters exhibit. What does one make of this collage of vocabularies?

A good example: H. I. introduces Nathan Jr. to his new home:

> Lookahere, young sportsman. That there's the kitchen area where Ma and Pa chow down. This here's the TV, two hours a day maximum, either—either educational or football, so's, y'know, you don't ruin your appreciation of the finer things. An' this here's the divan, for socializin' and relaxin' with the family unit. Yessir, many's the day.... (33–34)

H. I.'s language mixes the safely external descriptions of a real estate ad or a furniture sales agent ("the kitchen area," "the divan, for socializin' and relaxin'") with sociologically clinical diction ("the family unit") and advice column prose about children's TV. H. I.'s speech seems in fact a pastiche of pop culture performance genres, shifting gears almost as if channel surfing among talk shows. These shifts are rapid, often oblique, producing sometimes a kind of whiplash in the viewer. What appears to be a random sequence of styles highlights some odd contrasts between dialects and clichés. What do we make of this "family unit," for whose leisure the divan is a facilitating commodity? In what sense is it a family, and how can it be conceived as a unit? Is this a "unit" as a part of some organizational flow chart, as in "the Chicago unit," or "the public relations unit"? And what is the tone of "finer" if it applies to both *Nova* and Monday Night Football?

These gaps would once have signaled an ironic intelligence, either H. I.'s or his storyteller's. Bakhtin theorizes extensively about these gaps that get articulated in the multiple dialects that we mentioned in chapter 4, but one key effect of these gaps in his account is unmasking and comment: "Incorporated into the novel are a multiplicity of 'language and verbal-ideological belief systems ... [that] are unmasked and destroyed as something false, hypocritical, greedy, limited" (*Dialogic Imagination* 311–12). It is exactly evaluation and commentary about class positions that seem to go missing in this postmodern comedy. It seems unlikely that the controlling irony in our scene would be H. I.'s, because his body and face convey a kind of awkward generosity that is clearly at odds with the sterility of the formula "the family unit." As he holds Nathan Jr. up to see each new feature of the trailer, H. I. gives no sign that he is aware of the gap between that generosity and the cliché. On the gap between *Nova* and Monday Night Football as examples of "the finer things": we are pretty sure this syntax does not function as a satiric equation, in comparison, say, to Pope's "husbands, or lapdogs" in *The Rape of the Lock* (III 158). But in the film text, in the enunciation of camera movement and editing, is there not some awareness of this flattening of distinctions? Commentary from the architect of the text's rhetoric is as tricky to locate here as in other complex film texts we have discussed, from *Nothing But a Man* and *The Silence of the Lambs* in chapter 2, to P. J. Hogan's *Peter Pan* in chapter 4. Nicolas Cage's sad-sack performance tends to take the sting out of any juxtaposition of clichés that does not swivel clearly around a particular target. Instead, *Raising Arizona*'s flamboyant contradictions here seem to be archetypally postmodern in Jameson's sense, fractured and displacing but not ironic, giving us this holy family, Ed and H. I. and Nathan Jr., sacred and profane and neither, in which H. I. functions as the innocent, generous, foolish visionary, even in his dependence upon shards of overheard vocabularies. Is there a function for suture amidst this bricolage? What kinds of threads, however oblique, could provide shape and syntax? They might have to be deferred and incomplete and modest in their claims, as we will see in the film's paradigmatic coda.

Other language codes are at work, too. There is Shakespearean cliché, as in "these were the happy days, the salad days as they say" (H. I. on the first hopeful months of their marriage), echoed when child-making and adoption are fruitless: "But I preminisced no return of the salad days" (16, 19). It's a fine question whether the film's implied, competent viewer remembers only Shakespeare, or also Cleopatra, or even Cleopatra's rueful memory of her youth, "When I was green in judgment" (*Antony and Cleopatra* I iv 74). Maybe the text notes and expects its audience to note H. I.'s offhand "as they say": well, no, it was Shakespeare and specifically Cleopatra who said. Another example occurs oddly offhandedly, when H. I. explains to Nathan Sr. who stole his baby: "*I* took him, sir, my wife had nothin' to do with it. I crept in yon window" (133). However distant the echoes have become at this point, there is still some further overlay of images here too (beyond the tips of the ladder and the baby shoes), of the battered H. I. and Romeo. How, then, are these echoes sutured together here, however indirectly, as memories of youth and hope for fruitfulness?

Biblical language surfaces in a similarly secondhand way, again as if H. I. is repeating words he's heard ("as they say"), not read. This secondhandedness, which is another kind of indirection, makes the targets of the film's parody less clear. H. I.'s generosity is not a target, but maybe his deferentiality is, or indeed the implied film viewer's class expectations for H. I. and Ed. In another example of tangled tones, H. I.'s words, "The doctor explained that her insides were a rocky place where my seed could find no purchase," are accompanied by rapid editing, quick-moving banjo music, and a serio-comic treatment of the anatomical drawings that illustrate the "rocky place" (18).[9] And a little later H. I. addresses his audience directly—"Now y'all who're without sin cast the first stone"—as he describes the decision to take one of the Arizona quints: "But we thought it was unfair that some should have so many while others should have so few" (22–23). H. I. combines Jesus' traditional words, injecting the (hardly postmodern) notion of "sin" with a murky appeal against nature's unfairness in order to justify a little redistribution of nature's bounty, nature aided and abetted, true, by fertility pills and more extensive medical attention than he and Ed could afford.

These shards of vocabularies, echoes and imitations, could suggest, not parody, but the postmodern pastiche that Jameson describes:

> Pastiche is, like parody, the imitation of a peculiar mask, speech in a dead language; but it is a neutral practice of such mimicry, without any of parody's ulterior motives, amputated of the satiric impulse, devoid of laughter. (65)

Certainly *Raising Arizona* provokes plenty of laughter, but I take Jameson's more significant point to be the absence of "ulterior motives" and specific targets, judged by "healthy linguistic normality" (65). But pastiche in this film is manifestly not neutral, in my view, and is more reasonably an example of Hebdige's subcultural styles with "an intrinsically subversive component" that seems "to work against the reader and resist any authoritative interpretation" (*Subculture* 125–26). Yes, *Raising Arizona*'s subversive impulse is not rigorously consistent. Sometimes H. I. seems to repeat language with no sense of its history, so that his innocence or even foolishness gets underlined (as with "yon window" or "the family unit"). At other moments, H. I. seems to understand his rhetoric and its rhythms. When he laments, "Those were the happy days, the salad days as they say," his retrospect is as melancholy about early happiness as Cleopatra's was. Or consider H. I. as visionary: when he dreams forth "the lone biker of the Apocalypse," the film's camera movements and soundtrack are somber, without the high-speed, oblique, and discontinuous editing that undercuts other sequences, especially the prologue.

---

9. Gilmore notes a visual joke in the way the gynecologist manipulates his cigar in this scene, as if "simultaneously explaining the problem of Ed's infertility and simulating sex" (16).

The same confusions of discourse, with the same puzzlements of tone, occur in other semantic fields in *Raising Arizona*. For example, the soundtrack's music quotes from a dazzling array of sources. On one hand, the film uses Beethoven's "Ode to Joy" from the 9th Symphony (in the prologue), wonderfully simplified for banjo player and a wordless human voice (hum, actually), and on the other hand, it uses "Home on the Range" (during Nathan Jr.'s homecoming) ("and the skies are not cloudy all day" [20:10]). And, as if to combine concert and folk music, we have one of the key Russian folk motifs from Stravinsky's "Petrouchka" at the beginning of the prologue and during the final credits (0:35 to 1:19, and 1:31:00).[10] Then there is the wacky note of the operetta playing on the television that Gale and Evelle are watching when Ed and H. I. return from their diaper-hunting expedition (50:35).

The film is also rich with quotations from and allusions to the discourse of film genres: the biker film, for example, and the road picture, as well as the Western (H. I. tells Ed, "I come from a long line of frontiersmen"). Nathan Arizona gives these traditions a peculiar twist when he says, of Leonard Smalls, "Big fella rides a Harley, dresses like a rock star" (132). And then there is that gas station restroom door bearing the mysterious inscription "P. O. E.," and beneath it "O. P. E.": a strange echo of General Jack E. Ripper from *Dr. Strangelove?* Behind all of these echoes lies the tradition of screwball comedy, with the title *Raising Arizona*'s revision of *Bringing Up Baby*.

The effect of the collision of these discourses is not, to my mind, "neutral" in the way Jameson claimed for postmodern pastiche. Just as critics like Paul Maltby and Linda Hutcheon have argued that postmodernism may offer a politics, and not only by default, behind the mask of "neutrality," perhaps *Raising Arizona*'s looping tones (and loopy tunes) offer a version of the *komos,* sutured across the gaps of the chiasmus, even if the revel song is now a "revel song," and nature is now "nature." To the extent that Cornford and Frazer's rituals *are* part of this text, then, the film may be about (among other things) the gap between nature and "nature." If the *komos* is a ritual of rebirth, then it is pertinent to ask

---

10. Gilmore draws attention to Pete Seeger's "Goofing Off Suite," first recorded in 1955, cited in the film's credits. Seeger's work includes these riffs on Beethoven's 9th Symphony and Russian folk music (without the link to "Petrouchka"), and further versions of Beethoven's 7th Symphony and Bach and Grieg motifs. The actual performances on *Raising Arizona*'s soundtrack are not Seeger's performances, but new versions of his versions—a whistle instead of a hum, say, or different guitar work, sometimes adding harmony that is missing in Seeger (Smithsonian Folkways CD, 1993).

what birth can mean in a Derridean version of that story. Remember that Derrida's text refers to the "ceremony" of the *pharmakos*. His narrative runs like this:

> The hemlock, that portion which in the *Phaedo* is never called anything but *pharmakon*, is presented to Socrates as a poison; yet it is transformed, through the effects of the Socratic *logos* and of the philosophical demonstration in the *Phaedo*, into a means of deliverance, a way toward salvation, a cathartic power. ("Plato's Pharmacy" 126)

What is the power of the logos in *Raising Arizona*, what demonstration of narrative's magic that transforms poison into the promise of new life, so that the lost newborn baby, a product of "nature," nonetheless drives the film's final, apocalyptic dream of hope?

Linda Hutcheon's model of postmodern film's compromised ideologies may be useful here:

> What happens when we get Woody Allen's *Stardust Memories* parodying and challenging, however respectfully, Fellini's modernist *8½*? What happens, perhaps, is something we should label as postmodern . . . : both a respectful—if problematized—awareness of cultural continuity and . . . an ironic contesting of the authority of that continuity. The postmodernist is in this sense less radical than the modernist; it is more willfully compromised, more ideologically ambivalent or contradictory. (*Politics of Postmodernism* 107)

Pastiche combines so many registers of languages in *Raising Arizona* that its parodies cannot be consistent, and the authority of its central prophet and the film's invisible narrator/enunciator must be thoroughly problematic, yes. But Hutcheon's notion of the willfully compromised authority, or revised authority, opens the door to a less austerely neutral or paralyzed postmodernism. Belief may be only "belief" in the comic narrative, but then the scare quotes are one of this film's rhetorical strategies. That strategy allows the archaic and the postmodern to function together, as threads in the Derridean chiasmus. The loops are sutured into place, but not closed, in the paradox of the distance that is closeness that we have tracked from chapter 2 in Merleau-Ponty's rich model of inter/subjectivity. The model here is *not* Jameson's. Oddly, perhaps almost mystically, the outcome of rupture was also hope in Derrida's "Structure, Sign and Play" essay, as he faced "the as yet unnamable which is proclaiming itself and which can do so, as is necessary whenever a birth is in the offing, only under the species of the nonspecies, in the formless, mute, infant and terrifying form monstrosity" ("Structure" 265). I'm not sure birth in *Raising Arizona* is unnamable, however. It may simply be waiting across the border in Utah.

Enough languages and tones surface throughout *Raising Arizona* to evoke a poststructuralism that plays with signifiers, moving among narrative logics and rhetorics, semantic fields and film genres. That play occasions many collisions of images and tones that provoke humor, certainly, much of it humor of anxiety and dislocation, even aggression and fear: Glenn's, for example, and much of Gale and Evelle's. Genuinely postmodern comedy would probably offer humor, play, without *komos*. On this key point, poststructuralist comedy, or at least Derridean comedy, might be different, since Derrida believed that the doubleness of the *pharmakon* did suggest the possibility of "deliverance, a way toward salvation, a cathartic power" ("Plato's Pharmacy" 126). Centerlessness for Derrida is more open-ended than for Jameson, certainly, or Hebdige: "The *pharmakon*, without being anything in itself, always exceeds [dialectics' philosophemes] in constituting their bottomless fund. It keeps itself forever in reserve even though it has no fundamental profundity nor ultimate locality" ("Plato's Pharmacy" 127–28). *Raising Arizona* seems to insist both on centerlessness and on belief, at least in "comedy," and this doubleness takes shape in its chiasmus. If so, suture will be its characteristic form and theme.

The final dream sequence is my example of this chiasmus, of how *Raising Arizona* has it both ways, is both archaic and postmodern, in Lyotard's and Hebdige's senses: without master discourse (or logocentric signifier), with a *telos* that is problematized as fantasy. H. I.'s role as dream-prophet seems to promise a *telos* articulated in a peculiarly self-mocking language that also promises, paradoxically, some secure ground. H. I.'s role includes his foolish and generous innocence (he's the armed robber who never uses live ammo), but also his folk wisdom, which trumps the innocence (the Biker *does* exist, and we remember H. I.'s relief that Ed sees the Biker too outside the bank). H. I.'s dream of family is a fantasy of a land, "if not Arizona, then a land, not *too* far away, where all parents are strong and wise and capable, and all children are happy and beloved" (139). He knows well that fantasy may be a temptation and an evasion: "I don't know, you tell me. This whole dream, was it wishful thinking? Was I just fleein' reality, like I know I'm liable to do?" H. I.'s reply is simply that "it *seemed* real, it *seemed* like us." But he wants more

FIGURE 5.2. Eyes wide closed (1:28:41)

certainty than seeming, and so casts about for some grounding for his dream. This final dream sequence is especially significant because in it suture is both form and theme, as the film stitches together gazes and gaps to launch a prophecy/fantasy about community.

H. I.'s dream of the future occupies a little more than the last three minutes of *Raising Arizona*. He "sees" it while his eyes are closed, as not only the opening shot emphasizes (see figure 5.2), but as the reestablishing shots affirm (1:28:38 and 1:29:15). So the sequence's fundamental visual logic asks about the status of dream's seeing (and we remember that H. I.'s previous dream-vision, of the Lone Biker, became real outside H. I.'s dream), or even more to the point, the nature of seeing with one's eyes wide shut. Everything that follows the first shot of H. I.'s closed eyes is, through the logic of the implied eyeline match, the object of H. I.'s attention. The remainder of the three-minute sequence underscores, in its mise-en-scène and editing, the gap of the missing reverse shot. Readers of chapter 2 may remember that in the history of thinking about suture, it was the missing reverse shot in *Psycho* that to Kaja Silverman sealed her case for the castrating effect of shot / reverse shot narration of human consciousness in film. To counter her argument, I traced Merleau-Ponty's idea of embodiments in a chiasmus, in which gaps are part of loops at a distance that are only partially empty. *Raising Arizona*'s coda returns us to those thoughts, filtered also by Derrida's notion of chiasmus as pharmacy. H. I. sees people seeing, and sees people seeing him see, without a reverse shot: the narrative logic here resembles, if I may continue to recall chapter 2, the second sequence from *Nothing But a Man*: once again, the missing reverse shot echoes like distant thunder throughout the scene. But this time, the inflection of the echo yearns for hope, in contrast to the ominous threat of violence between Duff and Josie in that prior moment. The rhetorics of absence are multiple, but in my view are still rhetorics of various kinds of embodiment.

In this case, how exactly does the *komos* of the missing reverse shot work? The camera announces a series of absences that function to define the loops of the film's chiasmus. The first absence is an excellent model for the working of the Derridean *komos*: missing reverse shots that suggest both seeing and blindness. The three shots of H. I.'s closed eyes (1:27:27, 1:28:38, 1:29:15) suggest that H. I. "regards" the following and intervening scenes from behind his eyelids, that he sees, indeed, with his eyes wide shut. Ordinarily reverse shots follow eyeline matches (though frequently obliquely angled maybe 30 degrees from the direct match, as I discussed in chapter 2). In this case, the eyes in the eyeline match are closed. The next two shots of H. I.'s closed eyes repeat the same pattern: a blind gaze that is never returned. What would a reverse shot at this point acknowledge? The promise of suture's bridge arcs forward into what? The irrelevant space behind the camera in H. I.'s bedroom? The ambiguity of the shots here that are indeed sutured across blindness functions as a way to explore the ambiguity of prophecy and community: what really happens behind, and more importantly in front of, H. I.'s eyelids? As H. I. wonders, is this sequence just "wishful thinking" (139)?

There is another missing reverse shot in this sequence as well, in this case a gap inside the vision's diegesis. The last minute of this sequence sets the camera behind an elderly H. I. and Ed greeting two younger couples (adults in their late thirties, perhaps) and twelve children (ranging in age from maybe four to ten). H. I. describes the scene as "an old couple bein' visited by their children—and all their grandchildren too," and a banner over the feast-laden table reads "WELCOME HOME KIDS" (139). One of the women comes up to the elderly watcher and says "Dad" (an addition not noted in the continuity script) (see figure 5.3). Barry Sonnenfeld's camera gets close to the older couple, hovering between them so that the viewer watches all the action occur between their figures: the outside door to the home opens in the middle of the frame, the girls dance a circle in the middle of that door, and the camera zooms backward from the banner so that its viewing position is still between the older couple, until the camera tilts down for a close-up on two empty chairs at the end of the table (1:30:25). The two elderly figures then block this image as they move to

FIGURE 5.3. "Dad" (1:29:46)

the center of the frame, and H. I.'s voice-over continues, "It seemed like a land ... not *too* far away, where all parents are strong and wise and capable, and all children are happy and beloved" (139; 1:30:25).

This long sequence, which consists of only two shots, implies the point of view (displaced over the shoulder, according to the editing convention I discussed in chapter 2) of the older Hi and Ed. But there is no moment when the camera cuts to watch the watchers; there is no confirmation of the gaze in a traditional reverse shot. Characters inside the frame see, gesture to, respond to H. I. and Ed, but there is no moment from those perspectives to look back at and register the gazers' gaze. This missing reverse shot emphasizes the power of suture to knit gazes together (inside the frame and also guiding the implied viewer's gaze) and to verify the nature of watching. The missing shot resonates throughout the scene, an absence that asks the question, what is its purpose? One answer lies in H. I.'s rhetoric ("where all parents are strong ... , and all children are happy"), which emphasizes the sequence as fantasy; maybe a reverse shot within the dream would violate its epistemology. Seeing the missing eye (of H. I. and Ed) would fill in a gap necessary to produce the loop of the pharmacy's chiasmus. Because healing requires loss, and medicine is poison, the missing suture emphasizes the "deep background" out of which the Derridean *komos* emerges ("Plato's Pharmacy" 128). But inside the dream there is no closing of the loop, and the *komos* never addresses the charge that it is a fantasy.

Raising Arizona closes its study of gaps and faith with a stunning suture of blindness and sight, in an acknowledgment of the missing

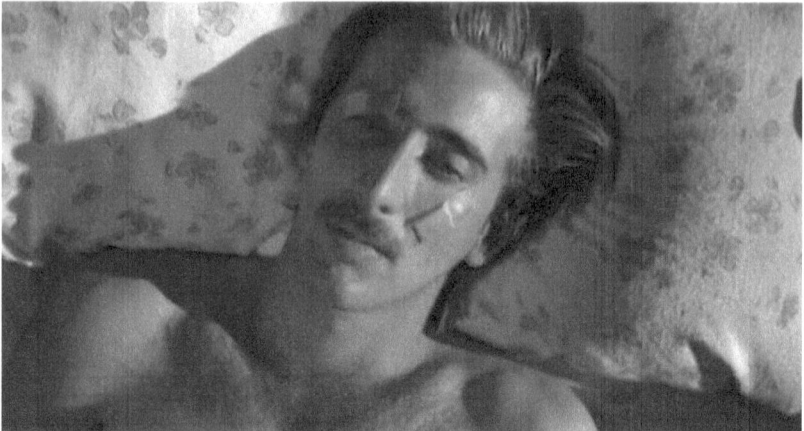

FIGURE 5.4. Awakening (1:30:45)

reverse shot. Like the successive missing downbeats in the bass figures of a Beethoven sonata that lead to an emphatic resolution of the suspense (however arbitrary, framed as convention), the completion of the reverse shot pattern, after sustained absence, carries extra weight. It defines a rhetoric of absence that differs from the one I discussed in *Nothing But a Man*. The pull of the missing reverse shot deepens when H. I. opens his eyes to gaze *at* another emptiness in offscreen space (see figure 5.4). As it probes the complexities of suture, this look—the last shot of the film—suggests what is at stake in the Derridean *komos* of *Raising Arizona*. H. I.'s gaze, framed by bandages beside each eye, completes the gazes inside his dream, meets them belatedly and obliquely, but does meet them, or at least their shadow. The daughter turning to H. I. on our right to say "Dad" invites H. I.'s acknowledging gaze, but that connecting gaze, when it finally occurs, also sutures across a large gap, thirty seconds of the film's running time, and it is a nice question if this loop gets closed. There is still no reverse shot, no gaze seeing H. I.'s gaze (even if such reverse shots are rare inside dream sequences in film: the absence matters). Other linkages are tenuous too; H. I. emphasizes in his frame narration that he is now looking "years, years away" into the future (138), and yet the specifics of the feast scene seem years past: boys in bow ties, girls in starched pinafores, one mother in a shirtwaist dress and bead necklace, the dads in Sunday best suits and sweater vests, the table set with checkered tablecloth and a Currier and Ives turkey and edged with Ethan Allen American traditional chairs: this "years away" is almost a parody of a Norman Rockwell Thanksgiving, and like H. I.'s character combines generosity and evasion.

H. I.'s final look thus knits his present to an ambiguously past future. Where in time and space is this community? Michael Miller's editing provides the answer with an appropriate twist. H. I. had asked, gazing at the feast, where this place might be, and replies, "I dunno." At that precise moment, the film cuts from H. I.'s dream-future cardigan and graying hair back to H. I. in bed. He opens his eyes, and after a beat delivers the punch line of the film: "Maybe it was Utah." This conclusion arcs from one desert to another, grounding its fantasy of H. I.'s children's children in a specific retro-future. The loops of the gaze in the story's coda, broken even in this final moment, demonstrate suture as chiasmus with lots of holes, with deep space between the threads. This pharmacy endlessly promises and endlessly vanishes. Perhaps it comes to seem unreliable, as Derrida observes in a different context later in his argument: "The pharmacy has no foundation" ("Plato's Pharmacy" 148). Utah, of course, is simply another desert land with a mythic story about gardens and a *telos* no more finished than unpainted Arizona's story. So how is rebirth possible amid these fragments?

Part of the answer lies in returning once more to notions of chiasmus and suture that underlie the thought of Merleau-Ponty and Derrida. In "Plato's Pharmacy," Derrida uses chiasmus primarily as a rhetorical trope, as a way to describe the crisscrossing of words and ideas (as in the double meanings of the *pharmakos* as medicine and poison). This crossing between and inside words certainly connects to the themes of this chapter and book, but in *On Touching—Jean-Luc Nancy* Derrida returns to Merleau-Ponty to meditate on chiasmus as a phenomenological process rather than a rhetorical one. Here the stitching together applies to the connections (or failure of connections) between/among consciousnesses. Sometimes the connections are more single-layered, what one might call elementary chiasmus, making use of elementary suture as a narrative device, and sometimes the connections (or failures of same) are more recursive, moving toward what I have called deep suture or deep intersubjectivity. What is important for this late Derrida work is the complexity of the late Merleau-Ponty text *The Visible and the Invisible*, in which the key elements of chiasm (whose appositive is "the intertwining") that Derrida takes up are its fragility, incompleteness, multiplicity, and promise (Merleau-Ponty, *Visible* 130). This is the Merleau-Ponty whose notion of community resides somewhere between the transcendental and the solipsist.

For Derrida it is important that in Merleau-Ponty connection between consciousnesses is always "imminent." And why does this matter? Derrida asks pointedly, "What counts more: is it imminence, always in suspense, or that after which imminence is chasing, driving it and keeping it ever disappointed and breathless?" (*On Touching* 212). What counts more, the promise or the incompletion? Derrida sees this poignancy in another moment from *The Visible and the Invisible*, where Merleau-Ponty puzzles about how we understand touching touching, one hand feeling the other hand and then feeling the first hand's grasp of the second hand: "This reflection of the body upon itself always miscarries at the last moment.... But this last-minute failure does not drain all truth from that presentiment" (of touching touching) (Merleau-Ponty, *Visible* 9; cited in Derrida, *On Touching* 356). Derrida defines the core issue here—"this non-coincidence as ever-imminent coincidence" (*On Touching* 213). Once again Derrida's thought turns toward the future, to the promise of the *pharmakon* that is forever in reserve. Once again, this is not Jameson's flat, neutral postmodernism.

Merleau-Ponty describes more fully this/these chiasmus/chiasms, always separate, always connected, always "encroaching":

> There is no coinciding of the seer with the visible. But each borrows from the other, takes from or encroaches upon the other, is in chiasm with the other. In what sense are these multiple chiasms but one: not in the sense of synthesis, of the originally synthetic unity, but always in the sense of *Uebertragung*, encroachment, radiation of being therefore——(*Visible* 261)

Merleau-Ponty hastens to dodge the transcendental bullet—the chiasms are not one "in the sense of ideality," but because they share the same "structural sense: the same inner framework" (*Visible* 261). These chiasms, always miscarrying at the last minute but not entirely, with the promise of imminence lurking, encroaching on the horizon of the other: this is the model for postmodern sutures in *Raising Arizona*. The dashes that end the citation above are Merleau-Ponty's, the text's own way of finishing the paragraph: open syntactically as well as phenomenologically.

The final dream sequence of *Raising Arizona* is my full-dress example of this complicated, profound model for community, a chiasmus in a postmodern *komos,* a paradigm for "non-coincidence as ever-imminent coincidence." But there are other examples for this style of intersubjectivity in the film. Some suturing is more single-layered, as I discussed in chapter 1: without the recursive chain of response to response, the promise of imminence is still resonant, but not encouraged by a narrative arc that might have stretched through responses to responses in deeper intersubjectivity. So, for example, when H. I. first sees Ed, "in the county lock-up in Tempe, Arizona," and says, "You're a flower, y'are. Just a little desert flower," this thirty seconds of film requires twelve shots, all exchanged looks between Ed and H. I. (except for one close-up of the flash bulb) (00:25–56). But despite all the suturing of looks, there is as yet no response between these two characters, or if so, only H. I.'s continuing movement toward the stony-faced Ed. Already the film's language posits its dilemma: how to discover the promise of the desert flower, the paradoxical bloom that H. I.'s shirt in this scene (red with extravagant blossoms) juxtaposes against sterility, outlined as H. I.'s shirt is outlined against the prison's white wall in the lineup room to sharpen his prison portrait. (A note on the paradox: if someone is a flower in this scene, it's H. I., not Ed, in her severe quasi-military uniform, complete with officer's cap [figures 5.5–5.6].) Somehow the narrative drives forward through the gaps of H. I.'s prison terms, so that soon he imagines "a brighter future lay ahead—a future that was only eight to fourteen months away" (12). Grace arcs across these gaps, and by the end of the film Nathan Arizona forgives the kidnapers of his son and children appear out of the barren land (even if it was Utah).

As the film explores the desert *komos,* the loops of the chiasmus do connect more extensively, and suture works more deeply, suggesting that coincidence with the other is not present now (certainly not fully) but might be imminent. These loops are still limited, but they do open doors to some level of feelings between previously separated characters, as when Nathan Sr., watching Ed and H. I. at the crib-side where they have just returned his son, realizes, "*You* took him, didn't you?" (133). Or a moment of moderately intersubjective enlightenment can wreak deserved punishment, as Glenn learns when he tells one ethnic joke too many, to the Polish highway patrol officer.

A good example of Merleau-Ponty's multiple chiasms is the almost two-minute sequence in the middle of the film when H. I. writes his farewell letter to Ed. Throughout the sequence, the camera floats, tracking and zooming at that same temperate pace that is the mark of the camera's enunciating presence (55:10–57:05). H. I.'s voice-over continues his confession—"I will never be the man you want me to be . . . I say all this to my shame"—while the camera moves from H. I.'s trailer to Gale and Evelle asleep; to the Short Stop clerk H. I. robbed, dozing over his girly

FIGURE 5.5. Ed the desert flower (RA 0:55)
FIGURE 5.6. H. I. the desert flower (at least, he's wearing them) (RA 0:57)

magazine; to Nathan Sr., also asleep; to Ed holding Nathan Jr. in bed; and to the Lone Biker (90–91). Each moment in this sequence is a significant component of H. I.'s story, but each character is asleep (except for the Biker) and deeply separated from H. I.: so the visual track and H. I.'s aural track (as he composes the letter) are separate loops, or multiple chiasms. Only the hypnotic pace of the camera, the agency of the film's lone enunciator, and H. I.'s voice bridge the cuts from one shot to the next, on simultaneous but separate, parallel tracks. (In the case of the Biker, the camera stays with him, but the Harley moves.) Suture brings the fragments closer together, but wholeness and connection are only imminent.

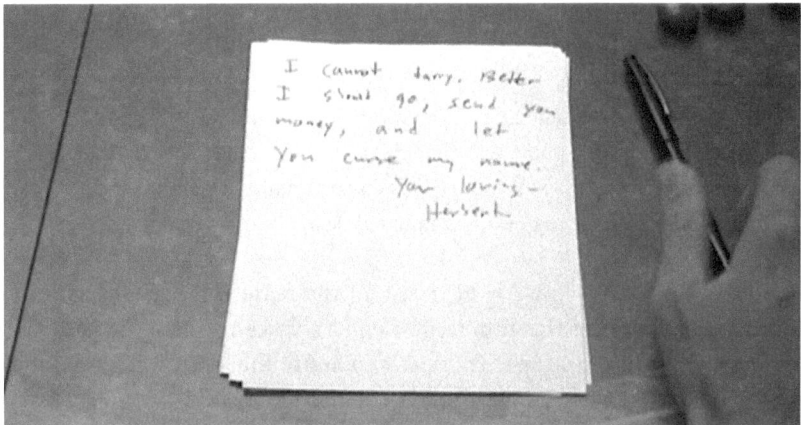

FIGURE 5.7. Cursing—or loving?—Herbert (57:08)

And as in the final dream sequence, the Coens withhold a key shot, in this case the reverse shot of H. I.'s face as he writes the letter. Instead, and paradoxically, in the voyeur's classic over-the-shoulder moment, the camera reveals, in H. I.'s signature, something private: the secret of "H": "Herbert" (not the name one expects for a tattooed robber of convenience stores) (92) (see figure 5.7). So the privileged viewer witnesses secrets and midnight confessions, crosses boundaries, and notes certain kinds of deeper connection, more complex kinds of intersubjectivity (H. I. responding to Ed's hopes for him/them, and his notion of how she will read his letter). What a mix (to cite Derrida again) of "fissions, interruptions, incompletion" (*On Touching* 212). Or, to return to Merleau-Ponty on the threads of complex intersubjectivity:

> To tell the truth even for the other is it properly visible as a seer?—No in the sense that it is always *a little behind* what the other sees.... *Posed* on the visible, like a bird, clinging to the visible, not *in* it. And yet in chiasm with it—(*Visible* 261; emphases in original)

Not immersed *in* the visible, and the other is always already there, so that one is always catching up: but one is close, connection is imminent, on the other side of the chiasm.

In a world of bricolage, community is always improvised, and suture across frames and families is fragile. Does the *komos* point to a nature, or to "nature," that knits the chiasmus? Why is the driving force in the narrative Ed's "logical" feelings (this is H. I.'s oxymoron) about having children? H. I. explained,

> And Ed felt that having a critter was the next logical step. It was all she thought about. Her point was that there was too much love and beauty for just the two of us, and every day we kept a child out of the world was a day he might later regret having missed. (16)

Of course, this paraphrase is H. I.'s, and the male voice has much more power to enunciate in this film than women's voices, so that viewers must ask some difficult questions. To what extent are the film's gender assumptions (H. I. speaks of the child as "he") the film's, in 1987? Does it see childbearing as a "logical" implication of marriage? Why *does* Ed want a child so much that despite some mockery by the film ("You go right back up there and get me a toddler!"), in the end she provokes Nathan Arizona's tears and generosity (29)? The screenplay that presents her this way was written by two men, and perhaps as a male writer I can only ask questions, such as, is the desire for children "natural," an ideological consequence, a residue of the archaic narratives of the *komos*? The conflict between story-worlds (different genders, different comedies) provides an excellent example of Brian McHale's move from epistemological questions in modernism to ontological ones in postmodernism: Which world is this? Which nature? Which gender? Which suture and chiasmus?

Maybe narratives of (re)birth can be both natural and "natural," and maybe the *komos* can be both archaic and Derridean, endlessly promising and vanishing, a chiasmus of hope and doubt. *Raising Arizona* points to these possibilities, I believe, and gestures, however blindly and parodically, toward a land of peace where all children are happy and beloved, which may be only as far away as Utah. Suture links, however obliquely and partially, fragments of story-worlds. Suture becomes an agent of the bricolage that uses well-worn ancient tools—"concepts from the text of a heritage which is more or less coherent or ruined," writes Derrida ("Structure" 55). The conventions of the *komos* are such "instruments," a "'means at hand' ... which one tries by trial and error to adapt" ("Structure" 255). The bricoleurs—the Coen Brothers, H. I., and Ed—acknowledge the usefulness of the *komos*. Its echoes in *Raising Arizona* raise the stakes for belief, or "belief," in community, its children, and the chiasmus of narratives that they must adapt into new forms and improvisations to tell their stories now.

EPILOGUE

Suture and Community in *Why Be Happy When You Could Be Normal?* and *(500) Days of Summer*

The thread that ties the studies of this book together is the thread (and threat) of the other, and the challenge in post-Enlightenment thought to what I have called deep intersubjectivity, the belief that a person can in some ways and degrees perceive the other's perceptions of his or her own perceptions of the other, and vice versa, in a recursive looping of subjectivities that is not entirely an illusion and that makes community possible (and also endangers community). Tracing out these issues has been the project of a group of recent books in the phenomenological tradition by Jean-Luc Nancy, Jacques Derrida, and J. Hillis Miller, but these writers are deeply aware of the other voices that surround their inquiry. Miller writes, in the chapter at the center of *For Derrida,* "Touching Derrida Touching Nancy,"

> How can I touch, in a shapely chapter, on the immense and immensely complex text [Derrida] wrote touching touching, the tactile, tactility, the contingent, the tangential as a theme in Nancy's immense work, and as a theme in Western philosophy from Aristotle to Husserl, Heidegger, Levinas, Didier Franck, Chretien, and by way of Immanuel Kant, Felix Ravaisson, Maine de Biran, and others? (245)

Clearly the immensity of the topic is daunting, and Miller despairs, like Derrida, of even beginning, given the importance of close reading to their work:

> A micrological reading of, say, Husserl's *Ideas II* would be more or less interminable.... Derrida says repeatedly that he has not even gotten

started yet.... Late in the book [*On Touching*] he formulates once more the project of this book and despairs, once more, of ever even beginning. (*For Derrida* 275)

Part of the difficulty is that these writers continue to worry at an unresolvable difficulty: how the isolated self ever encounters the other and others, and how reliable are the results of these encounters (conversation, romantic love, jealousy, marriage, political action, terrorism, institutional life, and budgets)? Narratives explore these encounters in both form and substance, and my examples of suture are about uses of the oblique and the indirect to embody webs of consciousnesses in all their isolation, fragility, and deludedness, but sometimes in connection that is, while always incomplete, yet somehow and partially reciprocal.

The threat is, of course, not only the touch of the other, but of radical aloneness. Existential phenomenologists have written extensively about this radical aloneness—especially Sartre, whom I discussed in chapter 2 and in *I Know That You Know That I Know*, and Levinas, who wrote, typically, "In separation ... the I is ignorant of the Other" (*Totality and Infinity* 62). The other is always absolutely exterior to the self, for Levinas, who saw his work as a response to the sometimes transcendental elements of Husserl and Heidegger—the Heidegger for whose lectures in the late twenties Levinas would queue early in the morning to secure a seat (Moyn 57). The response to this challenge of radical isolation has varied in the phenomenological tradition. For Paul Ricoeur, language provided the connection (though I'm simplifying Ricoeur's idea): "Finally, to mediate the opening of the Same onto the Other and the internalization of the voice of the Other in the Same, must not language contribute its resources of communication, hence of reciprocity, as is attested by the exchange of personal pronouns mentioned so many times in the preceding studies?" (*Oneself* 339).

But for Derrida, language could never be the bridge, was never truly "reciprocal." Any bridge would be possible/impossible, and deeply paradoxical, but it would also begin as an embodiment (which may include language). And hence the importance for Derrida of Merleau-Ponty, despite all the "errors" he uncovers as he "deconstructs" his thought (Miller, *For Derrida* 289). (Since for Miller the always necessary close readings uncover aporias, we can do a little close reading of his own language—see that list of important writers above who touch on touching, and notice an important aporia: Merleau-Ponty's name is missing.) The key elements in Merleau-Ponty's thought about "sensoriality" are expressed, Derrida believes, in the chiasmus: of the open/closed, the possible/impossible: "This noncoincidence [of touch, of bodies] as ever-imminent coincidence, this irreversibility that is always on the verge of becoming reflexive reversibility" (*On Touching* 213). Nancy continues to question "in what sense the other's sensoriality is implicated in my own," (cited by Derrida, *On Touching* 214), and he cannot decide any more than Merleau-Ponty can the degree to which "all these are 'figures' of thought" (Merleau-Ponty, *Visible* 273). But Derrida figures the figure of chiasmus is the way to grasp the contradictions here: at one moment, he emphasizes "this point of the chiasmus where nothing seems to count but reciprocity," and yet the chiasm is "activity and passivity coupled," and also is what Derrida sees that Merleau-Ponty sees, "the crystallization of the impossible" (*On Touching* 215). In the face of the "wholly other," Derrida could give up. But he does not, and continues to try to conceive some form of imperfect but authentic intersubjectivity.

Hillis Miller, like Derrida, searches for the traces of community, or communities, especially for what seems like the shadow of a shadow after Auschwitz and the postmodern, because questioning the ontology of the touch questions all. It might be useful for a theory of suture to look briefly at his recent project to rethink community after Derrida's death, extending what had been their joint interest in the thought of Jean-Luc Nancy. To address very briefly some of the threads of this discussion, Miller reflects on Nancy's paradoxical notion of a community made up of radically "singular" and isolated subjects: "No solid ground for doing things with words is offered by the community joining a 'set, a group of "exposed" singularities that are wholly other to one another'" (*Conflagration* 23). In this setting, as Nancy sees it, "no transparent 'intersubjective' communication, no social bond, can be counted on to certify for me the sincerity of speech acts uttered by another person," and so speech acts—promises, marriage oaths, wills—can only be "self-generated and self-sustained," that is, "are a kind of lifting oneself by one's own bootstraps over that abyss to which Nancy and Blanchot give the name 'death'" (*Conflagration* 23).

In contrast to this paradigm, Miller suggests a notion of "communities," not "community," which are "overlapping and interrelated," "no one of which exists in total isolation from the others" (*Conflagration* 30). Throughout the issue is alterity and any access to language or conventions or narratives that might provide, not "transparent intersubjectivity," but some moderate degree of mediated, opaque, indirect, but not altogether misleading opening to the other's consciousness for subjects who live with other subjects.

To adapt Miller, alterity and chiasmus: these are the deep themes at stake in this study of suture and intersubjectivities. And here is its epilogue: after a hundred years of complexly indirect narration of these intersubjectivities, in the increasing difficulty of my symptomatic examples, what problematics look most important in the stories of possible/impossible communities? James's late novels were not the first to make use of suture's indirections—free indirect discourse can get pretty complicated in *Mansfield Park*—but James intensified and extended the over-the-shoulder strategies of free indirect discourse in an unprecedented degree. Obliqueness became an aesthetic of elaboration in James, perhaps as one current in the movement of what looking back we call modernism that shaded into postmodernism, as the core difficulty moved from the epistemological to the ontological, to echo Brian McHale once again. Indirect narration of intersubjectivities raised the difficulty of perceiving others and their experience of us beyond the epistemological (how to know) to the ontological (what is the nature of being in each loop of the chiasmus): what McHale calls "pluralizing the fictional world itself" ("Postmodern Narrative" 457). So the oblique became even more intricate and mediated.

I have traced versions of the oblique in film, fiction, and a play, noting how the gaps between and among subjects have become more difficult to bridge, so that the links among consciousnesses are more fragile, and the cure of the medicine/poison in the *komos* is even more miraculous than it was in Socrates' tale (remember that Derrida finds, or finds that Plato finds, some redemption in that assignment to drink the hemlock) ("Plato's Pharmacy" 126). In this coda, I'd like to look briefly at two recent examples of narrative practices that problematize the building of communities now. The first topic is selfhood in self-narration, and the second is telling the story of desire amidst the shambles of the master narrative. My text examples are not unique in the first years of this twenty-first century. In fact, they reflect strategies that recur in other works, and they allow a useful demonstration of how the conventions of suture still operate.

The self as fiction and the fictions of selfhood have been topics of important work in the last thirty years by scholars like Paul John Eakin, Leigh Gilmore, Sidonie Smith, and Julia Watson (and this work is the reason I have included self-writing in a book with "fiction" in its subtitle). The coherent narratives of a coherent self have fragmented for many reasons, as Smith and Watson summarize:

> Both the unified story and the coherent self are myths of identity. For there is no coherent "self" that predates stories about identity, about "who" one is.... We are always fragmented in time, taking a particular or provisional perspective on the moving targets of our pasts, addressing multiple and disparate audiences. (61)

Each of the elements of self-narration is fragile and fragmentary: memory, the body, conventions of narrative rhetorics, social spaces for the performance of self and story, the rhetoric of those spaces, "identity" as languages. Each of these elements also carries an ideological imprint, and Jeanette Winterson's *Why Be Happy When You Could Be Normal?* (2011) confesses to those traces in multiple ways. The themes of gender and class run through Winterson's story of growing up adopted in the working-class town of Accrington north of Manchester, as in her discovery of Oxford after the narrow rooms and shops of her North: "I had no idea that there could be such a beautiful city or places like the colleges, with quadrangles and lawns, and that sense of energetic quiet that I still find so seductive" (135). (The theme here seems primarily class, but gender looms as well if one remembers Virginia Woolf—whom Winterson mentions reading—and that Oxbridge beadle in *A Room of One's Own*.) Selfhood is especially fractured in much contemporary life writing under the pressures of ideology and all those uncertainties in self-writing as we now understand it. What happens to the narrative of subjects, and to the phenomenology of intersubjectivity amid all these moving pieces? And how might suture function in such a story?

For Winterson, the dominant principle for her story is the palimpsest (my word, not hers), the multiple layers of time and experience written on the surface of her tale. The principle applies initially to the shape of the story's *syuzhet*: "I told my version—faithful and invented, accurate and misremembered, shuffled in time" (6). Winterson refers here initially to her first, and autobiographical, novel, *Oranges Are Not the Only Fruit*, but also to the current text, with its extensively scrambled story line. Winterson cites a line from an earlier book, "'Everything is imprinted forever with what it once was,'" and describes her guiding perception: "the sense of something written over yes, but still distinct" (157). And here is the palimpsest method:

> Flash forward to 2007, and I have done nothing about finding my past. It isn't "my past," is it? I have written over it. I have recorded on top

of it. I have repainted it. Life is layers, fluid, unfixed, fragments. I could never write a story with a beginning, a middle and an end in the usual way because it felt untrue to me. That is why I write as I do and how I write as I do. It isn't a method; it's me. (156)

But time is not the only narrative element that gets written on top of its versions and repetitions (of abandonment and loss, for example). The self is "non-linear," and other selves are too, so that Winterson's narrator encounters others through a collage of her own experiences ("events separated by years lie side by side imaginatively and emotionally") and of the other's (153). Intersubjectivity and community are also fragmented and layered.

How deeply indirect has intersubjectivity become in *Why Be Happy*? Consciousness of others as subjectivities is a key element when a character narrator tells his or her story, as I discussed in *I Know That You Know That I Know* with the examples of *Moll Flanders* and *Great Expectations,* and the narrator's adoptions of the other's version of herself; sometimes the other's subsequent espousals (always partial) of one's gestured revisions—deep intersubjectivity, that is—become a major theme in Winterson. Adoption is especially fraught in a story about adoption, often adoption as violation (in Mrs. Winterson's version of her new child she "was a Devil baby" who cried all the time; Mrs. Winterson "had a thing that was all body" [20–21]). Adoption is always the long way around, though Winterson finds her way back to a kind of acceptance of family and mother ("[Mrs. Winterson] was a monster but she was my monster") (229). Incorporation of the other into one's consciousness is also oblique in this story, so the style of interconnection in *Why Be Happy* is widely separated loops of responses. For example, in writing a children's book, Winterson invents a "Creature Sawn in Two" and begins talking to her own "vicious disagreeable creature," but the communication is tricky because "her preferred responses were non sequiturs": "Our conversations were like two people using phrasebooks to say things neither understands; you think you asked the way to church, but it translates as 'I need a safety pin for my hamster'" (173–75). So espousals by the other of one's own body and story are oblique and distorted, as Mrs. Winterson rages over her daughter's first book and its versions of their life together, and Winterson replies, "I can't remember a time when I wasn't setting my story against hers" (7, 9). Yet somehow "we get our language back through the language of others" (9).

In *Why Be Happy,* suture works as a set of chiastic strategies to narrate intersubjectivity, tracing the recursive loops of response to response, or semi-response to semi-response, in the non sequiturs to adoptions. But this narrator foregrounds the barriers of gender and sexual identity, and class and family in such an extended way that readers can be forgiven for wondering what is left besides alterity. When Winterson writes about this story of "my beginnings" that "it is a true story but it is still a version," can she offer, at the end of her text, a partially defamiliarized story in response to an earlier story (Mrs. Winterson's) that is also a response to a yet earlier story (Jeanette's own first account in *Oranges*) (229)? If so, then the loops of stories become a version of another deeply sutured intersubjectivity.

Finally, a brief glance at the second problematic: narrating desire faces difficulties of fragmentation and diffusion similar to those of self-narration. As an example, Marc Webb's *(500) Days of Summer* (2010) confronts the loss of coherence provoked by confusions over master narratives and conventions for performing gender. At the beginning of the film (which occurs at the end of the story, on day 488 of 500), the narrator says, "This *is* a story of boy meets girl.... You should know upfront that it is not a love story" (2:05). Lacking the comforts of genre and the rhetorical conventions of gender, Tom flails around in the clichés of romantic comedy, in fact in a parody of those clichés, starting with the narrator's bass voice, so knowing and dominant. A fuller example is the argument after the bar fight; when Summer denies they have a "relationship," Tom explodes, "You're not the only one who gets a say in this, and I say we're a couple" (47:06). *He* wants commitment, in a Joseph-Andrews-like inversion of the convention. And his fundamental question throughout echoes across the ages: what does Summer want? He cannot answer, and she cannot. In the park scene that opens and semi-concludes the film, Tom asks why Summer danced romantically with him at Millie's wedding (no engagement ring: 1:05:40) when she was involved with someone else who became her fiancé by the rooftop party the following Friday (ring on her finger then). She answers, "Because I wanted to" (1:23:59). We know Tom's interpretive skills are sometimes inadequate—after all, this is the guy who (granted, as a boy) misread *The Graduate* as a romantic comedy—but Webb suggests neither character understands what drives their stories.

Genre is deeply confusing in this film because the controlling stories, especially the master narratives about gender and romance and power, no longer guide, at least in any conventional way. The stories now, or this one anyway, are full of non sequiturs and gaping holes. Mary Anne Doane observed, about the classical Hollywood "woman's film," "It is as though the insistent attempt at the inscription of female subjectivity and desire, within a phallocentrically organized discourse such as the classical Hollywood text, produced gaps and incoherences which the films can barely contain" ("The 'Woman's Film'" 69). Gaps and incoherences are perfect descriptions of the structure of this story and its characters. Summer's desire remains a mystery to Tom, and the film's scrambled *syuzhet* is a symptom of *his* sexual anxiety, of his hysteria.

Laura Mulvey diagnosed another aspect of the gender conventions of film form: classical narrative's "cinematic codes create a [masculine] gaze, a world and an object, thereby producing an illusion cut to the measure of [male] desire" (25).[1] Tom's gaze functions exactly in this way, typically looking at Summer sideways, in the necessarily oblique way that enables desire. The difference between the conventional Hollywood film that Mulvey describes and *(500) Days of Summer* is the film's foregrounding of Tom's self-delusions and the operation of his gaze. Home, for example, is simply a simulacrum, a set in an IKEA store, where he and Summer pretend, but the pretense is itself something of a pretend for Tom. In this case, the film is not the disease, but a diagnosis of the disease (as is mostly true of the Hitchcock films that Mulvey discusses in her famous essay, *Rear Window* and *Vertigo*).[2] The film distances itself from Tom's misunderstandings and self-deceptions. For example, Tom knows himself through masquerade, obliquely. When Summer and he first sleep together, he expresses his joy in the form of a music-and-dance number worthy of the Technicolor glories of *Singin' in the Rain*, and he expresses his despair when they break up by role-playing from Bergman and Antonioni films (figure E.1). When Tom sees himself as *The Seventh Seal*'s Knight playing chess, he does not recognize the defamiliarizing, over-the-top gesture of his fantasy. But Webb's implied viewer does. Desire for Tom (and its shadow of loss) are masquerade and obliqueness.

Suture works in several ways to diagram and foreground Tom's struggle to tell the story of desire (his and others'). Shot / reverse shot linkages often get collapsed in split-screen frames, with subjects and

---

[1]. Mulvey's essay (1975) was just the first in a long series of interventions over the subject of the gender of the gaze in film. A wonderful later example is E. Ann Kaplan's response in *Women and Film: Both Sides of the Camera* (1983), in which she asks, "Is the gaze male?" Another interesting essay in this conversation is Marian Keane's "A Close Look at Scopophilia: Mulvey, Hitchcock and *Vertigo*" (1986), which finds much of Mulvey's reasoning flawed.

[2]. Of course, Mulvey didn't argue that they were a diagnosis of the disease. The book that took that step forward in feminist film criticism was Tania Modleski's *The Women Who Knew Too Much: Hitchcock and Feminist Film Theory*.

FIGURE E.1. Tom plays Bergman's knight (*[500] Days of Summer*, 54:11)

objects of the gaze placed on either side of the shot, for example. One sequence labels one side of the frame "Expectations" and the other side "Reality," so that the screen presents Tom's fractured consciousness, divided between hope and disappointment. "Expectations" is on the left, "Reality" on the right, and the conventional Hollywood viewer reads from left to right, from illusion to disillusion. The split-screen phone call at 1:00:50 between Tom and McKenzie is another version of this kind of suture, with the added advantage of its witty, bromantic glance back at *Pillow Talk*. The film's editing captures how Tom and Summer remain opaque to each other, how one consciousness perceives the other and the other's perception of oneself in very limited ways. In that early and late park bench scene, Summer and Tom talk to each other, in two-shots that shift from left to right, imitating the action of shot/reverse shots, but including both faces in each shot means watching the oblique confront the oblique. Each looks at the other sideways, especially Tom, and neither understands the other.

This is the story Summer tells: "One day I woke up and I knew... what I was never sure of with you" (1:23:26). But what Summer knows now, and what she never knew about Tom, never gets clarified. She was reading *Dorian Gray* in a deli one day, a guy comes up to talk to her about it, and now they're married. Summer says, "It just happened" (1:23:59). Her desire is something of a conundrum to her, to Tom, and to the implied viewer of the film's scrambled editing. Does Tom move forward toward enlightenment, as apparently Summer does (at least she made a commitment)? Here the Fielding novel echo comes from *Tom Jones,* whose hero Tom, the son of Summer, continues his mock odyssey to find a home, journeying back to a post-Edenic Paradise Hall.[3] Webb's Tom seems to have moved beyond IKEA as home and is returning to architecture, his true profession. This latter-day mock-hero has also moved on from Summer to Autumn. So the counter for his story resets to "1": maybe the plot will repeat itself, or maybe things will be different this time. The loops of the chiasmus work both ways.

Suture directs us indirectly, in my argument, to the story of stories about the lives of others that we live with and near and not near, to stories about communities and their successes and their failures and mostly, of course, a combination of the two. Understanding how those stories navigate our closeness and distance is not easy, and as Hillis Miller and Nancy (and others like Levinas) know, alterity always looms in the gaps. Merleau-Ponty gives an intricately observed account of what is at stake here:

> Should a response respond too well to what I thought without having really said it—and suddenly there breaks forth evidence that yonder also, minute by minute, life is being lived; somewhere behind those eyes, behind those gestures, or rather before them, or again about them, coming from I know not what double ground of space, another private world shows through, through the fabric of my own, and for a moment I live in it; I am no more than the respondent for the interpellation that is made to me. To be sure, the least recovery of attention persuades me that this other who invades me is made only of my own substance: how could I conceive, precisely as *his, his* colors, *his* pain, *his* world, except as in accordance with the colors I see, the pains I have had, the world wherein I live? But at least my private world has ceased to be mine only; it is now the instrument which another plays. (*Visible* 11)

So the other that Merleau-Ponty experiences here is in one moment of skepticism "made only of my own substance," and yet at another

---

3. This approach to *Tom Jones* is indebted to *Occasional Form: Henry Fielding and the Chains of Circumstance,* by J. Paul Hunter, who writes about Tom in the shadow of Homer (the epigraph for Fielding's novel is from *The Odyssey*), "*Tom Jones* engages a comic epic vision—which does not ask Tom to be Ulysses but only a modern imitation of a modern version of his lesser son" (the modern version—in 1749—was Fenelon's *Telemaque*) (139).

moment has so invaded his subjectivity that "my private world has ceased to be mine only." This almost miraculous vision, "coming from I know not what double ground of space," when "another private world shows through, through the fabric of my own," encapsulates Merleau-Ponty's hopefulness, and so is a good place to conclude. I promised that this argument would end with a comic turn toward, if not belief, at least belief in belief.

Communities are difficult to found and breathe life into and reform. The strategies of suture that tell their stories embody those difficulties, and honor the efforts of those who can sustain.

APPENDIX

The Ricochet Effect

Narrative Theory and Boundary Ethics

Since eavesdropping is a generic feature of much children's literature, narrative theory has begun to address it (eavesdropping) and the ethics of boundaries as children's literature has become a more deeply theorized subfield of literary studies in recent years. In this appendix I want briefly to address the theoretical contexts for the narratological and ethical issues here, especially as suggested by my grid for the ricochet effect. This appendix will be useful for readers who might want the specifics in the theoretical controversy that has swirled around Barrie's boundary crossing.

Recent narratological theory has addressed the phenomenon of what U. C. Knoepflmacher and Mitzi Myers call "crosswriting" in children's stories, which is "a dialogical mix of older and younger voices [that] occurs in texts too often read as univocal" ("From the Editors" vii). Knoepflmacher and Myers offer one approach to this polyvocality: they stress "creative cooperation" among these voices, whereas my model of eavesdropping amidst the ricochet of competing stories is less optimistic (vii). But one useful result of this work has been to problematize artificial boundaries between "child" and "adult" as well as overly simple definitions of those words. *Transcending Boundaries,* the title of one collection of scholarly essays, points to its interest in the new possibilities of a more fluid sense of audience for "children's literature," especially when allied in the last fifty years or so to a kind of postmodernism that seeks to complicate traditional categories. And the benefits for mainstream narrative of this fluidity are unmistakable. Brian Richardson has identified the rich possibilities of "multiple implied readers" in a single text for a variety of rhetorical, often overtly ideological purposes, since "political censorship produces its share of double codings"

(259). Unlocking these codes requires, of course, an expert audience, authorial and real-world.

Barbara Wall also revised Seymour Chatman's diagram for narrative structure in *The Narrator's Voice: The Dilemma of Children's Literature*, and my revision resembles hers. Wall multiplies kinds of consciousness also, identifying two narratees in a children's text (child and adult), two implied readers (child and adult), and two real readers (child and adult). Wall outlines various relationships among these personae, from "single address" by the narrator to "double" and "dual address," but she is most critical of Barrie's "double" address to two narratees, adults and children, because it is unstable and "untrustworthy" (22–25). Perry Nodelman also addresses this exfoliating narrative structure in children's literature in *The Hidden Adult: Defining Children's Literature* but draws different conclusions than Wall does. Nodelman, for example, sees various kinds of "shadow texts" at work in stories written for children to read or hear, shadows that real-world children will be "somewhat aware of" cast by the writer's unconscious, a culture's ideology, even by the implied child reader in the text as a fiction that seeks to satisfy the desire of the adult reader (real-world and implied) for a dream-child to guide, even to intimidate, the real-world child at his or her side (Nodelman 204–5, 63).

The issue of eavesdropping crops up well before these recent writers, too. Per Krogh Hansen cites Hans Christian Andersen's awareness of the two age groups in his audience, whose relationship he also figured with an overhearing image: "[The oral presentation] was told for children, but also the older should be able to listen" (Hansen and Lundholt 101; also cited in Richardson 259). Hansen sees in Andersen's characteristic stance his attention to "perhaps the hidden adult narratee, listening to the story and envying the child" (Hansen and Lundholt 116). But here the adult's eavesdropping role respects the separate experience of the child. In these examples, I find some kind of boundary still at work between the younger child audience and the adult eavesdropping, whether as implied or real audiences. Other nineteenth-century observers noticed this phenomenon, using other images to figure the "over the head" signal from narrator to different groups, usually older readers, once again implied or real. Barbara Wall quotes an essay from 1855 by William Calder Roscoe for an early example: "Many books ostensibly written for children are spoiled because the author always has a side glance at a wider audience. The possible verdict of an adult reader exercises a disturbing influence on his work" (20).

Where *is* the adult in this narrative labyrinth? One answer has been to look at the adult's role in the flesh-and-blood audience. Perry Nodelman, for example, writes about the function of children's literature for the adults who write, edit, and market them; it articulates "specifically adults' ideas about what children should be" (63). Nodelman here echoes Jacqueline Rose's claim that in some degree the major audience for children's literature is the adults who write and read it because those adults need to hear children hearing certain stories, mostly edited to avoid the anxieties of those adults. In this context, says Rose, "innocence [is] not a property of childhood, but ... of adult desire" (xv). What traces of this adult desire surface inside the text written for children? Who reads them in what ways? How deeply are they buried?

Those traces are readable in Barrie because the adult audience is not "hidden," to use Perry Nodelman's word (and maybe this transparency is another reason Barrie's Peter Pan tales are not "children's literature"). Outside the text, adults and children (usually that prepubescent middle-childhood child) are both in the theater, on stage, or sitting together with their book, watching each other listen. Innocence is already a performance, defamiliarized in complex ways at each level of audience for those who can understand the codes and signs of the performance. Most problematically, genuine animosity sometimes gets aimed at children, as in the novella's version of the "Do you believe in fairies?" sequence, when Peter pleads with his audience, "Clap your hands; don't let Tink die" (I cite the original as laid out on the page for the paragraphing emphasis):

> Many clapped.
>> Some didn't.
>> A few little beasts hissed. . . .
>> [Tink] never thought of thanking those who believed, but she would have liked to get at the ones who had hissed. (*Peter Pan* 185)

Barbara Wall offers the most unsentimental close reading of this narrator's multiple address to multiple audiences. In this scene, Wall says, "There is no suggestion of a 'wink.' The narrator exhibits, if momentarily, feelings of dislike towards a narratee he suddenly envisages as threatening" (28).

And so the ethical issues of these boundaries arise. A new sense of multiple voices and hybrid forms seems to some theorists a move toward freedom, toward the openness and creativity of postmodernism, perhaps including a new fluidity of gender identities. Carrie Wasinger, for example, celebrates the "slippage between narrative categories [that] encourages readers to identify with the child-figure's androgyny," and indeed, "invites the reader into a fantasy of his/her *own* indeterminacy" (223). Lots of boundaries have indeed moved or disappeared since 1911, and so mild profanity invades PG-13 movies, and then PG. Can *The Tigger Movie* be far behind? Even the most Bakhtinian theorists of children's literature, however, like Perry Nodelman, who promotes the multiplicity of voices in children's texts, or James Kincaid, who celebrates Peter Pan as the principle of play, seem albeit grudgingly to identify some buffer zone beyond which younger children (again, whether in implied audiences or real ones) should not hear stories about sexual intimacy, or about abandonment, violence, violation, and despair.

Peter Hollindale is the other critic who recognizes, minus some of our narratological language, Barrie's "layers of narrative address" and how unstable their alignments are (*Peter and Wendy* x). Hollindale links these instabilities of narrative boundaries to Jacqueline Rose's claims that Barrie's violation of genre protocols amounts to "molestation" of the (real) child reader. But Hollindale thinks Rose is "hypersensitive" about such boundaries, many of which "have largely fallen since 1900," and as a result Barrie is "very much a twentieth century writer for children" (xxiv). Hollindale admits that the adult reader needs to apply "some deft editing" when reading aloud to children, but the examples he chooses are safer moments of confusing parody or sentimental whimsy, not the moments of aggression against younger readers, or the moments of sadness or cynicism about family or erotic life (xxi). He ignores the really dangerous bullets ricocheting in the parlor.

A productive, liberating fluidity in addressing adult and child audiences thus runs into an ethical barrier. William Golding, whose *Lord of the Flies* is specifically a rewriting of Barrie's beloved *The Coral Island* and to some degree of *Peter Pan,* suggested in 1962 that children simply are not in the room with adults any more: "Perhaps in the twentieth century the sort of fables we must construct are not for children on any level" (*Hot Gates* 86). Adrienne Kertzer also describes limits to that liberating fluidity: her example is the way Isabella Leitner rewrote her Holocaust memoir, *Fragments of Isabella* (1978), for smaller children. The new version pays a price in "the erasure of the anger, fury and grief of the daughter-survivor who cannot forget the murder of her mother in the gas chambers of Auschwitz" (172). Kertzer, interestingly, does not meditate on the younger audience for this new, edited version or on the rhetoric of the editing, but mourns the losses it imposes, she believes, on the next volume Leitner wrote for adults, as if she developed a taste for retreating from the brutal honesty of her earlier adult memoirs. That is, Kertzer's interest lies with the adult audience and the depth (or lack thereof) in its reading experience. Leitner is more conservative than Barrie, because she censors her own tale rather than confront her young audience with an account of her mother's murder at Auschwitz.

The primary beneficiaries of this new freedom for children's literature to cross narrative boundaries seem to me to be the older child audience, what people now call "YA" or "Young Adult" readers, and the adult audiences who want to play the roles of younger readers, perhaps nostalgically remembering (or thinking they remember) their reading experiences at age eight. Some authors, like Jules Feiffer or Toni Morrison, who primarily address adult audiences, have adopted a different stance to address younger audiences, sometimes very successfully, but these texts do not typically breach the rules of an almost unspoken decorum about tones and content for younger children. My daughter began listening to Feiffer's *I Lost My Bear* with delight when she was about three, and at ten read it to herself with equal, if different, delight, but in neither case did she or I feel targeted as readers (implied or flesh and blood) by a narrator's anger or adult knowingness.

It is this crisscrossing of audience boundaries that my diagram and the concept of the ricochet effect address. It may be worth noting that commentary on these issues sometimes conflates levels of narrative form. For example, when Hansen above comments on "the hidden adult narratee," the adult is not a narratee in the text, but a member of the authorial audience, the text's implied reader who understands the conventions of the tale and the innocence of the child as narratee and narrative audience. Further, real-world membership in these audiences is complex: it's too easy to simplify age assumptions, as if all adults understand literary and cultural conventions and ironies, when in fact adults may belong to both narrative and authorial audiences in different degrees and for different topics. And none of us knows just when "younger" children become "older," because the process occurs at different times and in different stages for different children. Some "younger" children will understand parts of Barrie's multiple codes, and many will not. Remember Toni Morrison's account in *The Bluest Eye* of children who, not understanding their words when eavesdropping on adults, "listen for the truth in timbre":

> Their conversation is like a gentled wicked dance: sound meets sound, curtsies, shimmies, and retires. Another sound enters but is upstaged by still another.... We do not, cannot know the meanings of all their words, for we are nine and ten years old. So we watch their faces, their hands, their feet, and listen for truth in timbre. (10)

However imprecise the labels, and at whatever narrative level the age differences apply (to narratees, to narrative or authorial audiences, to flesh-and-blood readers and viewers), at some point the boundary issue becomes acute especially for the younger flesh-and-blood child audience.

Barrie was willing to violate the no-fly zone that separates younger children's audiences from older audiences, especially in *Peter and Wendy*. His address to multiple audiences has occasioned the strongest ethical criticism of Barrie's narrator, because the address to the older audience is not soundproofed for the younger one, and the eavesdropping between them can create various effects, from the careless and irresponsible to the coyly seductive to the covertly aggressive and even abusive.

In general, critical responses to these narrative "confusions" or boundary crossings in Barrie have taken three directions. One is to focus on the real adult reader with the cultural training and perspective to understand gender indeterminacy, issues of class and family structure, complexities of erotic allegiances, and the wounds of abandonment. The second is to focus on a child reader who either simply does not understand these matters, or who *will* at some level, and will flee or repress the terrors they evoke. The first reader joins the authorial implied audience, and the second joins the narrative implied audience, at least initially.

A third path has been to reduce the complexity of the characters Barrie constructs. Perry Nodelman offers an example of this last strategy when he oversimplifies Peter Pan by seeing Peter's childhood as "asexual," as articulating "a nostalgia for childhood as a place before or beyond sexual desire," an adult version of which Nodelman argues that Eve Kosofsky Sedgwick identified in Barrie's *Sentimental Tommy* (1896), written just before *Tommy and Grizel* (1900) and thus a reasonable context for Barrie's conception and writing of *Peter Pan* between 1900 and 1904 (Nodelman 275). But in fact, Sedgwick does not see Barrie's Tommy novels as at all "before or beyond sexual desire," and such an approach would be a serious evasion of what is at stake in the Peter Pan tales. Instead, Sedgwick argues that the Tommy novels are complex articulations of homosexual panic that are almost as painful as the novella that is her focus in that chapter, Henry James's "The Beast in the Jungle." Tommy Sandys is a tormented and tormenting contradiction who pursues his beloved Grizel but is unable to consummate their marriage. Like May Bartram, Grizel seeks an impossible erotic relation: "He did not love her. 'Not as I love him,' [Grizel] said to herself. 'Not as married people ought to love'" (*Tommy and Grizel* 468). To see Barrie's Peter (or Tommy) as asexual is to miss Barrie's rich overtones about this "cocky" (*Peter and Wendy* 91) character's confused search for "female companionship" (95), his yearning to complete the story of "Cinderella," and his interest in what it is, exactly, that Tinker Bell and Tiger Lily want from him: that is, his repeated approaches toward and retreats from erotic implications. It is exactly this pattern of approach and retreat that Sedgwick found so symptomatic of homosexual terror (199). It is a pattern that links Tommy and Peter, but not at all as figures that have transcended sexuality, but quite the reverse. And this pattern of approach and retreat has a thematic echo in Barrie's use of eavesdropping and the ricochet effect.)

We need to confront Jacqueline Rose's view on its own ethical terms, admitting the resonances of the deep wounds and losses in erotic and family life that sound throughout the Pan stories. *Molestation* is the wrong word now, as I wrote in chapter 4, because it implies a sexual agenda in the speaker, but Barrie's narrative complexities do invite younger children as well as older children and adults to overhear sad, angry, and painful voices. Barrie's narrative choices, it should be clear by now, are not confusions or mistakes, nor do they manifest what Carrie Wasinger calls "the collapse of distinct narrative categories" (223). To the contrary, Barrie's narrator is a profound and specific construct, with both formal and thematic coherence, and not only in *Peter and Wendy*. The same boundary issues appear elsewhere in his Pan stories, especially in *Peter Pan in Kensington Gardens* when read in its original context as stories told to a little boy inside *The Little White Bird*. Rose is excellent on this latter example, where "sexuality ... operates in a similar mode of difficulty and confusion" (25): "similar" in its function in the inserted Pan stories and in *The Little White Bird*'s frame tale.

So, Rose was right, if narratologically imprecise. My effort has been to provide a framework to talk specifically about who is overhearing whom and when, from narratees inside the diegesis, to implied readers narrative (naïve) or authorial (sophisticated), to flesh-and-blood audiences. Eavesdropping is not new, indeed, as we have seen above, but Barrie's work, especially his Pan prose, may be almost unique in its combination of voices without boundaries or guardrails for younger children. Given the fact that Barrie had never before written stories for children, perhaps this coincidence of whimsy and anger is almost an accident. That explanation would work for *The Little White Bird* (1902), but it serves less well for *Peter and Wendy* (1911), by which time Barrie was fully aware of the children in *Peter Pan*'s audiences.

It's useful to compare Barrie's narrative settings with the setting in which Bruno Bettelheim said children at about age five begin to hear fairy tales from their parents with more understanding. For Bettelheim, fairy tales are at their core about the deep terrors of a child's life—"deep despair, escape from some great danger"—and most terrifying of all, about that fear than which "there is no greater in life ... —that we will be deserted, left all alone" (143, 145). And "the younger we are, the more excruciating is our anxiety when we feel deserted" (145). In Bettelheim's view, the purpose of the tale and its telling is always consolation for the child, and here "the ultimate consolation [is] that we will never be deserted" (145). The storytelling setting, he writes, is always "interpersonal," shaped by the parent-figure to console the child after a journey into the darkest fears (151). And the darkest fear of all is the core anxiety of *Peter Pan*, the terror of abandonment, of the Boys who were Lost.

What is the source of this anxiety in *Peter Pan*? Did Peter choose abandonment or not? Is the way he always returns to Neverland a confirmation of playful freedom, as some writers we've cited believe, or is it a sad, even grim eternal return, a *Groundhog Day* with no deliverance? And what is in fact Barrie's narrator's tone toward those listeners who really deserve to be smacked? Now we can measure a little more precisely the arcs of the ricochets of anger and sadness and the ethical boundaries crossed by Barrie's "cross-writing." The final choice in *Peter and Wendy* is particularly clear when we look at the last line of *When Wendy Grew Up* (a kind of Act VI to *Peter Pan*), performed once in 1908 and unpublished until 1956, when Wendy thinks ahead if *her* daughter has a daughter who could fly away with Peter: "And in this way I may go on for ever and ever, Nana, so long as children are young and innocent" (*Peter Pan* 163).

But in 1911 in *Peter and Wendy*, concluding a now-even-more-famous story, Barrie's narrator revises this sentence into a form that no one will have read before but one that will also become famous, with a new, deeply ambiguous final adjective: "And thus it will go on as long as children are gay and innocent and heartless." There is little consolation for the audience of alert—even if heartless—children or of alert adults in *Peter Pan*. The cycle of the lost will continue in all its ambiguity.

WORKS CITED

(500) Days of Summer. Dir. Marc Webb. Screenplay by Scott Neustadter and Michael Weber. Perf. Zooey Deschanel and Joseph Gordon-Levitt. Twentieth Century Fox, 2009.

Ackerman, Robert. *The Myth and Ritual School: J. G. Frazier and the Cambridge Ritualists*. New York: Garland, 1991.

Ahmed, Sara. *Queer Phenomenology: Orientations, Objects, Others*. Durham: Duke University Press, 2006.

Armstrong, Paul B. *The Challenge of Bewilderment: Understanding and Representation in James, Conrad and Ford*. Ithaca: Cornell University Press, 1987.

———. "Phenomenology." *The Johns Hopkins Guide to Literary Theory and Criticism*. 2nd ed. Ed. Michael Groden, Martin Kreisworth, and Imre Szeman. Baltimore: Johns Hopkins University Press, 2005. 731–35.

———. *The Phenomenology of Henry James*. Chapel Hill: University of North Carolina Press, 1983.

———. *Play and the Politics of Reading: The Social Uses of Modernist Form*. Ithaca: Cornell University Press, 2005.

Austen, Jane. *Emma*. Ed. Stephen Parrish. New York: W. W. Norton, 1972.

———. *Pride and Prejudice*. Ed. Vivian Jones. London: Penguin Books, 2003.

Bakhtin, Mikhail. *The Dialogic Imagination: Four Essays*. Ed. Michael Holquist. Trans. Caryl Emerson and Michael Holquist. Austin: The University of Texas Press, 1981.

———. *Rabelais and His World*. Trans. H. Iswolsky. Bloomington: Indiana University Press, 1984.

Banfield, Anne. *Unspeakable Sentences: Narration and Representation in the Language of Fiction*. Boston: Routledge, 1982.

Barber, C. L. *Shakespeare's Festive Comedy*. Princeton: Princeton University Press, 1959.

Barrie, J. M. *Alice Sit-By-the-Fire*. 1905. New York: Scribner, 1919.

———. *The Little White Bird*. 1902. London: Hodder and Stoughton, 1913.

---. *Peter Pan in Kensington Gardens / Peter and Wendy*. Ed. Peter Hollindale. Oxford: Oxford University Press, 1991.

---. *Peter Pan and Other Plays*. Ed. Peter Hollindale. Oxford: Oxford University Press, 1995.

---. Preface. *The Coral Island*. 1913. *Peter Pan*. Ed. Anne Hiebert Alton. Peterborough: Broadview Editions, 2011. 380–83.

---. *Sentimental Tommy*. 1896. New York: Scribners, n.d.

---. *Tommy and Grizel*. New York: Scribners, 1900.

Bazin, Andre. *What is Cinema?* Vol. 1. Trans. Hugh Gray. Berkeley: University of California Press, 1967.

Bell, Millicent. *Meaning in Henry James*. Cambridge: Harvard University Press, 1991.

Bettelheim, Bruno. *The Uses of Enchantment*. New York: Random House, 1975.

Birkin, Andrew. *J. M. Barrie and the Lost Boys*. 1979. New Haven: Yale University Press, 2003.

Bolton, Matthew. "The Rhetoric of Intermediality: Adapting Means, Ends, and Ethics in *Atonement*." *Diegesis* 2.1 (2013): 23–53.

Bordwell, David. *Making Meaning: Inference and Rhetoric in the Interpretation of Cinema*. Cambridge: Harvard University Press, 1989.

---. *Narration in the Fiction Film*. Madison: University of Wisconsin Press, 1985.

Brooks, Peter. *The Melodramatic Imagination: Balzac, Henry James and the Mode of Excess*. New Haven: Yale University Press, 1976.

Browne, Nick. "The Spectator-in-the-Text: The Rhetoric of *Stagecoach*." *Film Quarterly* 29 (1975): 26–38.

Brownell, W. C. Rev. of *The Portrait of a Lady*, by Henry James. Repr. in *The Portrait of a Lady*. Ed. Robert D. Bamberg. New York: Norton, 1995. 660–64.

Butler, Christopher. *Postmodernism: A Very Short Introduction*. Oxford: Oxford University Press, 2002.

Butte, George. *I Know That You Know That I Know: Narrating Subjects from "Moll Flanders" to "Marnie."* Columbus: The Ohio State University Press, 2004.

Cameron, Sharon. *Thinking in Henry James*. Chicago: University of Chicago Press, 1989.

Carroll, Noel. *Theorizing the Moving Image*. Cambridge: Cambridge University Press, 1996.

Cavell, Stanley. *Contesting Tears: The Hollywood Melodrama of the Unknown Woman*. Chicago: University of Chicago Press, 1996.

---. *Pursuits of Happiness: The Hollywood Comedy of Remarriage*. Cambridge: Harvard University Press, 1981.

---. *The World Viewed: Reflections on the Ontology of Film*. Enlarged ed. Cambridge: Harvard University Press, 1979.

Chanter, Tina. "Wild Meaning: Luce Irigaray's Reading of Merleau-Ponty." *Chiasms: Merleau-Ponty's Notion of Flesh*. Ed. Fred Evans and Leonard Lawlor. Albany: State University of New York Press, 2000. 219–36.

Chatman, Seymour. *Coming to Terms*. Ithaca: Cornell University Press, 1990.

---. *Story and Discourse*. Ithaca: Cornell University Press, 1978.

Citizen Kane. Dir. Orson Welles. Screenplay by Henry Mankiewicz and Orson Welles. RKO, 1941. Warner Home Video, 2011.

Coats, Karen. "Child-Hating: *Peter Pan* in the Context of Victorian Hatred." *J. M. Barrie's Peter Pan In and Out of Time*. Ed. Donna White and C. Anita Tarr. Lanham: Scarecrow Press, 2006. 3–22.

Coen, Ethan, and Joel Coen. *Raising Arizona: The Screenplay*. New York: St. Martin's, 1988.

Cohen-Solal, Annie. *Sartre: A Life*. Trans. Anna Cancogni. New York: Pantheon Books, 1987.

Cohn, Dorrit. *Transparent Minds*. Princeton: Princeton University Press, 1978.

Cornford, Francis Macdonald. *The Origins of Attic Comedy*. 1914. Ed. T. H. Gaster. Ann Arbor: University of Michigan Press, 1993.

Dastur, Francoise. "World, Flesh, Vision." *Chiasms: Merleau-Ponty's Notion of Flesh*. Ed. Fred Evans and Leonard Lawlor. Albany: State University of New York Press, 2000. 23–50.

Davidson, Jim. "The Making of *Nothing But a Man*." *CommonQuest: The Magazine of Black/Jewish Relations* 3 (1998): 1–14.

Dayan, Daniel. "The Tutor-Code of Classical Cinema." *Film Quarterly* 28 (1974): 22–31.

Derrida, Jacques. *On Touching—Jean-Luc Nancy*. Trans. Christine Irizarry. Stanford: Stanford University Press, 2005.

———. "Plato's Pharmacy." *Dissemination*. Trans. Barbara Johnson. Chicago: University of Chicago Press, 1981. 61–171.

———. "Structure, Sign and Play in the Discourse of the Human Sciences." *The Structuralist Controversy*. Ed. Richard Macksey and Eugene Donato. Baltimore: Johns Hopkins University Press, 1972. 247–65.

Dixon, Wheeler Winston. *It Looks at You: The Returned Gaze of Cinema*. Albany: State University of New York, 1995.

Doane, Mary Ann. "Film and Masquerade: Theorising the Female Spectator." *Film Theory and Criticism*. 4th ed. Ed. Gerald Mast, Leo Braudy, and Marshall Cohen. New York and Oxford: Oxford University Press, 1992. 758–72.

———. "The 'Woman's Film': Possession and Address." *Re-Vision: Essays in Feminist Film Criticism*. Ed. Mary Ann Doane, Patricia Mellencamp, and Linda Williams. Frederick: University Publications of America, 1984. 67–82.

Doyle, Laura. *Bodies of Resistance: New Phenomenologies of Politics, Agency and Culture*. Evanston: Northwestern University Press, 2001.

Egan, Michael. "The Neverland as Id: Barrie, *Peter Pan*, and Freud." *Children's Literature* 10 (1982): 37–55.

Eisenstein, Sergei. *The Eisenstein Reader*. Trans. Richard Taylor and William Powell. Ed. Richard Taylor. London: British Film Institute, 1998.

Erasmus, Desiderius. *The Praise of Folly and Other Writings*. Trans. and ed. Robert M. Adams. New York: W. W. Norton, 1960.

Evans, Fred, and Leonard Lawlor. "Introduction: The Value of the Flesh." *Chiasms: Merleau-Ponty's Notion of Flesh*. Ed. Fred Evans and Leonard Lawlor. Albany: State University of New York Press, 2000. 1–20.

Freud, Sigmund. *Jokes and Their Relation to the Unconscious.* Trans. James Strachey. New York: W. W. Norton, 1960.

Gawande, Atul. *Complications.* New York: Henry Holt, 2002.

Genette, Gerard. *Narrative Discourse.* Trans. Jane Lewin. Ithaca: Cornell University Press, 1980.

Gilmore, Richard. "*Raising Arizona* as an American Comedy." *The Philosophy of the Coen Brothers.* Ed. Mark T. Conard. Lexington: University of Kentucky Press, 2009. 7–26.

Girard, Rene. *The Scapegoat.* Trans. Yvonne Freccero. Baltimore: The Johns Hopkins University Press, 1986.

Gledhill, Christine. "The Melodramatic Field: An Investigation." *Home Is Where the Heart Is.* Ed. Christine Gledhill. London: British Film Institute, 1987. 5–39.

Goffman, Erving. *Stigma: Notes on the Management of Spoiled Identity.* New York: Simon and Schuster, 1963.

The Golden Bowl. Dir. James Cellan Jones. Screenplay by Jack Pulman. Perf. Cyril Cusak, Gayle Hunnicutt, and Barry Morse. 1972. *The Henry James Collection.* Disc 5. BBC Worldwide, 2009.

The Golden Bowl. Dir. James Ivory. Screenplay by Ruth Prawer Jhabvala. Perf. Nick Nolte, Uma Thurman, and Kate Beckinsale. Lionsgate, 2000.

Golding, William. *The Hot Gates and Other Occasional Pieces.* New York: Harcourt, Brace, 1965.

Gopnik, Adam. "The Real Work: Modern Magic and the Meaning of Life." *The New Yorker* 17 March 2008. 62–69.

Gubar, Marah. "On Not Defining Children's Literature." *PMLA* 126.1 (2011): 209–16.

Gunn, Daniel. "Free Indirect Discourse and Narrative Authority in *Emma.*" *Narrative* 12 (2004): 35–54.

Halberstam, Judith. "The Transgender Gaze in *Boys Don't Cry.*" *Screen* 42 (2001): 294–98.

Hammond, N. G. L., and H. H. Scullard, eds. *The Oxford Classical Dictionary.* 2nd ed. Oxford: Oxford University Press, 1970.

Hansen, Per Krogh, and Marianne Lundholt, eds. *When We Get to the End: Towards a Narratology of the Fairy Tales of Hans Christian Andersen.* University Press of Southern Denmark, 2005.

Hardy, Thomas. *The Complete Poems.* Ed. James Gibson. New York: Macmillan, 1976.

Hatley, James. "Recursive Incarnation and Chiasmic Flesh." *Chiasms: Merleau-Ponty's Notion of Flesh.* Ed. Fred Evans and Leonard Lawlor. Albany: State University of New York, 2000. 237–50.

Hawthorn, Jeremy. *The Reader as Peeping Tom: Non-Reciprocal Gazing in Narrative Fiction and Film.* Columbus: The Ohio State University Press, 2014.

Heath, Stephen. "Notes on Suture." *Screen* 18 (1978): 48–76.

Hebdige, Dick. *Hiding in the Light.* London: Routledge, 1988.

———. *Subculture: The Meaning of Style.* London: Routledge, 1979.

Hibbs, Thomas S. "The Human Comedy Perpetuates Itself: Nihilism and Comedy in Coen Neo-Noir." *The Philosophy of the Coen Brothers.* Ed. Mark T. Conard. Lexington: University of Kentucky Press, 2009. 27–40.

Higson, Andrew. *English Heritage, English Cinema*. New York: Oxford University Press, 2003.

Hill, Rodney. "Small Things Considered: *Raising Arizona* and *Of Mice and Men*." *Post-Script: Essays in Film and the Humanities* 8 (1989): 18–27.

Holmes, Martha Stoddard. "Peter Pan and the Possibilities of Child Literature." *Second Star to the Right: Peter Pan in the Popular Imagination*. Ed. Allison Kavey and Lester Friedman. New Brunswick: Rutgers University Press, 2009. 132–50.

Hunter, J. Paul. *Occasional Form: Henry Fielding and the Chains of Circumstance*. Baltimore: Johns Hopkins University Press, 1975.

Hutcheon, Linda. *The Politics of Postmodernism*. London: Routledge, 1989.

———. *A Theory of Adaptation*. New York: Routledge, 2006.

Ian, Marcia. "How to Do Things with Words: Making Language Immaterial in *The Wings of the Dove*." *Henry James on Stage and Screen*. Ed. John R. Bradley. Basingstoke and New York: Palgrave, 2000. 212–39.

The Innocents. Dir. Jack Clayton. Screenplay by Truman Capote. Perf. Deborah Kerr and Michael Redgrave. Twentieth Century Fox, 1961. Criterion DVD, 2006.

Irigary, Luce. "The Invisible of the Flesh: A Reading of Mearleau-Ponty, *The Visible and the Invisible*, 'The Intertwining—The Chiasm.'" *An Ethics of Sexual Difference*. Trans. C. Burke and G. C. Gill. Ithaca: Cornell University Press, 1993. 151–84.

Jack, R. D. S. *The Road to the Never Land*. 1991. Glasgow: Humming Earth, 2010.

James, Henry. *The Ambassadors*. Ed. Harry Levin. London: Penguin, 2003.

———. *The Complete Plays of Henry James*. Ed. Leon Edel. London: Hart-Davis, 1949.

———. *The Golden Bowl*. Ed. Virginia Smith. Oxford: Oxford University Press, 1983.

———. *Letters*. Vol. 4. Ed. Leon Edel. Cambridge: Harvard University Press, 1984.

———. *What Maisie Knew*. Ed. Paul Theroux. London: Penguin, 1985.

———. *The Wings of the Dove*. Ed. John Bayley. London: Penguin, 2003.

James, Ian. *The Fragmentary Demand: An Introduction to the Philosophy of Jean-Luc Nancy*. Stanford: Stanford University Press, 2006.

Jameson, Frederic. "Postmodernism, or the Cultural Logic of Late Capitalism." *New Left Review* 146 (1984): 53–92.

Jack, R. D. S. *The Road to the Never Land*. Aberdeen: Aberdeen University Press, 1991.

Jeong, Seung-Hoon. *Cinematic Interfaces: Film Theory After New Media*. New York: Routledge, 2013.

Kaiser, Walter. *Praisers of Folly: Erasmus, Rabelais, Shakespeare*. Cambridge: Harvard University Press, 1963.

Kaplan, E. Ann. *Women and Film: Both Sides of the Camera*. New York: Methuen, 1983.

Kavey, Alison. Introduction. *Second Star to the Right: Peter Pan in the Popular Imagination*. Ed. Alison Kavey and Lester Friedman. New Brunswick: Rutgers University Press, 2009. 1–12.

Kaye, Richard A. "Portraits of Lady Chatterleys: Jamesian Triangles, Lawrencian Eros and the Triumph of Cinematic Adaptation in *The Wings of the Dove*." *Henry James on Stage and Screen*. Ed. John R. Bradley. Basingstoke and New York: Palgrave, 2000. 240–60.

Keane, Marian E. "A Close Look at Scopophilia: Mulvey, Hitchcock and *Vertigo*." *A Hitchcock Reader*. Ed. Marshall Deutelbaum. New York: Wiley, 2009. 234–60.

Kertzer, Adrienne. "'What Happened?' The Holocaust Memories of Isabella Leitner." *Transcending Boundaries: Writing for a Dual Audience of Children and Adults*. Ed. Sandra Beckett, New York: Garland, 1999. 167–82.

Kincaid, James. *Child-Loving: The Erotic Child and Victorian Literature*. New York: Routledge, 1992.

Knoepflmacher, U. C. "Children's Texts and the Grown-up Reader." *The Cambridge Companion to Children's Literature*. Ed. M. O. Grenby and Andrea Immel. Cambridge: Cambridge University Press, 2009. 159–73.

———, and Mitzi Myers. "From the Editors: 'Cross-Writing' and the Reconceptualizing of Children's Literary Studies." *Children's Literature: Special Issue on Cross-Writing Child and Adult*. New Haven: Yale University Press, 1997. vii–xvi.

Lacan, Jacques. "The Mirror Stage as Formative of the Function of the I." *Ecrits: A Selection*. 1966. Trans. Alan Sheridan. New York: W. W. Norton, 1977. 1–7.

Last Year at Marienbad. Dir. Alain Resnais. Screenplay by Alain Robbe-Grillet. Perf. Delphine Seyrig and Georgio Albertazzi. 1961. Fox Lorber, 1999.

Lawrence, D. H. *Women in Love*. New York: The Viking Press, 1960.

Leavis, F. R. *The Great Tradition*. 1948. Harmondsworth: Penguin, 1966.

Lentricchia, Frank. *After the New Criticism*. Chicago: University of Chicago Press, 1980.

Levinas, Emmanuel. "Intersubjectivity: Notes on Merleau-Ponty." Ed. Michael Smith. *Ontology and Alterity in Merleau-Ponty*. Ed. Galen Johnson and Michael Smith. Evanston: Northwestern University Press, 1990. 51–66.

———. *Totality and Infinity: An Essay on Exteriority*. Trans. A. Lingis. Pittsburgh: Duquesne University Press, 1969.

Lyotard, Jean-Francois. *The Postmodern Condition: A Report on Knowledge*. Trans. G. Bennington and B. Massumi. Minneapolis: University of Minnesota Press, 1984.

Mackail, Denis. *Barrie: The Story of J. M. B.* New York: Scribners, 1941.

Maltby, Paul. *Dissident Postmodernists: Barthleme, Coover, Pynchon*. Philadelphia: University of Pennsylvania Press, 1991.

Martin, Michael T., and David Wall. "Close-Up: *Nothing But a Man*." *Black Camera* 3.2 (2012): 85–204.

McHale, Brian. *Postmodernist Fiction*. London: Methuen, 1987.

———. "Postmodern Narrative." *Routledge Encyclopedia of Narrative Theory*. Ed. D. Herman, M. Jann, and M.-L. Ryan. London: Routledge, 2005. 456–60.

———. "Transparent Minds Revisited." *Narrative* 20.1 (2012): 115–24.

Merleau-Ponty, Maurice. *Adventures of the Dialectic*. 1955. Trans. Joseph Bien. Evanston: Northwestern University Press, 1973.

———. "The Child's Relation with Others." Trans. William Cobb. *The Primacy of Perception*. Ed. James Edie. Evanston: Northwestern University Press, 1964. 96–155.

———. "The Film and the New Psychology." *Sense and Non-Sense*. Trans. Hubert Dreyfus and Patricia Dreyfus. Evanston: Northwestern University Press, 1964. 48–59.

———. *Humanism and Terror*. Trans. John O'Neill. Boston: Beacon Press, 1969.

———. *In Praise of Philosophy and Other Essays*. 1953. Trans. J. Wild, J. Edie, and J. O'Neill. Evanston: Northwestern University Press, 1970.

———. *Phenomenology of Perception*. Trans. Colin Smith. London: Routledge, 1962.

———. *The Primacy of Perception*. Ed. James Edie. Evanston: Northwestern University Press, 1964.

———. *Signs*. 1960. Trans. Richard McCleary. Evanston: Northwestern University Press, 1964.

———. *The Visible and the Invisible*. 1964. Trans. Alphonso Lingis. Evanston: Northwestern University Press, 1968.

Miller, J. Hillis. *The Conflagration of Community: Fiction Before and After Auschwitz*. Chicago: University of Chicago Press, 2011.

———. *For Derrida*. New York: Fordham University Press, 2009.

———. *Literature as Conduct: Speech Acts in Henry James*. New York: Fordham University Press, 2005.

———. *Versions of Pygmalion*. Cambridge: Harvard University Press, 1990.

Miller, Jacques-Alain. "Suture (Elements of the Logic of the Signifier)." 1966. Trans. Jacqueline Rose. *Screen* 18 (1978): 24–34.

Mitchell, Lee Clark. "'Based on the Novel by Henry James': *The Golden Bowl* 2000." *Henry James Goes to the Movies*. Ed. Susan M. Griffin. Lexington: The University Press of Kentucky, 2002.

Modelski, Tania. *The Women Who Knew Too Much*. New York and London: Methuen, 1988.

Morrison, Toni. *The Bluest Eye*. New York: Holt, Rinehart, 1970.

Moyn, Samuel. *Origins of the Other: Emmanual Levinas Between Revelation and Ethics*. Ithaca: Cornell University Press, 2005.

Mulvey, Laura. "Visual Pleasure and Narrative Cinema." 1975. *Visual and Other Pleasures*. Bloomington: Indiana University Press, 1989. 14–26.

Munns, David. "'Gay, Innocent and Heartless': *Peter Pan* and the Queering of Popular Culture." *J. M. Barrie's Peter Pan In and Out of Time*. Ed. Donna White and C. Anita Tarr. Lanham: Scarecrow Press, 2006. 219–42.

Nadel, Alan. "Ambassadors from an Imaginary 'Elsewhere': Cinematic Convention and the Jamesian Sensibility." *Henry James Goes to the Movies*. Ed. Susan Griffin. Lexington: The University Press of Kentucky, 2002. 193–209.

Nodelman, Perry. *The Hidden Adult: Defining Children's Literature*. Baltimore: Johns Hopkins University Press, 2008.

Nothing But a Man. Dir. Michael Roemer. Screenplay by Michael Roemer and Robert Young. Perf. Ivan Dixon and Abbey Lincoln. 1964. New Video, 2004.

Ohmer, Susan. "Disney's *Peter Pan*: Gender, Fantasy and Industrial Production." *Second Star to the Right: Peter Pan in the Popular Imagination*. Ed. Alison Kavey and Lester Friedman. New Brunswick: Rutgers University Press, 2009. 151–87.

Olkowski, Dorothea, ed. *Feminist Interpretations of Merleau-Ponty*. University Park: Pennsylvania State University Press, 2006.

Oudart, Jean-Pierre. "Cinema and Suture." Trans. Kari Hanet. *Screen* 18 (1978): 35–47.

Palmer, Alan. *Fictional Minds*. Lincoln: University of Nebraska Press, 2004.

———. *Social Minds in the Novel*. Columbus: The Ohio State University Press, 2010.

Palmer, R. Barton. *Joel and Ethan Coen*. Urbana: University of Illinois Press, 2004.

Peter Pan. Dir. Clyde Geronimi, Wilfred Jackson, and Hamilton Luske. Voice perf. Bobby Driscoll, Kathryn Beaumont, and Hans Conried. Walt Disney Films, 1953.

Peter Pan. Dir. P. J. Hogan. Screenplay by P. J. Hogan and Michael Golderberg. Perf. Jeremy Sumpter, Rachel Hurd-Wood, and Jason Isaacs. Universal Studios, 2003.

Phelan, James. *Narrative as Rhetoric*. Columbus: The Ohio State University Press, 1966.

———. *Reading People, Reading Plots*. Chicago: University of Chicago Press, 1989.

Plath, Sylvia. *Ariel*. New York: Harper and Row, 1965.

Pope, Alexander. "The Rape of the Lock." *The Poems of Alexander Pope*. Ed. John Butt. New Haven: Yale University Press, 1963.

Poulet, Georges. "Criticism and the Experience of Interiority." *The Structuralist Controversy*. Ed. Richard Macksey and Eugenio Donato. Baltimore: The Johns Hopkins University Press, 1970. 56–72.

Prince, Gerald. *Dictionary of Narratology*. Lincoln: University of Nebraska, 1987.

———. "Introduction to the Study of the Narratee." *Reader-Response Criticism: From Formalism to Post-Structuralism*. Ed. Jane Tompkins. Baltimore: Johns Hopkins University Press, 1980. 7–25.

———. "The Narratee Revisited." *Style* 19 (1985): 299–303.

Rabinowitz, Peter. *Before Reading*. 1987. Columbus: The Ohio State University Press, 1998.

———. "Truth in Fiction: A Reexamination of Audiences." *Critical Inquiry* 4.1 (1977): 121–41.

Raising Arizona. Dir. Joel Coen. Written by Ethan Coen and Joel Coen. Cinematography by Barry Sonnenfeld. Perf. Nicolas Cage and Holly Hunter. Twentieth Century Fox, 1987.

Raw, Laurence. *Adapting Henry James to the Screen*. Lanham: The Scarecrow Press, 2006.

Rear Window. Dir. Alfred Hitchcock. Written by John Michael Hayes. Perf. Cary Grant and Grace Kelly. Paramount, 1954.

Reckford, Kenneth. *Aristophanes' Old-And-New Comedy*. Chapel Hill: University of North Carolina Press, 1987.

Richardson, Brian. "Singular Text, Multiple Implied Readers." *Style* 41.3 (2007): 259–74.

Ricoeur, Paul. *Husserl: An Analysis of His Phenomenology*. Trans. Edward Ballard and Lester Embree. Evanston: Northwestern University Press, 1967.

———. *Oneself as Another*. Trans. Kathleen Blamey. Chicago: University of Chicago Press, 1992.

Rose, Jacqueline. *The Case of Peter Pan, or The Impossibility of Children's Fiction*. 2nd ed. Philadelphia: University of Pennsylvania Press, 1993.

Rothman, William. "Against the System of Suture." *Film Quarterly* 29 (1975): 45–50.

Sadoff, Dianne. *Victorian Vogue: British Novels on Screen*. Minneapolis: University of Minnesota Press, 2010.

Salt, Barry. "Film Style and Technology in the Forties." *Film Quarterly* 31 (1977): 46–57.

Sartre, Jean-Paul. *Being and Nothingness*. Trans. Hazel Barnes. New York: Simon and Schuster, 1966.

Sedgwick, Eve Kosofsky. *The Epistemology of the Closet*. Berkeley: University of California Press, 1990.

Seeger, Pete. *Darling Corey and Goofing-Off Suite*. 1950, 1955. Washington DC: Smithsonian Folkways Recordings, 1993.

Segal, Erich. *The Death of Comedy*. Cambridge: Harvard University Press, 2001.

Shakespeare, William. *Anthony and Cleopatra*. New York: New American Library, 1964.

———. *A Midsummer Night's Dream*. New York: New American Library, 1963.

The Silence of the Lambs. Dir. Jonathan Demme. Screenplay by Ted Tally. Based on the novel by Thomas Harris. Perf. Jodie Foster and Anthony Hopkins. Twentieth Century Fox, 1991. DVD, 2006.

Silverman, Kaja. *The Subject of Semiotics*. New York: Oxford University Press, 1983.

Smith, Judith E. "Civil Right, Labor, and Sexual Politics on Screen in *Nothing But a Man* (1964)." *Black Camera* 3.2 (2012): 164–93.

Smith, Sidonie, and Julia Watson. *Reading Autobiography: A Guide for Interpreting Life Narratives*. 2nd ed. Minneapolis: University of Minnesota Press, 2010.

Sobchack, Vivian. *The Address of the Eye: A Phenemenology of Film Experience*. Princeton: Princeton University Press, 1992.

Spurling, Laurie. *Phenomenology and the Social World: The Philosophy of Merleau-Ponty and Its Relations to the Social Sciences*. Boston: Routledge, 1977.

Stacey, Jackie. *Star Gazing: Hollywood Cinema and Female Spectatorship*. London: Routledge, 1994.

Stam, Robert, Robert Burgoyne, and Sandy Flitterman-Lewis. *New Vocabularies in Film Semiotics*. London: Routledge, 1992.

Teahan, Sheila. *The Rhetorical Logic of Henry James*. Baton Rouge: Louisiana State University Press, 1995.

Van Ghent, Dorothy. *The English Novel: Form and Function*. New York: Harper and Row, 1953.

Wall, Barbara. *The Narrator's Voice: The Dilemma of Children's Fiction*. New York: St. Martin's Press, 1991.

Wall, David C., and Michael Martin. "*Nothing But a Man*: Cinematic Principles and Practice at Work." *Black Camera* 3.2 (2012): 101–27.

Wasinger, Carrie. "Getting Peter's Goat: Hybridity, Androgyny and Terror in *Peter Pan*." *J. M. Barrie's Peter Pan In and Out of Time*. Ed. Donna White and C. Anita Tarr. Lanham: The Scarecrow Press, 2006.

Weisbuch, Robert. "Henry James and the Idea of Evil." *The Cambridge Companion to Henry James*. Ed. Jonathan Freedman. Cambridge: Cambridge University Press, 1998. 102–19.

Williams, Linda. "Discipline and Fun: *Psycho* and Postmodern Cinema." *Alfred Hitchcock's "Psycho": A Casebook*. Ed. Robert Kolker. Oxford: Oxford University Press, 2004. 164–204.

Williams, Merle. *Henry James and the Philosophical Novel: Being and Seeing*. Cambridge: Cambridge University Press, 1993.

Wings of the Dove. Dir. Iain Softley. Screenplay by Hossein Amini. Perf. Helena Bonham Carter, Linus Roache, and Alison Elliott. Miramax, 1997.

Winterson, Jeanette. *Why Be Happy When You Could Be Normal?* New York: Grove Press, 2011.

Zunshine, Lisa. "Can We Teach the 'Deep Intersubjectivity' of Richardson's *Clarissa?*" *New Windows on a Woman's World: A Festschrift for Jocelyn Harris*. Otago Studies in English, 9. Dunedin: University of Otago, 2005. 88–99.

———. *Why We Read Fiction: Theory of Mind and the Novel*. Columbus: The Ohio State University Press, 2006.

INDEX

500 Days of Summer (Webb), 213–16, 215

abandonment, 14, 120–21, 126, 139–46, 148, 150, 161. *See also* absences; mothers
absences: Derrida and, 180–82, 188–89, 195; gaps as, 7; Lacan and, 3, 7, 10–11, 22–25, 29–33, 175; of mothers, 121, 125–26, 128–29, 139–46, 150, 152–54, 161, 169–70, 185–86; politics of, 71–72; postmodernism and, 176–79, 181–89; shot / reverse shot structure and, 11–12, 38–39, 43–44, 54n16, 118–19, 200. *See also* film theory; narrative theory; suture
Absent One, 22–26, 31, 54n16, 112, 154, 174–75
adaptation theory, 100–101, 102n11, 123–24, 127, 162
The Address of the Eye (Sobchack), 32n9
African Americans, 11–12, 20, 38–51. *See also Nothing But a Man* (Roemer); race
Ahmed, Sara, 82, 112
Alice Sit-By-The-Fire (Barrie), 60
Allen, Woody, 189n7, 195
Althusser, Louis, 21–22, 25, 27, 29, 43–44
The Ambassadors (James), 90n7
Andersen, Hans Christian Andersen, 220

anxiety, 54–56, 99–100, 105, 155–62, 183n6, 189, 219–26
Armstrong, Paul, 17, 31n8, 75, 82–83, 86n1
Aron, Raymond, 69–70
"The Art of Feeling in Henry James" (Ross), 90n7
As I Lay Dying (Faulkner), 45
Atonement (film), 101
audiences: authorial, 23n2, 44, 52, 56–57, 94, 113–14, 125, 129, 131–32, 143–44, 152–53, 155, 157–58, 169, 220; eavesdropping and, 60, 139–54, 219–26; ethics and, 219–26; flesh-and-blood, 23, 25–26, 28n4, 30, 43–44, 52–55, 57, 67, 102, 107, 124–25, 128, 131–34, 136–37, 148, 150–51, 155, 159, 220, 224; implied, 23, 53, 55–56, 67–68, 124–25, 128–29, 133–34, 136–37, 139–46, 150, 158–59, 169, 173–74, 214, 219–20; narrative theory's work and, 10, 56–57, 123–28; ricochet effect and, 3, 8–9, 14, 121, 145n10, 146–61, 174. *See also* narrative theory
Austen, Jane, 2, 4–7, 59–60, 75, 210
authorial audiences, 23n2, 44, 52, 56–57, 94, 113–14, 125, 129, 131–32, 143–44, 152–53, 155, 157–58, 169–71, 220
The Awkward Age (James), 74n1, 78

Babel (Iñarritu), 177
Bakhtin, Mikhail, 142, 181n3, 182, 191, 221
Ballantyne, R. M., 121
Banfield, Ann, 13, 98
Barber, C. L., 181n3
Barrie, J. M., 9, 14, 60, 97, 119, 123–54, 157–61, 220. See also *specific works*
BBC films, 13–14, 111–17
"The Beast in the Jungle" (James), 224
Beckett, Samuel, 178
Before Reading (Rabinowitz), 131
Being and Nothingness (Sartre), 6
Bell, Millicent, 73
Beloved (Morrison), 181n4
Bettelheim, Bruno, 225
"Beyond the Shot" (Eisenstein), 22
Birkin, Andrew, 127, 161
Black Camera, 38n13, 42
Bleak House (Dickens), 9, 177
Blood Simple (Coen Brothers), 181
The Bluest Eye (Morrison), 81, 223
body, the. See embodiment
Bolton, Matthew, 101
Booth, Wayne, 30
Bordwell, David, 22, 26–30, 46n14, 51, 53–54
Boucicault, Nina, 161
The Boy Castaways of Black Lake Island (Barrie), 123, 125
Boys Don't Cry (film), 27
"The Boy Who Wouldn't Grow Up" (Barrie), 126–27
Bresson, Robert, 55, 68
bricolage, 180, 190, 205–6. See also postmodernism
Broadway Melody (film), 33
Brook, Peter, 101
Brooks, Peter, 89n6, 110
Browne, Nick, 13, 46n14, 53–54, 58
Brownell, W. C., 73–74
Burgoyne, Robert, 30
Butler, Christopher, 180n2, 189
Butler, Judith, 81, 184

Cage, Nicholas, 192
Cahiers du Cinema, 21
Cambridge Ritualists, 177, 194
carnivalesque, 181n3, 182, 188
Carroll, Noel, 22, 26–27, 29–30
Carter, Helena Bonham, 107–8
Cartesian Meditations (Husserl), 18
Cassavetes, John, 10
Cavell, Stanley, 33, 89n6, 110
Cellan Jones, James, 111–17
Chanter, Tina, 80
Chatman, Seymour, 13, 31, 46n14, 131–32, 147–48, 150, 154–55, 158, 220
chiasmus: comedy and, 177–80, 189–206; definitions of, 78–79; Derrida and, 8, 15–16, 18, 176–78, 185, 188, 190, 195, 201–2, 208–9; feminist criticisms of, 81–83; in Merleau-Ponty, 4, 11, 18, 21, 29–30, 35–36, 42, 45, 66, 69–70, 75, 79–83, 85, 99, 175, 177, 195, 203–4, 216–17; shot / reverse shot structure and, 16, 113–17, 214–15; suture and, 5, 9, 36–37, 39–41, 47–48, 51–52, 153–54, 175, 177, 201, 203
children's literature, 14–15, 122–39, 147–54, 219–26. See also *specific critics and works*
"The Child's Relation with Others" (Merleau-Ponty), 34
Cinematic Interfaces (Jeong), 32n9
Citizen Kane (Welles), 61, 61–62, 118
Clark, Lee Mitchell, 117
class, 39–41, 44, 50, 191
Clayton, Jack, 102, 117–18
close-ups, 33, 39, 41–44, 47, 66, 107, 112–13, 166, 198, 203
Coats, Karen, 149
Coen, Joel and Ethan, 9–10, 15–16, 175, 180–89. See also *specific works*
Cohn, Dorrit, 5n2, 60, 98
comedy, 9, 16, 176–206
Coming to Terms (Chatman), 13
community, 17, 197, 201–6, 211–12
consciousness: embodiment and, 3–4, 17; layers of, 27–29, 92–93, 175;

misperceptions of, 5; narrating agency and, 8, 13–14, 47–48, 130–31; neuroscientific views of, 5–6, 122n4; ontology and, 21, 33–35, 68–69, 81–83; recursivity and, 7–9, 12–13, 32–33, 46, 71–72, 84, 122n4, 137–38, 151–52, 212; suture and, 2–3, 6–7, 16–17, 21–31, 45–46, 73–84, 92–100, 123, 178–79, 207–8; transparency and, 93–100, 110. *See also* deep intersubjectivity; eavesdropping; intersubjectivity; looking; recursivity; touch; voyeurism
Constructivism (perception model), 28
Contesting Tears (Cavell), 89n6
continuity editing, 21, 100–101
Coppola, Francis Ford, 6
The Coral Island (Ballantyne), 15, 121, 145, 222
Cornford, Francis, 176–78, 181–82, 185–86, 188, 190, 194
cultural work, 102, 109

Davidson, Jim, 38
Dayan, Daniel, 10–11, 21–22, 24–27, 29–31, 33, 35, 43–44, 51, 53
"The Dead" (Joyce), 148
de Beauvoir, Simone, 81
deep intersubjectivity, 3–18, 29–46, 69–76, 84–100, 124, 138–39, 151–52, 201–17. *See also* intersubjectivity; narrative theory; recursivity; suture
defamiliarization, 8, 26, 29, 44, 53–55, 60, 97, 213
Demme, Jonathan, 11–12, 58–69
Derrida, Jacques, 8–9, 15–18, 75, 80–81, 121–22, 175–90, 195–209
desire, 12, 15–16, 175, 212–16. *See also* absences; sexuality; vulnerability (to the other)
The Disappearance of God (Miller), 32n9
discourses (competing), 190–96
Disney, Walt, 15, 164, 165n14
Dixon, Wheeler Winston, 32n9
Doane, Mary Ann, 104, 213–14
Doisneu, Robert, 104
A Doll's House (Ibsen), 136

Doyle, Laura, 32–33, 69, 81–82, 184
Dr. Strangelove (Kubrick), 194

Eakin, Paul John, 210
eavesdropping, 60, 65–66, 97, 121, 139–61, 173–74, 219–26. *See also* children's literature; voyeurism
editing (in film), 4, 8–11, 20–31, 39–40, 45, 60, 173, 215–16. *See also* film theory; shot / reverse shot
Egan, Michael, 136–37
Eisenstein, Sergei, 22
elementary suture, 4–5, 8, 175, 201
Eliot, George, 130
Elliott, Alison, 108
embodiment: absence and, 175, 177; consciousness and, 3–6, 79–80; feminism and, 10–11, 81–83, 178, 184–85; gender and, 184–86; ideology and, 43–44; phenomenology and, 3, 69–72, 75, 82, 177; of a rhetoric, 47–48, 53–54; shot / reverse shot structure and, 103–10; suture and, 7–8, 16–18, 69–72. *See also* class; gender; phenomenology; race; vulnerability (to the other)
Emma (Austen), 59–60
enunciator, 7, 45–48, 52–60, 97, 117, 125, 195, 204, 206
eros, 14–15, 158, 163. *See also* desire; families; sexuality
espousal, 4, 15–17, 37, 51, 78–79, 83–85, 86n1, 99–100, 122, 212
establishing shots, 24, 53
ethics (in children's literature), 219–26
Evans, Fred, 80
evasion, 9, 14, 21, 27, 43, 50–53, 66–67, 95–96, 123–24, 135, 166–70
Evers, Medgar, 38
eyeline matching, 11–12, 41, 67, 173

Faces (Cassavetes), 10
families, 14–15, 158, 163–64, 166–67, 170–71, 224. *See also* abandonment; audiences; children's literature; mothers; sexuality
Feiffer, Jules, 222–23

feminism, 10–11, 21, 69–72, 80–83, 178, 184–85, 213–14
Fictional Minds (Palmer), 76n2
FID (free indirect discourse), 8; in Austen, 59–60; in Barrie, 145–54, 174; in Henry James, 12–13, 46–48, 74–76, 92–100; narrative theory and, 46n14, 58, 92–100; shot / reverse shot structure and, 51–52, 96–97, 100–101; as suture, 9, 12, 50, 83, 123; the uncanny and, 77–78, 146. *See also* chiasmus; narrative theory; shot / reverse shot; suture; *specific authors and works*
fidelity, 100–102, 162. *See also* adaptation theory
Fielding, Henry, 215–16
"Film and the Masquerade" (Doane), 104
"The Film and the New Psychology" (Merleau-Ponty), 33, 50
Film Quarterly, 22
film theory: adaptations and, 13–14, 100–101, 102n11, 123–24, 127, 162; eyeline matching and, 11–12, 41, 67, 173; feminist criticism and, 21, 213–14; intersubjectivity and, 31n8, 32–37, 102, 111–20; Lacan and, 3, 11–12, 20; Merleau-Ponty and, 29–31, 33, 50; mise-en-scène and, 44–48, 60, 103–6, 111–12, 172; narrators in, 13–14, 51–69, 111–17; Peter Pan stories and, 14; shot / reverse shot and, 9, 11–12, 16, 24, 33, 38–54, 113–17, 198–200; suture and, 6, 8, 10, 20–31, 34, 43–44, 180–89. *See also* narrative theory; *specific authors and works*
Finding Neverland (Forster), 123
Ford, John, 13
For Derrida (Miller), 121, 207
Forster, Marc, 123
For Whom the Bell Tolls (Hemingway), 132
fragmentation, 35, 124, 128, 181, 204–5, 210–11, 213–16
Fragments of Isabella (Leitner), 222
Frazer, J. G., 177–78, 194
Freud, Sigmund, 182, 189

Friends (television show), 76n2, 90
Frohman, Charles, 161

Gadamer, Hans Georg, 31n8
gaps: abandonment and, 126; community and, 213–16; Oudart and, 21–26; as presence and absence, 7–8, 11–12, 80–81, 191, 197–98; touch and, 121. *See also* absences; chiasmus; Lacan, Jacques; suture
Garber, Marjorie, 164
Gawande, Atul, 1–4, 11, 21, 72
gaze, the: film theory and, 32n9, 213–14; gender and, 59, 61; in James, 84–92; *komos* and, 198–99; race and, 41–44; recursivity and, 40–41, 46, 67, 71–72, 75–76, 84–86; subjectivities and, 4–5, 12, 22–23. *See also* deep intersubjectivity; film theory; intersubjectivity; looking
gender: comedy and, 183–84, 206, 213–14; film theory and, 21–22, 69–72; the gaze and, 59, 61, 103–5; performances of, 212–16, 221; phenomenology and, 10–11, 39–40, 50; sexuality and, 144–45, 150, 162–64, 166–67, 169–71, 184, 213; transgendering and, 26–27. *See also* embodiment; feminism
Genette, Gerard, 93n9
genre, 177–89, 194, 212–16. *See also* children's literature; comedy; melodrama
Gilmore, Leigh, 183n6, 193n9, 194n10, 210
Girard, Rene, 16, 178–79, 187
Gledhill, Christine, 89n6, 110
The Godfather (Coppola), 6
Goffman, Erving, 18, 178–79, 187
The Golden Bough (Frazer), 185
The Golden Bowl (BBC), 13–14, 102, 109, 111–17, 116, 119
The Golden Bowl (Ivory), 110–11, 114
The Golden Bowl (James), 12, 45, 73, 78, 89–95, 99–100, 175
Golding, William, 222
"Goofing Off Suite" (Seeger), 194n10
Gopnik, Adam, 52–53

Great Expectations (Dickens), 177, 212
Gubar, Marah, 128n6
Gunn, Daniel, 13, 46n14, 58–60, 93n9, 98

Halberstam, Judith, 22, 27
Hammerstein, Oscar, 36
Hansen, Per Krogh, 220, 223
Hard Core (Williams), 107
Hardy, Thomas, 149
Harrison, Jane, 177
Hatley, James, 80
Hawthorn, Jeremy, 46n14, 57, 63, 67, 156
Heath, Stephen, 21–22, 24, 27
Hebdige, Dick, 180n2, 189–90, 196
Hedda Gabler (Ibsen), 136
Hegel, G. W. F., 17
Heidegger, Martin, 18, 86n1, 208
The Hidden Adult (Nodelman), 15, 220
Hiding in the Light (Hebdige), 180n2
Hill, Rodney, 186
Hitchcock, Alfred, 24, 26, 55–57, 101, 156
Hogan, P. J., 15, 123, 127, 161, 164, 166–67, 170–72, 192
Hollindale, Peter, 129, 149–50, 222
Holmes, Martha Stoddard, 154
Home Is Where the Heart Is (Gledhill), 89n6
Hook (Spielberg), 123, 144, 171–72
Hopper, Hedda, 165n14
Humanism and Terror (Merleau-Ponty), 70–72, 82
humor, 188–89, 193
Hunter, J. Paul, 216n3
Husserl, Edmund, 17–18, 32n9, 71, 75, 78, 121, 208
Hutcheon, Linda, 102n11, 189, 194–95

Ian, Marcia, 108
Ibsen, Henrik, 136, 153
Ibsen's Ghost (Barrie), 136
idealism. *See* transcendental, the
identity at a distance, 11, 34

ideology, 21–22, 27, 29–31, 33, 43–44, 195, 211, 219–20
"I Have a Dream" (King), 38
I Know That Your Know That I Know (Butte), 5, 18, 75, 102, 208, 212
I Lost My Bear (Feiffer), 223
imminence, 203–5
implied narrators, 31, 46n14, 150, 155
improvisation, 180, 182, 190
Iñarritu, Alejandro, 21, 177
indirection. *See* FID (free indirect discourse); over-the-shoulder view; ricochet effect; shot / reverse shot
The Innocents (Clayton), 102, 117–18
interpellation, 21–22, 25, 33
intersubjectivity: comedy and, 177–78; community and, 201–3, 206–17; deep, 3–12, 18, 29–30; Merleau-Ponty and, 18, 23; recursiveness and, 7–9, 12–13, 32–33, 46, 71–76, 84, 122n4, 201, 203, 207, 212; suture and, 4–5, 18, 21–31, 37, 49–50, 129–30. *See also* consciousness; deep intersubjectivity; other, the; reciprocity; subjectivity; touch
"The Intertwining—The Chiasm" (Merleau-Ponty), 36
intimacy, 12, 42, 48, 69, 79, 84, 90–92, 97–100, 110, 119, 139, 222
Intolerance (Griffith), 9
Irigaray, Luce, 37, 80–81
irony, 189, 191
Isaacs, Jason, 166–67
Iser, Wolfgang, 23n2
It Looks At You (Dixon), 32n9
Ivory, James, 110, 114

Jack, R. D. S., 125, 138
James, Henry, 9–10, 12–14, 46–48, 69, 73–119, 122, 153, 178, 210, 224. *See also specific works*
James, Ian, 80–81
Jameson, Fredric, 190, 192–93, 195–96
Jeong, Seung-Hoon, 32n9
joking, 183n6, 189, 189n7
Joyce, James, 12, 148

Kaplan, E. Ann, 214n1
Kavey, Alison, 124n5
Kaye, Richard, 109
Kerr, Deborah, 118
Kertzer, Adrienne, 222
Kincaid, James, 139n9, 221–22
King, Martin Luther, Jr., 38
King Lear (Shakespeare/Brook), 101
Knoepflmacher, U. C., 219
komos, 9–10, 16, 176–82, 185–87, 190, 194–202, 205–6, 210
Kuleshov effect, 22, 33, 35

Lacan, Jacques, 3–4, 7, 10–12, 16, 20, 22, 27–32, 34–35, 76n3, 78, 175
Last Year at Marienbad (Resnais), 63, 64
"La Suture (elements de la logique du significant)" (Miller), 21
Lawlor, Leonard, 80
Lawrence, D. H., 2, 157
Leavis, F. R., 73
Leitner, Isabella, 222
Les Temps Modernes, 81
Levinas, Emmanuel, 17, 35–36, 78, 80, 121, 208, 216
L'invitee (de Beauvoir), 81
Literature as Conduct (Miller), 74n1
The Little White Bird (Barrie), 123–25, 162–63, 225
looking: Absent One and, 22–23, 25–26, 31, 54n16, 112, 154, 174–75; gender and, 103–4; in Henry James, 84–100; recursivity and, 3–5, 7, 11–12, 24–25, 32–33, 40–41, 44–45, 67, 71–72, 84–86, 91–93, 122n4, 137–38; representations of, 84–92; shot / reverse shot and, 7, 24–31, 40–41; suture theory and, 11–12, 22–31; voyeurism and, 56–57, 60, 97, 103–5, 205. *See also* gaze, the; misperception; shot / reverse shot; surveillance
Lyotard, François, 16, 179–80, 189, 196

Mackail, Denis, 161
Making Meaning (Bordwell), 46n14
Maltby, Paul, 194

The Maltese Falcon (film), 51
Mansfield Park (Austen), 210
Martin, Michael T., 38n13
masquerade, 84–89, 104
master narratives, 16, 179–80, 210
master shots, 41–42, 48
McHale, Brian, 5n2, 180, 190, 206, 210
melodrama, 89–90, 108, 110, 168, 170
Memento (Nolan), 177
Merleau-Ponty, Maurice: chiasmus and, 4, 7, 18, 21, 35–36, 42, 45, 50, 66, 75, 79–83, 85, 99, 110, 175, 177, 189, 195, 197–98, 201, 203–4, 216–17; Derrida and, 75, 80–81, 201–2, 205, 208–9; espousal and, 4, 15–17, 37, 51, 78–79, 83–85, 99, 122; intersubjectivity and, 5, 23; Lacan and, 11, 29, 33–35, 76n3; phenomenology of, 31–37, 76–77, 98; Sartre and, 6, 71–72, 86. *See also specific works*
A Midsummer Night's Dream (Shakespeare), 180–82
Miller, Jacques-Alain, 4, 10, 19, 21–22, 25, 35
Miller, J. Hillis, 13, 17–18, 32n9, 60, 74n1, 77–78, 121, 146, 181n4, 189, 207–10, 216
Miller, Michael, 201
Miller's Crossing (Coen Brothers), 181
mimicry, 58–59, 152
mise-en-scène, 44–48, 60, 103–6, 111–12, 166–67, 172
misperception, 5, 12, 98–100, 122, 159–60. *See also* intersubjectivity; looking; vulnerability (to the other)
Mitchell, Lee Clark, 111
Modleski, Tania, 214n2
molestation, 14, 122, 124, 153–54, 160, 160n12, 222, 224–25
Moll Flanders (Defoe), 212
montage, 22, 24, 34
Morrison, Toni, 81, 181n4, 222–23
mothers, 139–50, 152, 158, 166–67, 169–70, 185–86
Mulvey, Laura, 21–22, 105, 214
Munns, David, 162
Myers, Mitzi, 219

NAACP (National Association for the Advancement of Colored People), 38
Nadel, Alan, 108
Nancy, Jean-Luc, 17, 80, 121, 207, 209, 216
narcissism, 140–41, 143, 145–46
narratees, 122, 124, 128–46, 150–51, 154–61, 221
Narrative as Rhetoric (Phelan), 131–32, 132n7
narrative theory: audiences and, 10, 23, 25–26, 43–44, 52, 56–57, 74, 94–95, 123–39, 146–54, 170–71, 173–76; children's literature and, 14–15, 122–39, 147–54, 219–26; deep intersubjectivity and, 6–7, 31–37, 74–76, 84–100; film theory and, 3, 9, 13–14, 20–31, 51–69, 118–20; free indirect discourse and, 92–100, 145–54; gender and, 10–11, 16, 21; genre and, 9, 74, 89n6, 212–16; implied narrators and, 31, 46, 46n14, 143, 150; narratees and, 122, 124, 128–46, 150, 154–61, 221; narrating agency and, 8, 10, 12–13, 31, 45–46, 58, 92–94, 98, 114, 122n4, 125, 152; palimpsests and, 211–12; phenomenology and, 3, 6–7, 9–10, 69–72, 74–75; ricochet effect and, 3, 8–9, 14, 121, 145n10, 153–61, 169–70, 174–76, 219–26; suture and, 2–3, 43–44, 73–84, 177. *See also* audiences; chiasmus; eavesdropping; FID (free indirect discourse); ricochet effect; suture
The Narrator's Voice (Wall), 220
networks (of subjectivities), 2–3, 12–13
The New Yorker, 52–53
Nodelman, Perry, 15, 220–21, 224
Nolte, Nick, 110–11
Nothing But a Man (Roemer), 9–12, 20, 38–51, 69–70, 72, 153–54, 175, 192, 198; images of, 39–41, 49

oblique, the. *See* chiasmus; FID (free indirect discourse); over-the-shoulder view; ricochet effect; shot / reverse shot
Occasional Form (Hunter), 216n3
Of Mice and Men (Steinbeck), 186

Ohmer, Susan, 165n14
Olkowski, Dorothea, 81
omniscient narrators, 157n11
"On Not Defining Children's Literature" (Gubar), 128n6
ontology, 6, 21, 33–35, 68–69, 76, 81–83, 121–22, 190, 206, 209–10
On Touching (Derrida), 17–18, 75, 201
Oranges Are Not the Only Fruit (Winterson), 211, 213
other, the: communities and, 17, 71–72, 197, 201–6, 211–12; deep intersubjectivity and, 3–4, 74–84; Derrida and, 175, 185; Levinas on, 35–36, 208, 216; mirror-stage and, 34; ontologies of, 5–6; stigma and, 178–79; touch and, 120–22, 153–54, 202, 209; vulnerability to, 17, 37, 41–42, 63, 84, 86, 138, 153–54. *See also* consciousness; intersubjectivity; looking; vulnerability (to the other)
Oudart, Jean-Pierre, 4, 10–12, 19, 21–29, 33, 45, 51, 53–55, 68, 174
overhearing. *See* eavesdropping
over-the-shoulder view, 51–52, 58; in film, 51–52, 58, 61–64, 103, 112–17; in narrative, 7–8, 72, 96–100; ricochet effect and, 159–60. *See also* FID (free indirect discourse); shot / reverse shot

palimpsests, 211–12
Palmer, Alan, 76n2
Palmer, R. Barton, 190n8
parody, 189–90, 192–93, 200–201, 213–16
passing, 179
pastiche, 190–93, 195–96
pedophilia. *See* molestation
Peeping Tom (Powell), 175
performance, 84–89, 109–11, 191, 213–16, 221
Peter and Wendy (Barrie), 121, 123–26, 128–54, 157, 162, 223, 225–26
Peter Pan (Barrie), 8, 15, 60, 120–23, 125, 153, 158, 161, 168–70, 221
Peter Pan (Disney), 15, 120, 144, 162, 164, 164–65, 165, 166–68, 169

Peter Pan (Hogan), 123, 166, 166–67, 170–71, 172–74, 192
Peter Pan in Kensington Gardens (Barrie), 125–27, 225
pharmakon, 9, 15–16, 176–77, 182, 185, 188, 195–96
Phelan, Jim, 96n10, 131, 132n7, 135, 137, 155
phenomenology: definitions of, 32n9; embodiment and, 39–40, 69–72, 75, 82, 177; feminist thought and, 80–82, 178, 184–85; film theory and, 22–31, 33; Merleau-Ponty and, 5, 31–37, 98; narrative theory and, 3, 6–7, 9–10, 74–75; solipsism and, 17–18, 36, 77, 80–81, 121, 201, 208; transcendental temptations in, 6, 17–18, 32, 69–72, 74–77, 82, 201. See also *specific theorists*
Phenomenology and the Social World (Spurling), 70n18
The Phenomenology of Perception (Merleau-Ponty), 18, 77, 81–83
Plath, Sylvia, 1, 4, 21, 72
"Plato's Pharmacy" (Derrida), 16, 176–77, 182, 195, 201
play (term), 16, 31n8, 182, 195–96
Play and the Politics of Reading (Armstrong), 31n8
politics. See class; comedy; community; feminism; gender; race
The Portrait of a Lady (James), 73–74, 78
postmodernism, 9, 15–16, 179–80, 180n2, 181n4, 189–206, 213–16, 221
Poulet, Georges, 17, 32n9, 78
POV (point-of-view) shots, 51–53, 56
Powell, Michael, 175
Prince, Gerald, 132n7, 146, 155, 158
Psycho (Hitchcock), 26, 197

Queer Phenomenology (Ahmed), 82, 112

Rabelais and His World (Bakhtin), 181n3, 182
Rabinowitz, Peter, 13, 23n2, 56, 129, 131–32, 155

race, 11–12, 38–42, 50, 69–70, 153–54, 179
Raising Arizona (Coen Brothers), 8–10, 15–17, 175–206; images of, 187, 197, 199–200, 204–5
The Rape of the Lock (Pope), 192
Raw, Laurence, 102
The Reader as Peeping Tom (Hawthorn), 57
Rear Window (Hitchcock), 46n14, 55–56, 56, 57, 63, 66–68, 131, 156, 214
reciprocity, 35–36, 40–41, 63–64, 79–80, 140
Reckford, Kenneth, 181n3, 183
recursivity, 4–5, 7–9, 24–25, 32–33, 40–41, 46, 67, 71–72, 75–76, 84–86, 122n4, 137–38, 151–52, 201–3, 207, 212
Resnais, Alain, 63
reversibility, 79–80, 83–84
Reynolds, Burt, 164
The Rhetorical Logic of Henry James (Teahan), 74n1
rhetoric(s), 3–13, 18, 30–36, 48, 53–54, 74, 78, 92, 101–2, 110–11, 143, 179, 200
Richardson, Brian, 219
ricochet effect, 3, 8–9, 14, 121–23, 138–39, 145n10, 153–61, 169–76, 219–26
Ricoeur, Paul, 17–18, 208
The Road to Never Land (Jack), 125
Roemer, Michael, 9–12, 20, 38–51
A Room of One's Own (Woolf), 211
Roscoe, William Calder, 220
Rose, Jacqueline, 14, 122, 124–25, 128, 150, 153–54, 160, 221–22, 224–25
Ross, Melanie, 90n7
Rothman, William, 22, 24–25

Sadoff, Dianne, 102, 107, 109
Salt, Benjamin, 22, 24, 29, 51–52
Sartre, Jean-Paul, 4, 6, 63, 66, 71–72, 84, 86, 208
The Scapegoat (Girard), 178, 185
scapegoats, 178–79, 185
Scenes from a Marriage (Bergman), 17

Screen, 22
second-person narration, 136–37
Sedgwick, Eve Kosofsky, 224
Seeger, Pete, 194n10
Segal, Erich, 180, 182
selfhood, 210–11
Sentimental Tommy (Sedgwick), 224
A Serious Man (Coen Brothers), 181
sexuality, 144–45, 150, 158, 162–71, 175–76, 213, 224
Shakespeare, William, 180–82, 192
shame, 37, 49, 63, 66, 71, 84, 86, 99, 105–7, 138
shot / reverse shot: absences and, 11–12, 24, 54n16, 61–62, 103, 173, 197–98; chiasmus and, 16, 113–17, 214–15; compositions of, 47–48, 59; free indirect discourse and, 51–52, 96–97, 100–101; *komos* and, 197–99; narrative theory's relation to, 9, 51–52; *Nothing But a Man* and, 38–51; Oudart and, 10; subjectivity's formation and, 24–31, 39–40, 45–46, 48–49, 52–55, 65–69. *See also* film theory; narrative theory; *specific works*
Signs (Merleau-Ponty), 37, 77
The Silence of the Lambs (Demme), 8–9, 11–12, 20, 58–69, 97, 124, 192; images of, 58–59, 65–67
Silverman, Kaja, 10–11, 22, 25–27, 29, 31, 33, 35, 37, 43–44, 51–53, 83, 197
skepticism, 35–36, 74–78, 80–81, 113–17, 190. *See also* solipsism
Smith, Judith E., 42
Smith, Sidonie, 210–11
Sobchack, Vivian, 32n9
Softley, Iain, 102–10
solipsism, 17–18, 36, 76–78, 80–81, 121, 201, 208
Sondheim, Stephen, 85
Sonnenfeld, Barry, 186, 198
"The Spectator-in-the-Text" (Browne), 46n14
spectatorship (in film), 22–23. *See also* audiences
The Spider's Strategem (Bertolucci), 53

Spielberg, Steven, 123, 144, 171–72
Spurling, Laurie, 70n18
Stacey, Jack, 30n7
Stagecoach (Ford), 13
Stardust Memories (Allen), 195
Star Gazing (Stacey), 30n7
stigma, 178, 187
Story and Discourse (Chatman), 131
storytelling (in Peter Pan tales), 127–39
"Structure, Sign, and Play in the Discourse of the Human Sciences" (Derrida), 16, 180, 195
Subculture (Hebdige), 180n2
subjectivity: absence and, 21–31; ideology and, 22–27; ontology and, 33–35, 68–69, 76, 81–83, 121–22; shot / reverse shot and, 24, 50–51, 54–55, 65–69. *See also* consciousness; deep intersubjectivity; intersubjectivity
The Subject of Semiotics (Silverman), 22
Sumpter, Jeremy, 167
supplement, 176, 188
surveillance, 44–45, 57
suture: absences and, 3, 11–12, 22–33, 38–39, 43–44, 49–50, 71–72, 118–19, 129–30, 153–54, 174–75; chiasm and, 5, 9, 36–37, 47–48, 51–52, 153–54, 177, 201, 203; comedy and, 176–80, 189–206; community and, 197; consciousness and, 2–3, 16–17, 73–84, 92–100; deep intersubjectivity and, 3–5, 31–37, 45, 92–100, 207–10; embodiment and, 3, 7–8, 18, 69–72; etymology of, 5, 14, 31–32; film theory and, 4, 6–10, 20–31, 34, 43–44, 180–89; free indirect discourse and, 92–100, 123; as presence, 31–39, 44–45, 50, 110, 174–75; ricochet effect and, 160–61; shot / reverse shot structures and, 41–49, 214–15; typologies of, 4–5, 9; wounds and, 1–3, 9, 21, 31–32, 71–72. *See also* chiasmus; deep intersubjectivity; Merleau-Ponty, Maurice
The Sweet Hereafter (Banks), 45

tags, 147
Tarantino, Quentin, 21

Teahan, Sheila, 74n1
temporality, 124–28, 130–31, 137–38, 162–63, 168, 172–73, 202, 211–12
A Theory of Adaptation (Hutcheon), 102n11
Thurman, Uma, 102, 110
Tom Jones (Fielding), 157, 216, 216n3
Tommy and Grizel (Barrie), 157, 224
tone, 13, 98, 133, 141–46, 148–51, 154, 158–59, 194
touch, 3, 15, 95, 120–22, 144–45, 153–54, 158, 202, 207–9
traceability, 91, 95, 112–17. *See also* consciousness; deep intersubjectivity; recursivity
tracking shots, 117
transcendental, the, 6, 17–18, 32, 69–77, 80–83, 201. *See also* phenomenology; solipsism
Transcending Boundaries (collection), 219
transparency (between consciousnesses), 93–100, 110–17, 221. *See also* consciousness; intersubjectivity
Transparent Minds (Cohn), 5n2, 98
The Trial of Joan of Arc (Bresson), 55, 68
"Truth in Fiction" (Rabinowitz), 131
The Turn of the Screw (James), 122, 155

"*Un Regard Oblique*" (Doisneu), 104
Unspeakable Sentences (Banfield), 13

Van Ghent, Dorothy, 73
Vanity Fair (Thackery), 157
Versions of Pygmalion (Miller), 146
Vertigo (Hitchcock), 24, 214
Vested Interests (Garber), 164
The Visible and the Invisible (Merleau-Ponty), 11, 18, 36, 73, 75, 79, 81, 189, 201–2
voyeurism, 56–57, 60–61, 97, 103–5, 139–46, 156, 167, 205
vulnerability (to the other), 5–6, 14, 37, 41–42, 63, 84–86, 123, 134–61, 169–70, 207–16

Waiting for Godot (Beckett), 178
Wall, Barbara, 159, 220–21
Wall, David, 38n13
Walsh, Emmet, 183
The War of the Worlds (Wells), 173
Wasinger, Carrie, 221, 225
Watson, Julia, 210–11
Webb, Marc, 213–16
Weisbuch, Robert, 75
Welles, Orson, 22–23, 61–62
Wells, H. G., 173
Wharton, Edith, 10
What Every Woman Knows (Barrie), 122
What Maisie Knew (James), 46, 50, 73, 78, 83–84, 97–100
When Wendy Grew Up (Barrie), 125, 226
Why Be Happy When You Could Be Normal? (Winterson), 8, 211–13
Why We Read Fiction (Zunshine), 76n2
Williams, Linda, 21–22, 107
Williams, Merle, 75–76, 86n1
The Wings of the Dove (James), 74, 85–89, 92–93, 95, 97–98
The Wings of the Dove (Softley), 103, 104–6, 106, 107, 108–9
Winterson, Jeanette, 211, 213
Women and Film (Kaplan), 214n1
The Women Who Knew Too Much (Modleski), 214n2
Woolf, Virginia, 136, 211
wounds: abandonment as, 121, 125–26, 174; surgical, 1–5, 11, 72; suture concept and, 2–3, 9; touching as, 15–16; vulnerability to the other and, 5–6, 11–12, 14–15
Wyler, William, 22–23

YA literature, 222
Young, Robert, 38–51

Zunshine, Lisa, 5–6, 5n3, 75, 76n2, 90, 122n4

THEORY AND INTERPRETATION OF NARRATIVE

James Phelan, Peter J. Rabinowitz, and Robyn Warhol, Series Editors

Because the series editors believe that the most significant work in narrative studies today contributes both to our knowledge of specific narratives and to our understanding of narrative in general, studies in the series typically offer interpretations of individual narratives and address significant theoretical issues underlying those interpretations. The series does not privilege one critical perspective but is open to work from any strong theoretical position.

Suture and Narrative: Deep Intersubjectivity in Fiction and Film
GEORGE BUTTE

The Writer in the Well: On Misreading and Rewriting Literature
GARY WEISSMAN

Narrating Space / Spatializing Narrative: Where Narrative Theory and Geography Meet
MARIE-LAURE RYAN, KENNETH FOOTE, AND MAOZ AZARYAHU

Narrative Sequence in Contemporary Narratology
EDITED BY RAPHAËL BARONI AND FRANÇOISE REVAZ

The Submerged Plot and the Mother's Pleasure from Jane Austen to Arundhati Roy
KELLY A. MARSH

Narrative Theory Unbound: Queer and Feminist Interventions
EDITED BY ROBYN WARHOL AND SUSAN S. LANSER

Unnatural Narrative: Theory, History, and Practice
BRIAN RICHARDSON

Ethics and the Dynamic Observer Narrator: Reckoning with Past and Present in German Literature
KATRA A. BYRAM

Narrative Paths: African Travel in Modern Fiction and Nonfiction
KAI MIKKONEN

The Reader as Peeping Tom: Nonreciprocal Gazing in Narrative Fiction and Film
JEREMY HAWTHORN

Thomas Hardy's Brains: Psychology, Neurology, and Hardy's Imagination
SUZANNE KEEN

The Return of the Omniscient Narrator: Authorship and Authority in Twenty-First Century Fiction
PAUL DAWSON

Feminist Narrative Ethics: Tacit Persuasion in Modernist Form
KATHERINE SAUNDERS NASH

Real Mysteries: Narrative and the Unknowable
H. PORTER ABBOTT

A Poetics of Unnatural Narrative
EDITED BY JAN ALBER, HENRIK SKOV NIELSEN, AND BRIAN RICHARDSON

Narrative Discourse: Authors and Narrators in Literature, Film, and Art
PATRICK COLM HOGAN

An Aesthetics of Narrative Performance: Transnational Theater, Literature, and Film in Contemporary Germany
CLAUDIA BREGER

Literary Identification from Charlotte Brontë to Tsitsi Dangarembga
LAURA GREEN

Narrative Theory: Core Concepts and Critical Debates
DAVID HERMAN, JAMES PHELAN AND PETER J. RABINOWITZ, BRIAN RICHARDSON, AND ROBYN WARHOL

After Testimony: The Ethics and Aesthetics of Holocaust Narrative for the Future
EDITED BY JAKOB LOTHE, SUSAN RUBIN SULEIMAN, AND JAMES PHELAN

The Vitality of Allegory: Figural Narrative in Modern and Contemporary Fiction
GARY JOHNSON

Narrative Middles: Navigating the Nineteenth-Century British Novel
EDITED BY CAROLINE LEVINE AND MARIO ORTIZ-ROBLES

Fact, Fiction, and Form: Selected Essays
RALPH W. RADER. EDITED BY JAMES PHELAN AND DAVID H. RICHTER.

The Real, the True, and the Told: Postmodern Historical Narrative and the Ethics of Representation
ERIC L. BERLATSKY

Franz Kafka: Narration, Rhetoric, and Reading
EDITED BY JAKOB LOTHE, BEATRICE SANDBERG, AND RONALD SPEIRS

Social Minds in the Novel
ALAN PALMER

Narrative Structures and the Language of the Self
MATTHEW CLARK

Imagining Minds: The Neuro-Aesthetics of Austen, Eliot, and Hardy
KAY YOUNG

Postclassical Narratology: Approaches and Analyses
EDITED BY JAN ALBER AND MONIKA FLUDERNIK

Techniques for Living: Fiction and Theory in the Work of Christine Brooke-Rose
KAREN R. LAWRENCE

Towards the Ethics of Form in Fiction: Narratives of Cultural Remission
LEONA TOKER

Tabloid, Inc.: Crimes, Newspapers, Narratives
V. PENELOPE PELIZZON AND NANCY M. WEST

Narrative Means, Lyric Ends: Temporality in the Nineteenth-Century British Long Poem
MONIQUE R. MORGAN

Understanding Nationalism: On Narrative, Cognitive Science, and Identity
PATRICK COLM HOGAN

Joseph Conrad: Voice, Sequence, History, Genre
EDITED BY JAKOB LOTHE, JEREMY HAWTHORN, JAMES PHELAN

The Rhetoric of Fictionality: Narrative Theory and the Idea of Fiction
RICHARD WALSH

Experiencing Fiction: Judgments, Progressions, and the Rhetorical Theory of Narrative
JAMES PHELAN

Unnatural Voices: Extreme Narration in Modern and Contemporary Fiction
BRIAN RICHARDSON

Narrative Causalities
EMMA KAFALENOS

Why We Read Fiction: Theory of Mind and the Novel
LISA ZUNSHINE

I Know That You Know That I Know: Narrating Subjects from Moll Flanders to Marnie
GEORGE BUTTE

Bloodscripts: Writing the Violent Subject
ELANA GOMEL

Surprised by Shame: Dostoevsky's Liars and Narrative Exposure
DEBORAH A. MARTINSEN

Having a Good Cry: Effeminate Feelings and Pop-Culture Forms
ROBYN R. WARHOL

Politics, Persuasion, and Pragmatism: A Rhetoric of Feminist Utopian Fiction
ELLEN PEEL

Telling Tales: Gender and Narrative Form in Victorian Literature and Culture
ELIZABETH LANGLAND

Narrative Dynamics: Essays on Time, Plot, Closure, and Frames
EDITED BY BRIAN RICHARDSON

Breaking the Frame: Metalepsis and the Construction of the Subject
DEBRA MALINA

Invisible Author: Last Essays
CHRISTINE BROOKE-ROSE

Ordinary Pleasures: Couples, Conversation, and Comedy
KAY YOUNG

Narratologies: New Perspectives on Narrative Analysis
EDITED BY DAVID HERMAN

Before Reading: Narrative Conventions and the Politics of Interpretation
PETER J. RABINOWITZ

Matters of Fact: Reading Nonfiction over the Edge
DANIEL W. LEHMAN

The Progress of Romance: Literary Historiography and the Gothic Novel
DAVID H. RICHTER

A Glance Beyond Doubt: Narration, Representation, Subjectivity
SHLOMITH RIMMON-KENAN

Narrative as Rhetoric: Technique, Audiences, Ethics, Ideology
JAMES PHELAN

Misreading Jane Eyre: A Postformalist Paradigm
JEROME BEATY

Psychological Politics of the American Dream: The Commodification of Subjectivity in Twentieth-Century American Literature
LOIS TYSON

Understanding Narrative
EDITED BY JAMES PHELAN AND PETER J. RABINOWITZ

Framing Anna Karenina: Tolstoy, the Woman Question, and the Victorian Novel
AMY MANDELKER

Gendered Interventions: Narrative Discourse in the Victorian Novel
ROBYN R. WARHOL

Reading People, Reading Plots: Character, Progression, and the Interpretation of Narrative
JAMES PHELAN